D0119747

SAINSBURY'S
REGIONAL WINE GUIDES

FRENCH
RED AND ROSÉ
WINES

OZ CLARKE

Published in the UK exclusively for
J Sainsbury plc, Stamford House, Stamford Street,
London SE1 9LL by Webster's Wine Guides,
Axe and Bottle Court, 70 Newcomen Street, London SE1 1YT

First published 1989

ISBN 1 870604 01 6

Typeset by Black Bear Press Limited, Cambridge, England
Colour separations by Spectrum Reproductions, Colchester, England
Printed and bound in Italy by Arnoldo Mondadori, Vicenza

Conceived, edited and designed by Webster's Wine Guides

CONTENTS

THE RED WINE REGIONS OF FRANCE

One of the best ways to appreciate the dominant position of France in the world of red wine is to visit all the other leading wine producers across the globe. Visit the producer of a leading Pinot Noir red in California's Napa Valley and as you congratulate him on his wine he will confide that he believes he has at last found a way to make French red Burgundy – in California. Savour the remarkable Cabernet Sauvignon wines of New Zealand's Hawkes Bay or Australia's Coonawarra and the way to send the producer into paroxysms of pleasure is to say you really feel Hawkes Bay or Coonawarra wines are the New World's closest equivalents to the great reds of the Médoc – in France.

All the internationally recognized classic red wine types originate in France. *All* the greatest red wine grape varieties are French. And *all* the methods of wine-making now accepted worldwide as the textbook procedures for production of great red wines are based on French tradition. Not only that, but the French methods of quality control, as laid out in the *Appellation d'Origine Contrôlée* (Controlled Appellation of Origin) are the basis for virtually all the quality control regulations in the rest of the world. The only thing the rest of the world can't get its hands on is France itself, and this book is dedicated to describing the unique qualities which make French red wines the most varied and the most exciting in the world.

If there is one thing which to me exemplifies the French red wine style it is balance – the balance between overripeness and underripeness, too much fruit flavour and not enough, too much new oak flavour and not enough. And this is the result of almost 20 centuries of trial and error, experimentation and refinement, which began with the Romans and are still continuing today. Generation after generation of winemakers have patiently matched grape varieties with the most suitable soils in the most suitable sites so that from far north to far south, the perfect ripening conditions have been found for all the great table wine grapes.

The north of France is rarely warm enough to produce exciting red wines, since black grapes do need more sun than white grapes to ripen fully. Yet there is a little pale Pinot Noir red made in Champagne and Alsace and a good deal of pink fizz comes out of Champagne.

Burgundy built its reputation on red wines, and though these start hesitantly near Auxerre just south of Paris, once we arrive at Dijon, red wine production is getting in to full swing with the Côte d'Or – a narrow slope of south-east facing land which produces many of the most famous red wines in the world – but in extremely limited quantities. South of the Côte d'Or is the Côte Chalonnaise – a less spectacular, but extremely good source of red Burgundy from the Pinot Noir, while the Mâconnais, although primarily a white wine producer, does produce a fair amount of red and rosé from Pinot Noir and Gamay grapes.

The Gamay's hour of glory, however, comes in Beaujolais. This is a large area just north of Lyon, consisting largely of granite slopes pushing out into the Saône valley from the Massif Central, and Beaujolais wine is the juiciest, fruitiest red that France has to offer. South of Lyon in the steep, positively cliff-like vineyards of the northern Rhône valley, the grape changes to the Syrah and fruitiness gives way to power and fiery force with some of France's grandest reds from Côte Rôtie, Hermitage and Cornas. But the valley spreads out beneath the hill of Hermitage and the flavours soften too as the Grenache blends in with the Syrah, the Carignan and the Cinsaut to produce enormous amounts of easy-fruited Côtes du Rhône and much smaller amounts of super-ripe Châteauneuf-du-Pape.

The whole of the south of France is dominated by red wine – although Provence is more famous for its rosé – and though there aren't many well-known names yet, we're going to see more and more of Corbières, Minervois, Fitou and Côtes du Roussillon as very reliable, good-value reds.

The western side of France is dominated by the Loire valley and Bordeaux. The Loire is primarily a white wine area, but there is fairly decent red Sancerre from the Pinot Noir, good to excellent red

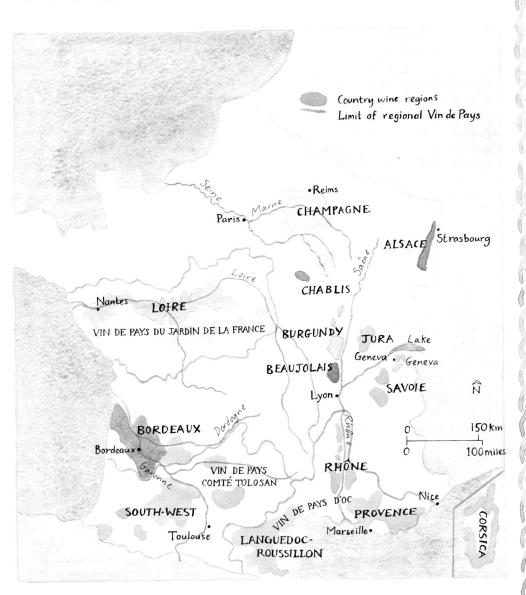

Country wine regions
Limit of regional Vin de Pays

Seine

• Reims

Marne

CHAMPAGNE

Paris •

ALSACE Strasbourg

Saône

Loire

CHABLIS

Nantes • LOIRE

VIN DE PAYS DU JARDIN DE LA FRANCE

BURGUNDY

JURA Lake

Geneva • Geneva

BEAUJOLAIS

SAVOIE

N̂

Lyon •

BORDEAUX Dordogne

Bordeaux •

0 ————— 150 km
0 ————— 100 miles

Garonne

VIN DE PAYS
COMTÉ TOLOSAN

RHÔNE

Rhône

Nice
•

SOUTH-WEST

VIN DE PAYS D'OC

PROVENCE

CORSICA

Toulouse •

LANGUEDOC-
ROUSSILLON

Marseille •

Chinon and Bourgueil from the Cabernet Franc and a world-famous rosé – Rosé d'Anjou.

Bordeaux could well lay claim to the title 'red wine capital of the world'. Though the region does make exciting dry and sweet whites, it is the reds, based on the Cabernet Sauvignon and Merlot grapes, which cover Bordeaux with glory. The Merlot dominates the clay-rich vineyards of St-Émilion and Pomerol, while the gravelly soils of the Graves and the Haut-Médoc, especially at Margaux, St-Julien, Pauillac and St-Estèphe, provide the perfect conditions for Cabernet Sauvignon to produce a string of stunning wines.

And between these great classic areas, there are the little backwaters of wine; the byways which usually get forgotten as the big producers surge to the fore. Well, we don't forget them. As well as covering all the major areas, in great detail, the minor areas also get their due, sometimes even a little more than they deserve, but that simply means that they've given me particular pleasure on some picnic lost in a high mountain valley or in some little country café as I tucked into the *plat du jour* heading south to the sun. Great and small, famous and unknown, they all add up to the magical world of France and its red wines.

MAKING RED
AND ROSÉ WINES

Wine is created by fermentation – yeasts turning grape sugar into alcohol. It's as simple as that, and if you bought a few bunches of ripe grapes, squashed them, put the resulting goo into a bucket and left it somewhere warm like the airing cupboard – well, a wine of sorts would almost certainly be produced. It might taste more like vinegar, but technically it would be wine.

Of course, if it was as easy as that, we'd all be doing it ourselves instead of spending our hard-earned money on the many different bottles which are now crowding the shelves. But this simple chemical reaction has been refined by hundreds of years of experience, and, more recently, by the application of high technology and microbiological know-how. Today the making of *good* wine is a complicated, high-tech affair, and more and more it is scientists who are in charge – rather than the guy who never went to wine school, but with something in his soul which spurs him on to make great wine time and again. We are now in the age of the white-coat winemaker. The result is more attractive, affordable wine than ever before, to balance the declining influence of many-flavoured brilliance from the old-style wine magicians.

The wine-making process begins when the grapes are brought in from the vineyard and are prepared for fermentation. With the exception of Beaujolais and a few other wines using the 'whole bunch' method of fermentation (also called carbonic maceration, see page 18), black grapes are put through a crusher to break their skins and release the juice. Usually a crushing machine also removes the stalks as these have a tough tannic taste, but in some areas – especially the Rhône –they are left on to produce a firmer wine. The resulting 'must' – pulpy mush of flesh and juice and skins (which give red and rosé wines their colour) – is pumped into a big vat, ready for fermentation. Traditionally, fermentation vats were made of wood but are now usually of stainless steel or glass-lined cement.

Yeasts are naturally present on grapes, but increasingly, cultivated yeasts are used to ensure a rapid start. At this stage, in the cooler areas of France, the addition of sugar is permitted if the grapes aren't fully ripe. Similarly, in the hottest regions, a little acid may be added if the grapes are overripe. A light red ferments for less than a week, whereas a full-bodied red takes around two weeks – sometimes even three or four – to extract all the flavour and colour from the skins. Since this happens most effectively between 77°F and 84°F (25°C and 29°C) big reds generally spend at least some time at this temperature. With rosés, the fermenting juice is drawn off the skins after a day or less, and fermentation then continues at low temperatures – between 59°F and 68°F (15°C and 20°C) – which produces a fresher, fruitier wine.

Throughout the process, skins – and any other debris like stalks and pips – surge upwards, pushed by the stream of carbon dioxide released during fermentation. At the top, they form a thick 'cap' which must be mixed back in continually – partly so that the wine can extract maximum colour and flavour. Formerly, the cap was pushed down with a large pole but today wine is taken from the vat base and pumped over it.

When red wine fermentation is finished – all the sugar having been converted to alcohol – the juice is drawn off the vat, and the residue of skins is pressed, to produce a dark, tannic wine called 'press wine'. This may be added to the free-run juice to create a deeper, tougher style, or it may be stored apart – it all depends on what the winemaker wants.

Technically, the wine is now made – but it is pretty raw stuff, in need of further care and attention. To begin with, it probably has a sharp, green-apple acidity. This is reduced through a second fermentation – the 'malolactic' – which converts that tart malic acid into mild lactic acid. Although the malolactic should happen naturally the following spring when the weather gets warmer, it is almost always induced, much earlier, either by raising the cellar temperature or by injecting the wine with malolactic bacteria. Almost all red wines undergo this fermentation – becoming rounder and softer.

If the wine is to be drunk young it is put in large tanks of stainless steel or concrete to rest a short while before bottling. Almost all rosé is treated this way. Red wine for ageing, however, is stored – ideally in small 225-litre oak barrels – for anything from nine months to over two years. If the barrels are new or only once-used, they impart a strong flavour of spice, herbs, perfume and vanilla as well as adding to the wine's tannic structure.

During this pre-bottling period, wine throws a deposit. Since this contains murky-flavoured dead yeast cells, it must be separated from the wine. This

▲Fermentation is closely monitored. Here, at Château Langoa-Barton, Haut-Médoc, the winemaker uses a hydrometer to measure the sugar content of the must.

◀Inside the co-operative at Juliénas, one of the Beaujolais *cru* villages. Fermentation is over; the light, fresh free-run wine has been drawn off and now the grapy residue from the vats is being piled into horizontal presses. The resulting wine – *vin de presse* – will be dark and tannic.

is done by racking – carefully transferring the wine to clean barrels. For cheaper wines, the same effect is achieved through filtration, but here some of the wine's body and flavour is always lost as well.

With top-quality wines, the last stage before bottling is 'fining' – removing any particles held in suspension by means of a clarifying agent. The agent – typically egg white or isinglass or gelatin – is added to the surface and, as it drops down through the wine, it collects all impurities with it. Most other wines are filtered; ones for immediate drinking often receive quite a fierce filtration to ensure no deposit forms in the bottle. Some of the best wines that have been fined are also filtered – but very lightly as preservation of their personality is all-important. In top red wines a slight deposit is inevitable.

For best results, bottling should be cold and sterile, with an inert gas like nitrogen filling the gap between wine and cork to prevent oxidation. But fine wines, destined to mature in bottle, need that tiny amount of air – not nitrogen – to continue the ageing process. Many everyday wines, however, are either 'hot-bottled' or pasteurized. Both treatments, which involve heating the wine, ensure its stability but, undoubtedly, detract from its personality.

So, that's the outline. Of course at every single stage, numerous fine-tunings occur and even the most technocratic winemaker indulges in little personal adjustments – otherwise all our wines would end up tasting the same, which would defeat the whole purpose of the exercise – and make this book redundant!

CLASSIFICATIONS

France has the most complex and yet the most workable system in the world for controlling the quality and authenticity of its wines. First and foremost it is based on the belief that the soil a vine grows in, and the type of grape variety employed, are crucial to the character and quality of the wine.

There are three levels of specific quality control for French wines above the basic *Vin de Table* – table wine – level. At the top is *Appellation d'Origine Contrôlée* (Controlled Appellation of Origin) usually abbreviated to AOC or AC. All the great classics and most other top wines belong in this group.

The second level is *Vin Delimité de Qualité Supérieure* (Delimited Wine of Superior Quality), usually abbreviated to VDQS. This is a kind of junior *appellation contrôlée*, and many wines – after a probationary period as VDQS – are promoted to AC. It is also used for oddballs which don't match AC requirements but are nonetheless interesting.

Third is a relative newcomer – *Vin de Pays* (Country Wine, see page 116). This was created in 1968 (and finalized in 1973) to give a geographical identity and quality yardstick to wines which had previously been sold off for blending. Many good wines are appearing under the *vin de pays* label at very fair prices. It is a particularly useful category for adventurous winemakers because the regulations usually allow the use of good quality grape varieties which are alien to an area and thus debarred from its AC. Some of southern France's most exciting new wines come into this class.

There are seven major areas of control in the AC regulations, which are mirrored to a greater or lesser extent in both VDQS and *Vin de Pays*:

LAND The actual vineyard site is obviously at the top of the list. Its aspect to the sun, elevation, drainage – all these crucially influence the grape's ability to ripen. The composition of the soil also affects flavour and ripening.

GRAPE Different grape varieties ripen at different rates given more or less heat and on different sorts of soil. Some wines are traditionally made from one grape variety – like Beaujolais from the Gamay, some are made from several – like Bordeaux's Cabernet Sauvignon and Merlot grapes. Over the centuries the best varieties for each area have evolved and only these are permitted.

ALCOHOLIC DEGREE A minimum alcoholic degree is always specified as this reflects ripeness. Ripe grapes give better flavour – and their higher sugar content creates more alcoholic fermentation.

VINEYARD YIELD Overproduction dilutes flavour and character – this is as true for vines as it is for pears and plums. So a sensible maximum yield is fixed which is expressed in hectolitres of juice per hectare.

VINEYARD PRACTICE The number of vines per hectare and the way they are pruned can dramatically affect yield and therefore quality. So maximum density and pruning methods are decreed.

WINE-MAKING PRACTICE The things you can or can't do to the wine – like adding sugar to help fermentation, or removing acidity when the crop is unripe. Each area has its own particular rules.

TESTING AND TASTING The wines must pass a technical test for soundness – and a tasting panel for quality and 'typicality'. Every year a significant number of wines are refused the AC.

You may also see words like *grand cru, grand cru classé* or *premier cru* on the label. Sometimes, as in Alsace and Burgundy, this is part of the AC.

But in the Haut-Médoc in Bordeaux, it represents a historic judgement of excellence. In the 1855 Classification 60 red wines from the Haut-Médoc – and one from the Graves (now in Pessac-Léognan) – were ranked in five tiers according to the prices they traditionally fetched on the Bordeaux market. Although there are some underachievers, there are at least as many overachievers, and, in general, the 1855 Classification is still a remarkably accurate guide to the best wines of the Haut-Médoc.

Sauternes was also classified in 1855, but Graves had to wait till 1953 for its reds and 1959 for its whites. Pomerol has no classification, though St-Émilion does – and it is revised every ten years to take account both of improving properties and of declining ones.

However, these Bordeaux classifications, though obviously influenced by the best vineyard sites, are actually judgements on the performance of a wine over the years – something which is often as much in the hands of the winemaker as inherent in the soil.

Alsace and Burgundy have a classification, enshrined in the AC, which delineates the actual site of the vineyards. So the potential for excellence is rewarded with either *grand cru* (the top in both areas) or *premier cru* (the second rank, so far only in Burgundy). Ideally this is the better method – although a bad grower can still make bad wine from a *grand cru.*

◀ Château Pichon-Lalande, a Pauillac property classified a Second Growth in 1855, still produces consistently remarkable wines.

THE CLASSIFICATION OF 1855

FIRST GROWTHS (*PREMIERS CRUS*)

Latour, *Pauillac*

Lafite-Rothschild, *Pauillac*

Margaux, *Margaux*

Haut-Brion, *Graves*

Mouton-Rothschild, *Pauillac* (since 1973)

SECOND GROWTHS (*2ÈME CRUS*)

Rausan-Ségla, *Margaux*

Rauzan-Gassies, *Margaux*

Léoville-Las-Cases, *St-Julien*

Léoville-Poyferré, *St-Julien*

Léoville-Barton, *St-Julien*

Durfort-Vivens, *Margaux*

Lascombes, *Margaux*

Gruaud-Larose, *St-Julien*

Brane-Cantenac, *Cantenac-Margaux*

Pichon-Baron, *Pauillac*

Pichon-Lalande, *Pauillac*

Ducru-Beaucaillou, *St-Julien*

Cos d'Estournel, *St-Estèphe*

Montrose, *St-Estèphe*

THIRD GROWTHS (*3ÈME CRUS*)

Giscours, *Labarde-Margaux*

Kirwan, *Cantenac-Margaux*

d'Issan, *Cantenac-Margaux*

Lagrange, *St-Julien*

Langoa-Barton, *St-Julien*

Malescot-St-Exupéry, *Margaux*

Cantenac-Brown, *Cantenac-Margaux*

Palmer, *Cantenac-Margaux*

la Lagune, *Ludon-Haut-Médoc*

Desmirail, *Margaux*

Calon-Ségur, *St-Estèphe*

Ferrière, *Margaux*

Marquis d'Alesme-Becker, *Margaux*

Boyd-Cantenac, *Cantenac-Margaux*

FOURTH GROWTHS (*4ÈME CRUS*)

St-Pierre, *St-Julien*

Branaire-Ducru, *St-Julien*

Talbot, *St-Julien*

Duhart-Milon-Rothschild, *Pauillac*

Pouget, *Cantenac-Margaux*

la Tour-Carnet, *St-Laurent-Haut-Médoc*

Lafon-Rochet, *St-Estèphe*

Beychevelle, *St-Julien*

Prieuré-Lichine, *Cantenac-Margaux*

Marquis-de-Terme, *Margaux*

FIFTH GROWTHS (*5ÈME CRUS*)

Pontet-Canet, *Pauillac*

Batailley, *Pauillac*

Grand-Puy-Lacoste, *Pauillac*

Grand-Puy-Ducasse, *Pauillac*

Haut-Batailley, *Pauillac*

Lynch-Bages, *Pauillac*

Lynch-Moussas, *Pauillac*

Dauzac, *Labarde-Margaux*

Mouton-Baronne-Philippe, *Pauillac*

du Tertre, *Arsac-Margaux*

Haut-Bages-Libéral, *Pauillac*

Pédesclaux, *Pauillac*

Belgrave, *St-Laurent-Haut-Médoc*

de Camensac, *St-Laurent-Haut-Médoc*

Cos Labory, *St-Estèphe*

Clerc-Milon-Rothschild, *Pauillac*

Croizet-Bages, *Pauillac*

Cantemerle, *Macau-Haut-Médoc*

A-Z OF WINES
GRAPES AND WINE
REGIONS

T he lists on the following pages cover all the *appellations contrôlées* for French red and rosé wines, plus a selection of the most important VDQS and *vins de pays*, so unless you are travelling in some *very* obscure corner of France you should find here a description of any wine you are likely to come across. There are also profiles of those Bordeaux châteaux which I consider to be the best. Often these are the most famous names, but not always! There are also entries on France's main red wine grape varieties and wine regions.

The wine entries all follow the same format, the left-hand column containing the name of the wine, the classification, the region and the main grape varieties (up to a maximum of four) in order of importance (see below for a sample explained in more detail). The right-hand column gives the wine description with, where appropriate, recommended producers and vintages.

If you cannot find the wine you want in the A-Z, it may mean that it is listed under a different name. In such cases consult the Index where alternative forms of the wine names may be found.

The largest red wine regions of France (Beaujolais, Bordeaux, Burgundy, Côte d'Or, Médoc, Rhône, St-Émilion and Pomerol) are each accorded a whole spread to themselves with maps and a list of the main wines and grapes of the region. The items in these lists can be found in their appropriate place in the A-Z. There is a similar section on *vins de pays*.

The name of the wine; in this case it's a claret (red Bordeaux) and these wines are generally known by the château name (ch. = château). Most wines are listed under their AC name.	**BEYCHEVELLE, CH.**	The classification; some wine regions (for example, Médoc, Côte d'Or, St-Émilion) have particular local systems of classification by which wines are allowed to style themselves *grand cru, premier cru* and so forth. The Médoc's famous classification dates from 1855. This wine is a Fourth Growth.
The *appellation contrôlée* (AC) name.	**St-Julien AC,** *4ème cru classé*	
The region; Haut-Médoc is a major sub-area of Bordeaux.	HAUT-MÉDOC, BORDEAUX	
	Cabernet Sauvignon, Merlot, Cabernet Franc, Petit Verdot	The grape varieties listed in order of importance.
The wine name and *appellation* (this wine is a Vin Délimité de Qualité Supérieure – VDQS).	**MARCILLAC VDQS**	
	SOUTH-WEST	The region.
The grapes in order of importance up to a maximum of four named varieties.	Fer, Gamay, Jurançon Noir	

◀ Languedoc-Roussillon in the south produces reliable, good-value reds.

11

AJACCIO AC
CORSICA
Sciacarello

Of all the Corsican ACs this is the only one which seems to break away from the Corsican mould of rather flaccid reds, head-banging rosés and stale fruitless whites. With the shining exception of Comte Peraldi, whose excellent white shows real class in both oak-aged and non-oaked versions, the whites are still all potential and little realization, as are the distinctly orange-hued rosés. However, the reds *do* show a bit of form, even if the rather sour edge of acidity still intrudes more than I'd like into the fairly plummy fruit. Again, Comte Peraldi is in a different league to the others, but there are rather rustic but tasty efforts from Clos Capitoro and Domaine de Paviglia.

ALOXE-CORTON AC
CÔTE DE BEAUNE, BURGUNDY
Pinot Noir

An important village at the northern end of the Côte de Beaune producing mostly red wines. Its reputation is based on the wines that come from the hill of Corton, which completely dominates the village and its impressive Château Corton-André (worth a visit if only to marvel at the tile-mosaic roofs of shimmering brown and gold). The hill is thick with vines from the east side, through the major south-facing swathe, to almost due west, and they reach right up to the tree-covered brow.

The large Corton vineyard is the Côte de Beaune's only red *grand cru*. It is also the cheapest – and most variable. The other vineyards of Aloxe-Corton used to offer some of Burgundy's tastiest wine at a fair price but the reds now rarely exhibit the delicious blend of ripe fruit and appetizing savoury dryness of which they are capable. Too often they are simply light and sweet. Although there are a number of *premiers crus* vineyards, these are hardly ever named on the label, but 'premier cru', denoting a blend of several *premier cru* wines, is quite common. Best years: 1987, '86, '85, '83, '82, '78. Best producers: Bize, Chandon de Briailles, Drouhin, Dubreuil-Fontaine, Latour, Senard, Tollot-Beaut, Voarick.

▼ An estate in Aloxe-Corton, the smallest village in the Côte de Beaune but famous for its *grand cru* Corton wines.

ALSACE PINOT NOIR
Alsace AC
ALSACE
Pinot Noir

It's bad luck on Alsace that, although the region boasts one of the greatest cuisines in France, it can't produce the great red wines many of the dishes cry out for. I don't remember a single visit to Alsace when I haven't gazed down at my plate groaning with hare, or pheasant, or venison . . . and sighed wistfully for a really full-bodied glass of red. Well, you have to go south to Burgundy, Beaujolais and the Rhône for that, because up in Alsace the only red grape they manage to ripen is the Pinot Noir – and only in the warmer years.

But I *do* like Alsace Pinot Noir, even if it is closer to pink than red: it often reveals a hauntingly spring-like perfume rare in a red wine, and a gentle soothing strawberry flavour that slips down pretty easily (chilling it for an hour isn't a bad idea). One or two producers are now putting the wine into new oak barrels to age, which is stretching things a bit since these wines don't have the guts to cope with oak-barrel ageing. In any case, I drink them for their bright, cherry-red fruit and that's the first thing to disappear if you leave the wine in an oak barrel for six months. Best producers: Cattin, Faller Frères, Hugel, Rolly Gassmann and co-operatives at Bennwihr, Éguisheim and Turckheim.

L'ANGÉLUS, CH.
St-Émilion AC, *grand cru classé*
BORDEAUX
Cabernet Franc, Merlot, Cabernet Sauvignon

Judging by the price, you would expect Château l'Angélus to be a leading *premier grand cru classé* – and the rich, warm, mouth-filling flavour would confirm this. Yet l'Angélus is only *grand cru classé*, St-Émilion's second quality category. It is an example of how one must not take wine classifications as gospel, because the influence of an energetic owner, a talented winemaker or investment in the winery can upgrade the quality of a vineyard's wine – just as surely as laziness, incompetence and penny-pinching can dilute it.

L'Angélus is well placed on the lower part of the *côtes* (slopes) to the west of St-Émilion, and the soil is rather heavy. Until 1979 this resulted in a fruity, though slightly bland, wine. But in the 1980s new oak-barrel ageing was introduced, adding a good, sturdy backbone to the easy-going fruit. 1985 and '86 showed glorious fruit and richness but also a gratifying firmness that will allow both to age beautifully.

D'ANGLUDET, CH.
Margaux AC, *cru bourgeois supérieur exceptionnel*
HAUT-MÉDOC, BORDEAUX
Cabernet Sauvignon, Merlot, Cabernet Franc, Petit Verdot

If you were in a cynical mood, you *could* take any remarks I make about Château d'Angludet with a substantial pinch of salt, because this was the first Bordeaux château I stayed at, did the vintage at, surreptitiously sampled the new wine of. . . So when I say that this English-owned property, set well back in the woods behind the village of Cantenac, makes one of my favourite wines, do bear with me. When I say the wine possesses a delicious, approachable burst of blackcurrant-and-blackberry fruit that makes you want to drink it as soon as it's bottled – yet ages superbly over a dozen years or more – be assured that I have put a great deal of personal effort (and consumption) into reaching that conclusion. And when I say that its price-quality ratio is one of the best in Bordeaux since the wine is always of Classed Growth standard but the price well below it – well, whenever *I* buy claret to lay down I start with d'Angludet. And in 1983 and '85 I only wish I'd bought twice as much.

ANJOU ROUGE AC
CENTRAL LOIRE
Cabernet Franc, Cabernet Sauvignon (Anjou); Gamay (Anjou Gamay)

Anjou is best known for its rosé wine, but increasingly the leading winemakers are turning their hand to red wine-making with considerable success. Anjou Rouge comes generally from Gamay or Cabernet Franc grapes. Gamay is the Beaujolais grape and using the Beaujolais method of vinification – carbonic maceration – the results can be similar, but usually a bit rougher. Cabernet Franc, however, although a bit thin and grassy in cool years, can be extremely good – attractively earthy but with a delightful, raw blackcurrant and raspberry fruit – and enough tannin to age for six to eight years. Best years: 1985, though '83 and '82 can still be good. Best producers: Château de Chamboureau, Clos de Coulaine, Colombier, Fougeraies, Richou, Rochettes.

ANJOU-VILLAGES AC
CENTRAL LOIRE
Cabernet Franc, Cabernet Sauvignon

Since the Anjou AC is such a catch-all – and one with a fairly poor reputation and price tag to boot – the better producers of red wines have been lobbying for years to get their wines upgraded. Well, they've at last managed it. Forty-six villages spread through Anjou can now use the AC Anjou-Villages for red wine only, using Cabernet Franc and Cabernet Sauvignon, and the next couple of years will let us see whether they're worth the extra. My feeling is that they *are* worth it, and already some extremely attractive dry, but piercingly fruity reds are beginning to surface. The title 'Anjou-Villages Val-de-Loire' is also allowed for those who want to add to their printing costs.

ARBOIS AC
JURA
Trousseau, Pinot Noir, Poulsard

Arbois, on the slopes above the Saône valley, is one of the main towns of the Jura region and one of its four ACs. You don't see much Arbois wine outside France and, to be honest, I'm not surprised: the chief grape, Trousseau, is a pretty brutish specimen, usually giving hefty thick-edged wines quite unlike what you'd expect from mountainside vineyards. The Poulsard grape is less disturbing, and can produce quite pleasant light reds and good, smoky rosés. Pinot Noir gives pale but tasty, perfumed reds. Some of the best wines come from the village of Pupillin and are called Arbois-Pupillin. Best producers: Bourdy, Henri Maire, Aubin and Pupillin co-operatives.

L'ARROSÉE, CH.
St-Émilion AC, *grand cru classé*
BORDEAUX
Merlot, Cabernet Sauvignon,
Cabernet Franc

One of those unknown properties that swept to international prominence so quickly you have to keep checking your tasting notes to see you haven't got the name wrong. But this small property, situated on a good slope just south-west of St-Émilion town, really is exciting: it makes a rich, chewy and wonderfully luscious wine, full of that buttery soft ripeness which is St-Émilion at its most sensual and delicious. A real hedonist's wine, even in a poor vintage like 1984, and especially in the big broad years of '85, '83 and '82.

AUDE
LANGUEDOC-ROUSSILLON

A large *département* which stretches inland from Narbonne on the Mediterranean, up the Aude valley to Carcassonne and the Limoux hills, and more excitingly south-west into the tumbling, tangled mountain wilderness of the Corbières. This is one of those southern French areas that tended to be dismissed with a disdainful sniff and some derogatory remark about wine lakes and oceans of plonk.

But over the last five years the Aude has emerged as one of the most exciting areas in France. Fitou became all the rage as suburbia's favourite gutsy red, and both Corbières and Minervois have been raised to AC status with impressive results. Although only a couple of VDQSs now remain, there is a lot of *vin de pays* activity. On average 150 million bottles of *vin de pays* are produced, almost all red or rosé. About two-thirds go under the Vin de Pays de l'Aude title, but there are 21 *vins de pays de zone* which include Coteaux de Peyriac with an enormous 35 million bottles, the somewhat off-putting Val de Cesse, and the sublimely come-hither Vallée du Paradis.

AUSONE, CH.
St-Émilion AC, *premier grand cru classé*
BORDEAUX
Merlot, Cabernet Franc

This elegant property, on what are arguably the best slopes in the whole of St-Émilion, is a success story of the '80s. It has always been judged the potential equal of Médoc First Growths, but all through the '60s and most of the '70s, the wine from this compact 17-acre (7-hectare) site was wispy and stale. Things began to change in 1975 when a new hot-shot winemaker, Pascal Delbeck, was appointed. The improvements have been dramatic. Wine after wine, particularly in 1978, '82 and '85, has tasted brilliant from its first moment, drawn fresh from the barrel in France; actual bottles of the wines in the shops, however, have been less reliably memorable. Even so, Ausone will probably be back on a par with the best of the Médocs by the 1990s.

▶ Arbois, makes a range of wines, mostly based on indigenous grapes. Fruitière Vinicole is the largest producer.

AUXEY-DURESSES AC
CÔTE DE BEAUNE, BURGUNDY
Pinot Noir

It was Auxey-Duresses which introduced me to the curious idea that Burgundy undergoes a third fermentation in the bottle. I had this Auxey-Duresses – 1966 of all things – and as I pulled the cork there was a distinct pop and a fetching little foam formed in the neck. A wise and thirsty friend said not to worry – just decant it into a jug and pour it back and forth while all the bubbles dispersed. Which of course I did, and we had a lovely bottle of Burgundy for lunch. However, I delved into several respected books and discovered that a 'third fermentation' like this was by no means uncommon. My wise friend said, 'Rubbish, it just shows the wine was badly bottled and hadn't finished its *second* fermentation properly'. Well I believe *him*. I mean, find me a scientist who will adequately explain a *third* fermentation!

Anyway, by such chances are names engraved indelibly on one's mind. As it happens, Auxey-Duresses is rather a backwater village up in the hills behind the world-famous Meursault and on the way to the even less well-known St-Romain. It *can* produce rather full, round, cherry-and-strawberry-fruited wines, but too often recently the wines have been over-sweet and a bit jammy. A pity, because Auxey-Duresses is excellent value when it's good. Best year: 1985. Best producers: Leroy, Diconne, Duc de Magenta, Roland, Thévenin.

BALESTARD-LA-TONNELLE, CH.
St-Émilion AC, *grand cru classé*
BORDEAUX
Merlot, Cabernet Franc, Cabernet Sauvignon, Malbec

I became really keen on this wine in the town of St-Émilion itself. Perusing a seriously overpriced wine list, I saw the 1975 Balestard. Now I don't like many '75s – they're far too tannic and fruitless – but this '75 was excellent, full and sturdy but packed with rather muscle-shouldered fruit. Since then I have frequently sought out the wine and it has always been satisfyingly reliable, full of strong, chewy fruit, and decently priced to boot. Obviously it has been popular for a fair old while, because the label reprints a poem which Villon wrote in the fifteenth century that describes Balestard as 'this divine nectar'. Nothing like an unsolicited testimonial! Best years: 1986, '85, '83, '82, '78, '75.

BANDOL AC
PROVENCE
Mourvèdre, Grenache, Cinsaut, Syrah

There's no doubt that Bandol is a lovely resort town and fishing port, and there's no doubt that many of the vineyards are spectacular, cut high into the cliffs and slopes which tumble down to the Mediterranean beaches. But there is some doubt as to whether Bandol still ranks as Provence's top red wine. As an AC the general standard for reds (and rosés too) is the highest in the French Riviera region, though there are certain properties in Côtes de Provence, Coteaux d'Aix-en-Provence and the Hérault which surpass Bandol's best.

The Mourvèdre grape (to a minimum of 50 per cent) is the grape which gives Bandol its character – gentle raisin and honey softness with a slight, tannic, plumskins nip and hopefully a tobaccoey, herby fragrance. Other grapes, in particular Grenache, Cinsaut and occasionally Syrah make up the blend. The reds spend at least 18 months in wood. They happily age for ten years, but can be very good at three to four. The rosés, delicious and spicy but really too pricy, should be drunk as young as possible. Best producers: Cagueloupe, Ray Jean, Mas de la Rouvière, Ste-Anne, Tempier, Terrebrune, Vannières.

BANYULS AC
LANGUEDOC-ROUSSILLON
Grenache, Cinsaut, Syrah and others

▼ Banyuls, one of the best-known red *vins doux naturels*, is aged either in huge glass jars or in casks – both stored outside in the hot Midi sun. From barrels some evaporation occurs so they are topped up regularly with younger wine.

One of those strange, rather heavy, fortified wines – *vins doux naturels* – which the French like well enough but which frankly don't have the style and character of the ones from Spain (sherry, Montilla, Málaga) and Portugal (port, Madeira). It is grown on rocky shelves and plateaux strung along the sheer Pyrenean coastline to within spitting distance of the Spanish border. The wine, either red or tawny, must be at least 50 per cent Grenache Noir.

It is sometimes made fairly dry, but this strong plum and raisin flavour tastes best in a sweet version and it is also best bottled young – a common problem in isolated areas is winemakers' reluctance to draw the wine off from their leaky old casks until it's half-dead. Banyuls *grand cru* is at least 75 per cent Grenache, has 30 months' wood-ageing and is a bit richer as a consequence. *Rancio* means that the wine has been intentionally oxidized and will have a tawny colour. I'd stick to the red. Best producer: Mas Blanc.

BATAILLEY, CH.
Pauillac AC, *5ème cru classé*
HAUT-MÉDOC, BORDEAUX
Cabernet Sauvignon, Merlot,
Cabernet Franc, Petit Verdot

A byword for value-for-money – which, in the rarified world of Pauillac Classed Growths, is an infrequent accolade indeed. Batailley, an elegant eighteenth-century château, half-hidden by its own park, is helped by being set back from the town of Pauillac and its cluster of world-famous properties. The wine should be a byword for reliability too, because every year since the mid-1970s it has been good, marked by a full, obvious blackcurrant fruit (even when very young), not too much tannin, and a luscious overlay of good creamy oak-barrel vanilla. Lovely to drink at only five years old, the wine nonetheless ages extremely well for 15. Best years: 1985, '83, '82.

BÉARN AC
SOUTH-WEST
Tannat, Manseng Noir, Cabernet
Sauvignon, Cabernet Franc

While the rest of south-west France has been dusting off its historic reputation as a fine wine region, and creating shock waves with some highly original flavours, Béarn hasn't managed to cash in. The reason is simple – the wines (750,000 bottles, 90 per cent red and rosé) just aren't special enough and as yet the local co-operatives which dominate the region haven't decided to up the quality. If they do, we should see some excellent results because the grape varieties are good. At the moment the juicy rosé is probably best, ideally drunk chilled. There are now good reds from some Jurançon producers like Domaine Cauhapé. Best of the others: Bellocq co-operative.

BEAUJOLAIS AC &
BEAUJOLAIS-SUPÉRIEUR AC
BEAUJOLAIS, BURGUNDY
Gamay

Most of the Beaujolais we drink nowadays goes under the label Beaujolais Nouveau or Beaujolais Primeur. But that's exactly as it ought to be. Nouveau (new) and Primeur (first) on the label show that the wine is young as can be, and that's precisely what makes Beaujolais such fun – it gushes from the bottle into the glass and down your throat with a whoosh of banana, peach and pepper fruit which sounds like a white wine, even tastes a bit like it, but is actually France's gluggiest red.

The Beaujolais AC is the basic *appellation* covering 54,000 acres (22,000 hectares) of vineyards between Mâcon and Lyon. In the north, towards Mâcon, most of the production qualifies either as Beaujolais-Villages or as a single *cru* (ten villages which definitely *do* produce superior – and more expensive wine: Brouilly, Chénas, Chiroubles, Côte de Brouilly, Fleurie, Juliénas, Morgon, Moulin-à-Vent, Regnié, St-Amour). In the south, towards Lyon, the wide field of vines produces simple AC Beaujolais, a lovely light red wine to be drunk without more ado within months of the vintage.

Beaujolais-Supérieur is an AC occasionally seen in France, but it merely implies a wine with an alcoholic strength one degree higher than straight Beaujolais. Since freshness is everything, extra strength isn't really the point. Best producers: Carron, Charmet, Château de la Plume, Garlon, Jambon, Labruyère, Mathelin, Texier.

BEAUJOLAIS NOUVEAU
Beaujolais AC
BEAUJOLAIS, BURGUNDY
Gamay

The wine they all love to hate. Well, I love to love it! This is the first release of bouncy, fruity, happy-fresh Beaujolais wine on the third Thursday of November following the harvest. So the wine will normally be between seven and nine weeks old, depending on the date of the vintage – the earlier the better. What started out simply as the celebration of the new vintage in the Beaujolais villages and the nearby metropolis of Lyon has now become a much-hyped beano worldwide. And I'm glad! November's a rotten month. I need a party and Beaujolais Nouveau day is always a good party. And it's affordable!

Also, it is worth defending Nouveau by saying that the quality is usually extremely good, since many of the best selections in the Beaujolais AC are used for Nouveau. And another thing. It usually improves by Christmas and New Year and *good* ones are perfect for Easter and the first picnics of summer! Best producers: Bouchard Père & Fils, la Chevalière, Drouhin, Duboeuf, Ferraud, Jaffelin, Loron, Sarrau.

BEAUJOLAIS

O f all the recommended soils on which to grow fine red wine, granite must come fairly low on the list. But then, of all the grape varieties you'd choose, the usually dark Gamay would also come fairly near the bottom. But there is a string of magic hills, flowing out of the haunted emptiness of the mountains of the Massif Central into the flat prosperity of the Saône valley above Lyon, which *are* made of granite. And their slopes are covered with the vines of just one red wine variety – and that is the Gamay. The hills are the dreamy, fantastical hills of

Beaujolais. And the wine is Beaujolais, perhaps the most famous red wine name in the world!

The Gamay grape's unique characteristic is its youthful fruit, and this is maximized by a special method of making the wine, called carbonic maceration. The grapes are not pressed. They are all piled into the vat still in their bunches. The ones at the bottom burst and the juice begins to ferment. That heats up the vat, and the grapes on top actually begin to ferment inside their skins. Since all the perfume and colour is on the inside of the grape's skin and all the acid and tough tannin is on the outside, the result is loads of bright colour and orchard-perfumed fruit and mouthwateringly little toughness. In fact, the result can seem more like a white wine than a rosé, and that's why we drink Beaujolais young and ever so slightly chilled.

The most unmistakeable form of this happy-juice-type wine is Beaujolais Nouveau, and a great deal of

Beaujolais crus (MORGON)
Beaujolais-Villages
Beaujolais

N

0   5km
0   3 miles

Mâcon •

ST-AMOUR
JULIÉNAS
CHÉNAS
FLEURIE   MOULIN-A-VENT
CHIROUBLES   • Lancié
Beaujeu •   Lantignié
• MORGON
REGNIÉ
Quincié •
CÔTE DE BROUILLY   • Belleville
Odenas • BROUILLY
• St-Étienne-des-Ouillières

Ardières

Saône

Azergues

Villefranche •

• Theizé
• Le Bois d'Oingt

Lyon ▽

Beaujolais is now drunk as Nouveau at only a few months old. However, the *appellation controlée* system has picked out certain communes as making better wine. These are allowed to use the title Beaujolais-Villages and most of them are in the north of the region. The wines are fuller and riper, but basically it is still the luscious, juicy Gamay fruit which attracts.

Then there are ten villages with especially good slopes which are called *crus* or 'growths' – Brouilly, Chénas, Chiroubles, Côte de Brouilly, Fleurie, Juliénas, Morgon, Moulin-à-Vent, Regnié and St-Amour. They don't use the name Beaujolais on their labels at all, but most of them are simply that much deeper and juicier than Villages, without being radically different. They should still be drunk within a year or so, except for the occasional wine from Morgon, Chénas and Moulin-à-Vent which can age for a surprisingly long time.

MAIN WINES
Beaujolais
Beaujolais Nouveau
Beaujolais Supérieur
Beaujolais-Villages
Brouilly
Chénas
Chiroubles
Côte de Brouilly
Fleurie
Juliénas
Morgon
Moulin-à-Vent
Regnié
St-Amour

MAIN GRAPES
Gamay

◄ Beaujolais – a region of gentle, tree-topped hills, green valleys and, everywhere, vineyards. About half the wine, made exclusively from the Gamay grape, is released as Beaujolais Nouveau – fruity-fresh, very young and very popular.

19

BEAUJOLAIS-VILLAGES AC
BEAUJOLAIS, BURGUNDY
Gamay

A grouping of 39 communes with vineyard sites superior to run-of-the-mill Beaujolais. When carefully made from ripe grapes, a Beaujolais-Villages can represent all the gushing, gurgling excitement of the Gamay grape at its best. Some Villages is successfully made into Nouveau and is often worth keeping six months to drink at its gluggy peak. The best year recently has been 1985, but '87 isn't at all bad. Many Beaujolais-Villages are now bottled under a 'domaine' name, and from the label you can tell which village produced the wine. The best are Beaujeu, Lancié, Lantignié, Leynes, Quincié, Regnié-Durette (which is in the process of becoming the tenth *cru*), St-Étienne des Ouillières, St-Jean d'Ardières. Best producers: Aucoeur, Crot, Dalicieux, Depardon, Duboeuf, de Flammerécourt, Jaffre, Large, Pivot, Tissier, Verger.

BEAUMES-DE-VENISE
Côtes du Rhône-Villages AC
SOUTHERN RHÔNE
Grenache, Syrah, Mourvèdre, Cinsaut

This sunbaked village has become a household name not because of its red Côtes du Rhône-Villages – of which the locals are rather proud – but because of the sweet Muscat de Beaumes-de-Venise which vineyard workers used to swig out in the fields, never dreaming that it would become a highly-priced social necessity for after-dinner-party drinking. Even so the red wine is extremely good, one of the meatier Côtes du Rhône-Villages, but with a ripe plummy fruit in warm years, and an exciting myrtle and musk perfume in cooler ones. The local co-operative is a highly efficient producer.

BEAUNE AC
CÔTE DE BEAUNE, BURGUNDY
Pinot Noir

Beaune is the capital of the whole Côte d'Or and gives its name to the southern section, the Côte de Beaune. It is a lovely place – with its ramparts, cobbled streets, narrow alleys, compact squares and magnificent historic buildings. Chief of all these is the group known as the Hospices de Beaune, whose Hôtel-Dieu, with its fabulous mosaic-tiled roofs and gables, houses a world-famous wine auction every November.

But Beaune is also one of Burgundy's most important wine villages and, in the old British wine trade, Burgundies of any provenance were often lumped together under the title 'Beaune' – simply because it was the best-known village. In those days the name 'Beaune' meant little on the label, but now it means a good deal, since Beaune is the most consistent village in Burgundy. Almost all the wines are red, with a delicious, soft red-fruits ripeness to them, no great tannin, and not much obvious acidity, plus a slight minerally element which is unique and very enjoyable.

Beaunes age well, gaining a savoury yet toffee-rich flavour over five to ten years, but they are also among the easiest of Burgundies to drink young. There are no *grands crus* but many excellent *premiers crus*, especially Boucherottes, Bressandes, Cent Vignes, Grèves, Marconnets, Teurons, Vignes Franches. Best years: 1987, '84, '83, '82 and '81. Merchants dominate the vineyard holdings but there are some independent proprietors – such as Besancenot-Mathouillet, Jacques Germain, Lafarge, Morot, Tollot-Beaut. Best merchants: Bouchard Père & Fils (since 1986), Chanson, Drouhin, Jadot, Jaffelin, Leroy, Moillard.

BELAIR, CH.
St-Émilion AC, *premier grand cru classé*
BORDEAUX
Merlot, Cabernet Franc

Belair is Château Ausone's neighbour on the steep, south- and south-east-facing slopes just below the town. This 32-acre (13-hectare) vineyard isn't just a neighbour, however. The two properties share the same winemaker and the same owner. Indeed, since the late 1970s they have also shared in a spectacular revival of fortunes: during the 1960s Belair was not a wine I'd have dug deep into my pocket to buy, but it is now exceptional and, of course, expensive. In the nineteenth century it was regarded as even better than Ausone; now, the position is reversed – just – with Belair giving a lighter but still firmly-textured, rich-fruited wine, which is just as enjoyable as Ausone – at half the price. Best years: 1986, '85, '83, '82, '79.

BELLET AC
PROVENCE
Folle Noire, Braquet, Cinsaut,
Grenache

I'm usually a great fan of the little, half-forgotten *appellations* which, one suspects, have only avoided oblivion after an against-the-odds struggle by one or two obstinate growers wedded to tradition. Now, Bellet seems to fit this category. It *is* a tiny grouping of small vineyards high in the hills behind Nice – only 125 acres (50 hectares) of vines – whose existence was so precarious that the authorities almost withdrew its AC status in 1947 – they probably couldn't find enough wine to submit to a tasting panel. And there *is* a local hero – the Bagnis family, whose Château de Crémat is the only substantial producer. The thing is, Bellet has Nice as its home market, and people on the razzle after a day on the beach don't seem to care much what their wine tastes like so long as it is supposedly rare and definitely too expensive.

BERGERAC AC
SOUTH-WEST
Cabernet Sauvignon, Cabernet
Franc, Merlot

Bergerac is the main town of the Dordogne and the overall AC for this underrated area east of Bordeaux. The production is pretty sizable – 15 million bottles a year, of which about half is red, and the rest divided between rosé and white. The style of red is generally like a light, fresh claret, a bit grassy but with a good raw blackcurrant fruit too. A few producers make a more substantial version, often with the Côtes de Bergerac AC, which stipulates a higher minimum alcohol level. Bergerac rosés can be exciting too, with far more dry, cutting fruit than most pink wines manage. In general, drink the most recent vintage, though a few estate reds can age three to five years. Many Bergeracs come from the highly efficient co-op. Best producers: le Barradis, Court-les-Mûts, la Jaubertie, Lestignac, la Raye, Treuil-de-Nailhac.

BEYCHEVELLE, CH.
St-Julien AC, *4ème cru classé*
HAUT-MÉDOC, BORDEAUX
Cabernet Sauvignon, Merlot,
Cabernet Franc, Petit Verdot

When you drive up the road from the city of Bordeaux a beautiful seventeenth-century château overlooking the Gironde estuary graciously announces your arrival in St-Julien – the most concentrated stretch of tip-top quality vineyards in all Bordeaux, with 95 per cent of the land occupied by the great Classed Growths. Beychevelle's name comes from *baisse les voiles* – lower the sails – since the Admiral of France once lived there and presumably every passing ship was expected to strike its sails in respect – or else!

Although it is ranked as a Fourth Growth, its quality is leading Second – and its price too. The wine has a beautiful softness even when very young, but takes at least a decade to mature into the fragrant cedarwood and blackcurrant flavour for which St-Julien is famous. When this occurs, Beychevelle is a sublime claret, always expensive, frequently worth the price. Best years: 1986, '85, '83, '82, with good '84 and '80.

BLAGNY AC
CÔTE DE BEAUNE, BURGUNDY
Pinot Noir

A tiny hamlet which straddles the boundary of Puligny-Montrachet and Meursault. Its red is sold as Blagny and can be fair value if you like a rough, rustic approach to Burgundy. Matrot is the best producer in this style. Leflaive, on the Puligny side, produces a lighter, more typically fragrant wine.

BONNES-MARES AC
grand cru
CÔTE DE NUITS, BURGUNDY
Pinot Noir

A large *grand cru* of 38 acres (15 hectares), of which 88 per cent is in Chambolle-Musigny and the rest in Morey-St-Denis. This is one of the few Burgundian great names which seems to have preserved its character through the turmoils of the last few decades – the introduction of strict *appellation contrôlée* laws for the export trade, the see-saw of the American market, changing fashions in vineyard and cellar – all of which produced wild inconsistencies in much top Burgundy. Bonnes-Mares managed to keep its deep, ripe, smoky plum fruit, which starts rich and chewy and gradually matures over 10–20 years into a flavour full of chocolate, smoke again, and pruny depth. Lovely stuff. 1985 is the best recent year, but '87, '80 and '78 are also good. Best producers: Drouhin, Dujac, Jadot, Roumier, de Vogüé.

BORDEAUX

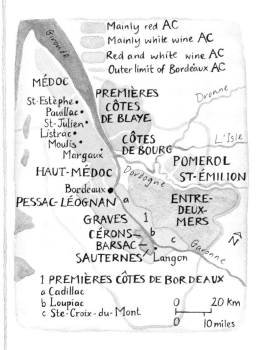

Mainly red AC
Mainly white wine AC
Red and white wine AC
Outer limit of Bordeaux AC

MÉDOC
St-Estèphe•
Pauillac•
St-Julien•
Listrac•
Moulis •
Margaux•
HAUT-MÉDOC
Bordeaux•
PESSAC-LÉOGNAN
GRAVES
CÉRONS—
BARSAC—
SAUTERNES

PREMIÈRES
CÔTES
DE BLAYE
CÔTES
DE BOURG
POMEROL
ST-ÉMILION
ENTRE-
DEUX-
MERS

Dronne
L'Isle
Dordogne
a
1
b
c
Garonne
Langon
Gironde

1 PREMIÈRES CÔTES DE BORDEAUX
a Cadillac
b Loupiac
c Ste-Croix-du-Mont

0   20 Km
0   10 miles

▲ A patchwork panorama of vineyards and villages bordering the Dordogne river in Fronsac.

Bordeaux carries a heavy responsibility, because just about every wine book describes it as the greatest wine region in the world. Is it? Yes, I have to admit that it is! And how does it do? Well, it shoulders that responsibility pretty impressively.

The remarkable thing about Bordeaux is that not only does it make what are quite possibly the world's greatest red wines, it also makes what are probably the world's greatest sweet white wines! There isn't much rosé, but what there is can be sublime, and it's really only in fortified wines and sparklers that Bordeaux fails to make the top rank.

Which leads on to the next thing. There's no doubt that some Burgundies are at least as great as top Bordeaux. But they are produced in minute quantities. All the *grands crus* of, say, Burgundy's Vosne-Romanée, only produce about 20,000 cases of wine a year. A single one of Pauillac's First Growths, Château Mouton-Rothschild, produces 25,000 cases. In red wines, dry whites and sweet whites, the best wines are produced in really significant quantities.

But it isn't only the top wines. Red Bordeaux has been the staple red wine of the northern Europeans for centuries, and the British love affair with it (they've even given it a special name, claret) is explained by the fact that the English owned Bordeaux from 1152 to 1453. It isn't the ritzy wines that have slaked half·a continent's thirst – it's straightforward Bordeaux Rouge and Bordeaux Blanc. And to provide that, alongside the superstars, in this vineland on the banks of the Dordogne and Garonne rivers and the Gironde estuary in the south-west of France, there are over 20,000 growers, working 247,100 acres (100,000 hectares) of land to produce about 500 million bottles of wine. *Every year.*

MAIN ACs	Listrac
Bordeaux	Margaux
Bordeaux Clairet	Médoc
Bordeaux Supérieur	Moulis
Canon-Fronsac	Pauillac
Côtes de Bourg	Pessac-Léognan
Côtes de Castillon	Pomerol
Côtes de Francs	Premières Côtes de Blaye
Fronsac	Premières Côtes de Bordeaux
Graves	St-Émilion
Graves de Vayres	St-Estèphe
Haut-Médoc	St-Julien
Lalande-de-Pomerol	

MAIN GRAPES

Cabernet Franc

Cabernet Sauvignon

Merlot

See also *Médoc*, pages 80–81, and *St-Émilion*, pages 104–105.

BORDEAUX AC
BORDEAUX
Merlot, Cabernet Franc, Cabernet Sauvignon and others

Simple AC Bordeaux is the most basic quality level of the region. But don't dismiss it. Indeed, straight red Bordeaux – often labelled as 'claret' in the UK – is one of the most reliable of all 'generic' labels, and often has a fresh, grassy fruit and attractive earthy edge. However, standards can vary: some Bordeaux Rouge is pretty raw stuff. There are many properties in the less fashionable areas which nevertheless want to sell wines under a château label and these may sport the Bordeaux AC. Wine from important communes with their own AC, like Pauillac or Margaux, may be de-classified to Bordeaux, while red or rosé wine made in the Sauternes/Barsac and Entre-Deux-Mers areas is also only allowed Bordeaux or Bordeaux Supérieur AC.

BORDEAUX CLAIRET AC
BORDEAUX
Cabernet Sauvignon, Cabernet Franc, Merlot

A very pale red wine, almost rosé in fact, which isn't much seen around Bordeaux any more. But it was once. The name 'claret', which we now apply to *any* red wine from the Bordeaux region, derives from *clairet*. What this means is that a few hundred years ago *all* Bordeaux reds were made in a light, quick-drinking style. As wine-making knowledge improved, the reds became darker and stronger, and Bordeaux Clairet almost faded away. Interestingly, a few very ritzy Classed Growth properties in the Médoc still make a little to have with their lunch. And the village of Quinsac, just south of Bordeaux in the Premières Côtes, specializes in Clairet. There are rumours that it is becoming fashionable again.

BORDEAUX SUPÉRIEUR AC
BORDEAUX
Cabernet Sauvignon, Cabernet Franc, Merlot, Malbec

This *appellation* covers the whole Bordeaux region, as does Bordeaux AC. The difference between them is that Supérieur must have an extra half a degree of alcohol for red and rosé and a lower yield from the vines – 40 hectolitres per hectare as against 50. This makes a considerable difference, because the riper fruit which gives the higher alcohol has more taste, and vines which are cropping 20 per cent less give a greater concentration of flavours. Almost all of the *petits châteaux* which represent the best value drinking in Bordeaux will be Bordeaux Supérieur. There are two areas – Côtes de Castillon and Côtes de Francs – which may tack on their own names after Bordeaux Supérieur. Their quality is generally far finer than their low price would suggest. 1985 is the best current vintage, although '86 is good in the Côtes de Castillon and Côtes de Francs.

BOURGOGNE AC
BURGUNDY
Pinot Noir, Gamay, Tressot, César

Bourgogne is the original French name we have anglicized as 'Burgundy'. As a generic *appellation*, from Chablis in the far north way down to Beaujolais in the south, it mops up all the wine which does not have a specific AC of its own. This means there are massive differences in quality and in style. Take the matter of the grapes used. Pinot Noir is thought of as the red Burgundy grape, and this is the variety used for the vast majority of Bourgogne Rouge. Yet around Chablis the local varieties César and Tressot occur (though very rarely), and down in the Mâconnais and Beaujolais Gamay can be used. As for quality, well, some of the less reputable Burgundy merchants buy wine from any source so long as the price is low. On the other hand, some unlucky but dedicated growers possess land only entitled to the simple Bourgogne AC yet on this they lavish the same care and devotion as they would on a famous *grand cru*.

Here's what you *should* find. Red Bourgogne is usually light, overtly fruity in a breezy, strawberry and cherry way, all up-front but if the perfume is there, no one minds if the flavour is a bit simple. It should be drunk young – two to three years' ageing is quite enough – and it shouldn't be fussed over too much; just enjoy it. The better merchants' blends usually come into this category. Sometimes, however, Bourgogne Rouge can be much more than this, the cherry and strawberry fruit deeper, thickened into a plummy richness, and perhaps with the creamy softness of some oak-barrel ageing added in.

Such wine will usually come from a single grower who has excluded some of his wine from the top label, either because it lacked the necessary concentration, or because the vines are just outside the specific *appellation* boundaries. It can be almost as exciting as the proprietor's full-blown Pommard, Gevrey-Chambertin or whatever – and half the price. In today's world of overblown Burgundy prices they may be the only way we can afford the joys of fine Burgundy. Another option is provided by the Caves Co-opératives of Buxy and of the Hautes-Côtes, both of whom now mature some of their wine in oak barrels – with impressive results. Best growers: Chanson, Coche-Dury, Germain, d'Heuilly-Huberdeau, Henri Jayer, Moillard, Morey, Parent, Rion, Rossignol. Best merchants: Drouhin, Jadot, Labouré-Roi, Leroy, Vallet and co-operatives at Buxy and Hautes-Côtes.

BOURGOGNE ROSÉ AC
BURGUNDY
Pinot Noir

Not much is made, but in overcropping years like 1982 many growers will try to give more concentration to their reds by drawing off some of the red wine before it has absorbed very much colour from the skins, and this can be a very pleasant pink.

BOURGOGNE GRAND ORDINAIRE AC
BURGUNDY
Gamay, Pinot Noir, César, Tressot

This really is bottom of the pile. If Bourgogne AC is the catch-all, then Bourgogne Grand Ordinaire AC is for the slops that splashed out of the vat. With a low minimum alcohol, and few growers likely to put much Pinot Noir in the blend, the usual result, I'm afraid, is a tough, fruitless travesty of the Burgundy name.

BOURGOGNE PASSE-TOUT-GRAINS AC
BURGUNDY
Gamay, Pinot Noir

Almost always red (with just a little rosé) this *appellation* is for a mixture of up to two-thirds Gamay with the rest Pinot Noir. In the Côte Chalonnaise and Côte d'Or, as vineyards are replanted, the percentage of Pinot Noir is increasing, which means here that the quality has improved in recent years and should now show a good sturdy, cherry fruit when very young, offset by a raspingly attractive, herby acidity from the Gamay, but softening over three to four years to a gentle, round-edged wine. Best growers: Chaley, Cornu, Rion, Thomas. Best merchants: Chanson, Leroy.

BOURGUEIL AC
CENTRAL LOIRE
Cabernet Franc, Cabernet Sauvignon

Bourgueil is a village just north of the Loire between Angers and Tours. The area is unusually dry for the Loire valley which explains why, in a region known for its easier-ripening white wines, Bourgueil is famous for red. Cabernet Franc is the main grape, with a little Cabernet Sauvignon, and in hot years the results can be superb. Although the wines can be rather peppery and vegetal at first, if you give them time – at least five years, preferably ten – they develop a wonderful fragrance which is like essences of blackcurrant and raspberry combined, with just enough earthiness to keep their feet firmly on the ground. Best years: 1985, '83, '82, '78, '76. Best producers: Audebert (estate wines), Caslot-Galbrun, Caslot-Jamet, Couly-Dutheil, Domaine des Raguenières, Druet, Lamé-Delille-Boucard.

BOUZY
Coteaux Champenois AC
CHAMPAGNE
Pinot Noir

A leading Champagne village on the Montagne de Reims growing the region's best Pinot Noir, usually made into *white* Champagne. However, in outstanding years, a little red wine also is made from Pinot Noir. It is light, high-acid, and often with a cutting, herby edge. But now and then, a waif-like perfume of raspberry and strawberry is just strong enough to provide a fleeting pleasure before the chalky tannins take over again. Best years: 1985, '83, '82. Don't age it on purpose, although it can keep for several years. Best producers: Bara, Georges Vesselle, Jean Vesselle.

BURGUNDY

Côte de Nuits
Côte de Beaune } Côte d'Or
Côte Chalonnaise
Mâconnais

0   20km
0   10 miles

N̂

HAUTES-CÔTES

Dijon

Vougeot
Nuits-St-Georges

Aloxe-
Corton
Beaune
Meursault

Bouzeron   Chagny
Rully
Mercurey   Saône
Dheune

Givry   Chalon-sur-
             -Saône
Montagny

Grosne

Mancey
Tournus

Lugny
Cluny   Viré
Clessé   Saône

Mâcon
Pouilly Loché
Fuissé   Vinzelles
St-Véran

►Gevrey-Chambertin is one of the most
famous villages in Burgundy's most
celebrated wine region, the Côte d'Or,
where what we generally think of as the
finest red Burgundy is made. Like many
of the best villages, Gevrey-Chambertin
possesses a number of particularly good
vineyards, classified as *grand cru* (in this
case eight); two of them –Chambertin
and Chambertin Clos de Bèze – can be
some of the greatest red wines in the
world.

Burgundy isn't just a wine name or even a wine region. It is a vast swathe of Eastern France which at one time was a Grand Duchy reaching right up to the North Sea, way down to below Lyon and across to the mountains guarding Switzerland and Italy. At the height of its influence Burgundy was as powerful and as wealthy as the Kingdom of France which eyed it fearfully from the west. What is now left of this grandeur is some inspiring architecture – and a tradition of eating and drinking which still makes gourmets the world over describe Burgundy greedily as the belly of France.

If Burgundy is indeed 'the belly of France', we'd better be a little more specific, because I don't think the Belgians, whose country once was part of Burgundy, will take too kindly to being described as Burgundian, although they're great eaters, and still purchase much of the best Burgundy wine. No, modern Burgundy is a rather slimmed down version – if that's the word.

It begins south of Paris near Auxerre where a few pleasant reds and some sparkling rosé are made, but doesn't really get into gear until the great Côte d'Or rises to the south of Dijon. The Côte d'Or – or Golden Slope – is incredibly small – a single sliver of south- to east-facing land running from Dijon to Chagny, which is in places, only a few hundred yards wide. Yet many of the most famous wines in the world are from these barely adequate acres.

The Côte d'Or is divided into two – the Côte de Nuits in the north, and the Côte de Beaune in the south. The Côte de Nuits is almost entirely red wine country. Gevrey-Chambertin, with its great vineyard Chambertin – Napoleon's favourite wine – is the first famous village, followed to the south by Morey-St-Denis, Chambolle-Musigny, Vougeot with its famous Clos de Vougeot, Vosne-Romanée, home of Romanée-Conti, the rarest and most expensive of Burgundies – and finally Nuits-St-Georges. The Côte de Beaune grows a considerable amount of white, but also produces wonderful reds in Aloxe-Corton, Beaune, Pommard and Volnay.

The Côte Chalonnaise lacks the cohesion of the Côte d'Or – no great long carpet of vines but rather vineyards taking their place on the best south- and east-facing slopes along with meadows and other crops. It's a relaxing area, and the wines, while good, rarely set out to scale the heights.

Burgundy finishes with the vast Mâconnais, whose fame lies in white wine, but there are a few reds and rosés from Pinot Noir or Gamay, which, while not memorable, at least are affordable.

MAIN WINES
Bourgogne
Bourgogne Grand Ordinaire
Bourgogne Passe-Tout-Grains
Bourgogne Rosé
Côte de Beaune ACs
Côte de Nuits ACs
Givry
Mâcon
Mâcon Supérieur
Mercurey
Rully

MAIN GRAPES
Gamay
Pinot Noir

See also *Côte d'Or*, page 46.

BROUILLY AC
BEAUJOLAIS, BURGUNDY
Gamay

'A bottle of Brooey' doesn't sound quite serious, does it? Well, why should it? Brouilly (which is pronounced approximately as above) is the largest of the Beaujolais *crus* (or special communes allowed to use their own name on their wine), which puts it in the top rank of Beaujolais. But it's still Beaujolais: it's still made from the juicy-fruity Gamay grape; it's still supposed to make you laugh and smile – not get all serious and pre-occupied; and you're still supposed to drink it in great draughts not dainty sips.

What makes Brouilly special is that it is the closest of the *crus* to the Beaujolais-Villages style (a lot of growers make both). Geographically, it is the most southerly of the *crus*: south of Brouilly the 'Villages' and the simple 'Beaujolais' vineyards stretch as far as the eye can see away towards Lyon. The wine is very fruity and in fact can make a delicious Nouveau (several local restaurants use it in this way). There is rarely much point in ageing it. Interestingly, 1985, '86 and '87 have all made some single-estate Brouilly which has improved with ageing, but this is the exception. Best producers: la Chaize, Duboeuf (Garranche, Combillaty), Fouilloux, Hospices de Beaujeu (especially Pissevieille Cuvée), Pierreux, Ruet, Tours.

BUGEY VDQS
SAVOIE
Gamay, Pinot Noir, Mondeuse, Poulsard

Frankly, Bugey is white wine country, but they do make a fair bit of red, so here goes. Bugey is one of those delectable 'lost' areas of France – somewhere west of the Rhône where it tumbles and tears down towards Lyon from Geneva. The vineyards are small: clumps of vines on little hillsides next to villages not marked on the map – that sort of thing. Fog, too, usually. The whites can be superb. The reds – they use Gamay and Pinot Noir with Poulsard and Mondeuse. All these grapes can make good wine – elsewhere – but in Bugey they rarely ripen and have a distinct flavour of damp vineyards and vegetable patches – hidden way up some unpronounceable valley!

BUZET AC
SOUTH-WEST
Cabernet Sauvignon, Cabernet Franc, Merlot, Malbec

From being an obscure south-western *appellation* squashed into the edge of the Armagnac brandy area, south of the river Garonne, Buzet has recently achieved a most welcome notoriety simply by offering the public what it wants! They use the Bordeaux mix of grapes, and so decided to make Bordeaux look-alike wines. As the prices of Bordeaux rose in the early 1980s, Buzet produced a string of delicious, grassy-fresh, blackcurranty reds – sharp enough to be reviving, soft enough to drink as soon as they were released – and at a lower price than Bordeaux. This kind of move into a market vacuum was facilitated by the fact that 95 per cent of the production is controlled by the co-operative which, luckily, knows what it is doing. Its Cuvée Napoléon, aged in oak, is extremely good to drink at five to ten years. There is very little rosé. Château de Padère is the only major independent property.

CABERNET FRANC

Cabernet Franc is often dismissed as a kind of 'minor' Cabernet Sauvignon, but this is grossly unfair. Where Cabernet Sauvignon ripens effectively – particularly in Bordeaux's Médoc and Graves – there is no doubt that the lighter, less intense character of the Cabernet Franc is overshadowed. But in cooler areas, or in areas where the soil is damper and heavier, Cabernet Sauvignon cannot ripen properly, and here Cabernet Franc comes triumphantly into its own. The Loire is the best example. In Anjou and Touraine, not only do all the best rosés (especially Cabernet d'Anjou) come from Cabernet Franc, but all the best reds as well. The finest Anjou, Saumur and Touraine reds are likely to be Cabernet Franc (although Gamay can be used) and have a strong, grassy freshness linked to a raw but tasty blackcurrant fruit. The best examples come from Saumur-Champigny, Bourgueil and Chinon, where, in a hot vintage, the intensity of orchard-fresh, sharp but juicy, raspberry and blackcurrant fruit is delicious, and so refreshing – a quality rarely associated with fine red wine.

In the Bordeaux region, St-Emilion and Pomerol growers prefer Cabernet Franc to Cabernet Sauvignon, blending it with Merlot to add toughness and backbone to the luscious, fat Merlot fruit. Many properties have 30 per cent Cabernet Franc; two of the greatest, Ausone and Cheval-Blanc, have 50 per cent and 66 per cent respectively. In the Médoc, vineyards are more likely to have 10–20 per cent. Here the soft, yet slightly grassy flavour of the grape calms down the proud, aggressive Cabernet Sauvignon, and makes it more supple and rounded.

CABERNET SAUVIGNON

The king of red wine grapes – not just in France, but worldwide. Yet it is to France that all other countries look to understand the variety's full glory – and in particular to Bordeaux, where many of the vineyards are regarded as perfect for Cabernet Sauvignon. The heartland of Cabernet Sauvignon is the Médoc, where it can make up as much as 85 per cent of the plantings in a single property, and usually provides at least 60 per cent in the top properties. On the gravel slopes of St-Estèphe, Pauillac, St-Julien and Margaux it ripens late and produces a small yield. This restrained but concentrated harvest of loose-bunched, thick-skinned grapes gives a wine dark in colour, strong in mouth-puckering tannin, yet potentially rich in the heady flavour of pure blackcurrant with a fragrance veering between cedarwood, cigar boxes and the shavings of a newly-sharpened pencil.

This transformation from tough, broody palate-scourer to something of incomparable delicacy may take up to 20 years or more to achieve, and would take even longer if Merlot and Cabernet Franc grapes were not also used to soften and broaden the flavour. Although Cabernet Sauvignon is often grown elsewhere in the world to produce a 100 per cent varietal wine, Bordeaux winemakers always blend it, and they're right: it can be too aggressive in feel and flavour by itself.

In the Graves it is still the dominant grape, but plays a minor role in St-Émilion and Pomerol since it needs warmer, drier soil to ripen well. Similarly, it is not much planted in the Loire region because the ripening season is too cool. Most of the other red wines of the south-west use Cabernet Sauvignon in varying proportions. And in Languedoc-Roussillon it is used to 'improve' the traditional varieties. As little as ten per cent makes a major difference to a blend. However, it is on the sun-baked hillsides of Provence that many growers are trying to emulate the supreme qualities of the Médoc by planting vineyards mostly in Cabernet Sauvignon; in Baux-en-Provence they even mix it with Syrah – to memorable, juicy-rich effect!

CAHORS AC
SOUTH-WEST
Malbec (Auxerrois), Merlot, Tannat

After Bordeaux Cahors is the leading red wine of the south-west, if only because it makes no attempt to ape Bordeaux and its flavours. But then, why should it? Cahors has been famous since Roman times, and indeed was often used by Bordeaux winemakers to provide colour and fruit for what (two centuries ago) was nearer Bordeaux rosé than red. The vineyards are on both sides of the river Lot, and the whole region is about as far from hustle-bustle as can be. Only red wine is produced, with Auxerrois as the main grape (70 per cent). This is called Malbec in Bordeaux, where they don't think much of it, but in Cahors it produces dark, tannic wine which has an unforgettable flavour of plummy richness, streaked with apple acidity. As it ages, it takes on a gorgeous tangle of tastes dominated quite superbly by tobacco spice and blackberry and sweet prunes! The vineyards are on slopes, where the toughest wines come from, but also on the valley floor which produces lighter, more mainstream flavours. There is a fast-improving co-operative, but otherwise single estates are best. I recommend the following producers: les Bouysses, Cayrou, Clos la Coutale, Clos de Gamot, Clos Triguedina, Gaudou, Haute-Serre, Quattre, Treilles.

CALON-SÉGUR, CH.
St-Estèphe AC, *3ème cru classé*
HAUT-MÉDOC, BORDEAUX
Cabernet Sauvignon, Cabernet
Franc, Merlot

The most northerly of all the Médoc's Classed Growths and the lowest in altitude, averaging less than 30 feet (10 metres) above sea level. What gives it Classed Growth quality is a spur of chalky, gravelly soil – usually found on higher ground. It is a classic example of microclimate making all the difference; because none of the neighbouring properties – struggling along on heavier clay soils – can produce wine which remotely matches Calon-Ségur. It used to be thought of as St-Estèphe's leading château, along with Montrose, but both have now been overtaken by Cos d'Estournel. Until the last few vintages, Calon-Ségur's problem was that its wine, though quite impressive, has been ever so slightly dull and, at the high prices demanded by Médoc Classed Growths, dullness isn't really on. Best vintages: 1986, '85, '82 (all too young but worth laying down till at least ten years' old). Second wine: Marquis de Ségur.

CANON, CH.
St-Émilion AC, *premier grand
cru classé*
BORDEAUX
Merlot, Cabernet Franc, Cabernet
Sauvignon, Malbec

If I had to plump for the most perfect, most recognizable, most reliably luscious St-Émilion – reeking of that toffee-butter-and-raisins mellow ripeness which only Merlot can impart – I'd go for Canon. This 'buttery' sweetness could seem a little shallow and one-dimensional, but not at Canon, because the wine is also deep, with a rich plummy fruit there to ride with the butter, and in good vintages it is impressively tannic to start with. In the last few vintages Canon has been as good as any wine in St-Émilion – in fact as good as almost any in all Bordeaux. It is possible to get great pleasure from it at only a few years old, but in good vintages hang on to your bottle for a dozen years or more. Best vintages: 1985, '83, '82, '79.

CANON-FRONSAC AC
BORDEAUX
Merlot, Cabernet Franc, Cabernet Sauvignon, Malbec

◀ Château Canon-de-Brem in Canon-Fronsac; its wines are two-thirds Merlot blended with one-third Cabernet Franc.

The heart of the Fronsac region, covering 750 acres (300 hectares) of hilly vineyard between the villages of Fronsac and St-Michel de Fronsac, just set back from the flat banks of the Dordogne river. The wines have a minimum of 11 degrees alcohol as against 10·5 degrees for Fronsac, and this means they can be quite strong and beefy when young. But they do age well and, after going through a rather gamy period at a few years old, usually emerge at ten years plus with a lovely, soft Merlot-dominated flavour and a good mineral tang sometimes a little reminiscent of Pomerol. Best years: 1985, '83, '82, '79, '78. Best producers: Canon (there are two, both good), Canon-de-Brem, Haut-Mazeris, Moulin-Pey-Labrie, Vrai-Canon-Bouché, Vrai-Canon-Boyer.

CANTEMERLE, CH.
Haut-Médoc AC, *5ème cru classé*
BORDEAUX
Cabernet Sauvignon, Merlot, Cabernet Franc, Petit Verdot

You head out of Bordeaux on the D2, through the suburbs, the shrubland, the damp meadows, and the occasional vineyard, and you're just beginning to wonder if you're on the wrong road for the great wineland of the Médoc, when the forests fall away and the land is thick with rows of neatly trained vines. There, on your right, is Château la Lagune then, on your left, Château Cantemerle. Cantemerle is a jewel set inside its little woodland glade. Drive up the long avenue shrouded over with age-old trees and stand in front of the turretted castle. Silence. Stillness. Fairyland? Not far off.

Cantemerle was placed last in the 1855 Classification – perhaps because of its sheltered, unnoticed forest existence. But the wine has always been better than that, and since Cordier, the large merchant house, took over in 1980, it has improved by leaps and bounds. In general, Cantemerle is almost muskily perfumed and relatively delicate, but the 1983 is a whopper – rich, concentrated, dark yet already showing an exotic fragrance – one of the most exciting wines of the vintage. Apart from the '83, which will benefit from 15 or more years' ageing, you don't have to age Cantemerle more than seven to ten years. Best years: 1985, '83, '82, '81, '78.

CARBONNIEUX, CH.
Pessac-Léognan AC, *cru classé de Graves*
BORDEAUX
Cabernet Sauvignon, Merlot, Cabernet Franc and others

Carbonnieux is a very important property. At 175 acres (70 hectares) it is the largest in the Graves region – but it is not very satisfying because its wine always seems to lack a bit of stuffing. That might not matter if the objective was to make a fruity, quick-drinking style, but the style is quite 'serious' – dry, rather reserved and closed when young, promising to open up with some maturity. There just isn't the weight or the concentration to achieve it. A pity.

CARIGNAN

I *like* Carignan. But I seem to be in a tiny minority. It's the dominant red grape in the south of France and forms the backbone for most anonymous French *vin de table*. Yet Carignan is ideally suited to modern wine-making. Traditionally, it produced a gigantic amount of tough, fruitless wine in many of the Midi's least-favoured vineyards, and its sprawling stranglehold over much of the south was a major reason for the comparative lack of ACs between Provence and the Pyrenees.

However, there is potential for a delicious spicy fruit in the Carignan, especially when the Beaujolais method of carbonic maceration is used to make the wine. This, combined with lower yields and better ripeness levels, means that the Carignan can at least achieve respectability in the sunny south, if not exactly nobility. But who wants nobility in a bottle of cheap, juicy Mediterranean red?

CASSIS AC
PROVENCE
Grenache, Cinsaut, Mourvèdre

This is really a white wine town, and rosé and red don't figure much on the quality stakes, although they represent almost half the production. The red is dull at best; the rosé can be lovely and can age for a surprisingly long time – but only from a single estate such as Clos Ste-Magdeleine or Mas Calendal.

CERTAN-DE-MAY, CH.
Pomerol AC
BORDEAUX
Merlot, Cabernet Franc, Cabernet Sauvignon, Malbec

A tiny property of 15 acres (six hectares) situated on the very best strip of land, heavy clay mixed with a little gravel, and Certan-de-May reflects this by producing richly plummy, exciting wines. It used to make wines which aged well but were always a little dull. Since the 1980s they are never dull and will probably age beautifully – if you have the willpower not to guzzle them in their first flush of fruit.

CHAMBERTIN AC & CHAMBERTIN CLOS-DE-BÈZE AC, *grands crus*
CÔTE DE NUITS, BURGUNDY
Pinot Noir

'Chambertin, King of Wines!' is how the old-timers described this powerful *grand cru* from Gevrey-Chambertin. 'Emperor of Wines' might have been more apt since this was Napoleon's favourite tipple. They say he drank it wherever he went – Russia, Egypt, Italy. . .Waterloo? Perhaps 1815 was a bad vintage! Well, maybe, but this *can* be a hell of a wine, the biggest, most brooding of all.

In a good year the wine starts off positively rasping with power, the fruit all chewy damson skins and tarry tannin. But give it time, five years, maybe ten, or even 20, and Chambertin transforms itself. The scent is exotic and rich, fleetingly floral, but more likely to envelop you with the powerful warmth of choice damsons and plums so ripe they would long have fallen from the tree – add to this the strange brilliance of chocolate, prunes, and well-hung game – and you have one of the most remarkable flavours red wine can create.

Chambertin and Clos-de-Bèze are neighbours on the stretch of slope at just below 1000 feet (300 metres), running from Gevrey-Chambertin south to Vosne-Romanée, which produces the greatest reds in Burgundy. Both wines are basically the same, and Clos-de-Bèze can simply call itself 'Chambertin' if it wants to. There is, however, a great difference in the quality of the different producers, because overproduction, resulting in feeble wines, is a recurrent problem. But good Chambertin or Clos-de-Bèze can be *so* good it is worth persevering. Best years: 1987, '85, '83, '80, '78, '76. Best producers: Camus, Damoy, Drouhin, Ponsot, Rebourseau, Armand Rousseau, Trapet.

CHAMBOLLE-MUSIGNY AC
CÔTE DE NUITS, BURGUNDY
Pinot Noir

Chambolle-Musigny is supposed to produce the most fragrant, perfumed red wines in all Burgundy. Well, yes and no. I have had a few bottles of Chambolle-Musigny Les Amoureuses or Les Charmes which really set my heart fluttering. Ah, those names! Les Amoureuses and Les Charmes are two of the village's leading vineyards, and their suggestion of coy, flirtatious femininity – all rustling silks and fans – is what many writers claim as the character of Chambolle-Musigny wines. The fact that 'Charmes' probably derives from the French for 'straw' or 'hornbeam tree' takes a bit of the romance out of it.

Even so, the potential for beautiful wines *is* there. The vineyards are excellently situated just south of Morey-St-Denis, between 800 and 1000 feet (250 and 300 metres) up. Both the *grands crus* – Musigny and Bonnes-Mares – are capable of great things, but that haunting fragrance of crushed rose petals and ripe cherries? No, I haven't found much of that in recent vintages. Best years: 1985, '83, '78. Best producers: Drouhin, Dujac, Grivot, Hudelot-Noëllat, Jadot, Mugnier, Roumier, Serveau, de Vogüé.

CHAMPAGNE ROSÉ AC
CHAMPAGNE
Pinot Noir, Pinot Meunier, Chardonnay

Quite the most chic of fizz a year or two ago, but the demand has cooled off a bit and we can now wipe our brows and see whether it was worth all the fuss. Well, it sometimes is! Good pink Champagne has a delicious fragrance of cherries and raspberries to go with the foaming froth and is a gorgeous tongue-tingler – usually to be drunk as young as possible, though a few wines, like Pommery and Taittinger, age really well over two to three years. It's usually made by taking an ordinary white Champagne and mixing in a little still red wine – the only time *that* practice isn't frowned on in AC-conscious France. Best years: 1985, '83, '82. Best producers: Charbaut, Krug, Laurent-Perrier, Moët & Chandon, Pommery, Roederer, Taittinger Comtes de Champagne.

CHAPELLE-CHAMBERTIN AC
grand cru
CÔTE DE NUITS, BURGUNDY
Pinot Noir

A small *grand cru* on the slopes just below Chambertin Clos-de-Bèze, which owes its name to the monks of Bèze building a chapel there in 1155. It's one of the marvellous things about Burgundy that you have this sense of history all around you, and you can stand among the vines of La Chapelle or Clos-de-Bèze knowing that this little field has been producing great wines without a break for 800 years or more. It also makes sense of the rigid and seemingly nit-picking regulations regarding which plots of land – or even strips of vine – are *grand cru*, or *premier cru*, or simple village wines: they've been working out which soil is best for over 20 generations! La Chapelle is not the most impressive *grand cru* because the wines are lighter than the others, although they can have a lovely perfume. This is partly due to a difference in soil type, but it's also that La Chapelle produces more wine per acre than any of its neighbours – the old problem. Best years: 1985, '83, '80, '78. Best producers: Damoy, Trapet.

CHARENTAIS, VIN DE PAYS
SOUTH-WEST
Merlot, Cabernet Sauvignon,
Cabernet Franc, Gamay

Vin de pays designated to mop up the excess wine no longer required for a shrinking Cognac production. This sounds pretty uninspired, but in fact the wines are increasingly good. Predominantly a white wine region, nevertheless the reds are reasonably refreshing, if a little acidic.

CHARMES-CHAMBERTIN AC
grand cru
CÔTE DE NUITS, BURGUNDY
Pinot Noir

We see more of this *grand cru* than any of the others based in Gevrey-Chambertin, because this large vineyard is, at 78 acres (31·6 hectares), more than twice as big as any of the others. It *can* be superb – not quite so startlingly grand as Chambertin, but big and broad, developing more quickly to a full, soft, chocolate and raspberry sweetness. Lovely wine, but it doesn't often make your spine tingle with excitement. Also, because the name Charmes-Chambertin is beguilingly come-hither, there are a fair few producers who decide to let the vines rip and produce all that they can. Result? Not charming that's for sure. Best years: 1985, '83, '80, '78, '76. Best producers: Bachelet, Leflaive, Rebourseau, Roty, Armand Rousseau, Taupenot, and Tortochot.

CHASSAGNE-MONTRACHET AC
CÔTE DE BEAUNE, BURGUNDY
Pinot Noir

This is a white wine village, isn't it? Well, almost all the wines we see from this village *are* white, and, indeed, almost half of Burgundy's greatest white wine vineyard – Le Montrachet – is in Chassagne-Montrachet. Yet over half Chassagne's wine is actually *red*. I have never quite understood why, since the red is frequently rather jammy and uncouth, while even the simplest Chassagne white can be exquisite – and is also far more expensive. I can only assume that once a Burgundian grower has planted a vineyard in one grape variety, he's blowed if he'll switch until he's got his money's worth from what he's planted. Good red Chassagne is always a little earthy, peppery perhaps and plummy, but there are few examples when all of these are in balance. Best years: 1986, '85, '83, '82. Best producers: Bachelet-Ramonet, Carillon, Clerget, Magenta, Gagnard-Delagrange, Lequin-Roussot, Albert Morey, Ramonet-Prudhon.

CHASSE-SPLEEN, CH.
Moulis AC, *cru grand bourgeois*
exceptionnel
HAUT-MÉDOC, BORDEAUX
Cabernet Sauvignon, Merlot,
Cabernet Franc, Petit Verdot

All owners of lesser Bordeaux properties who gaze wistfully at the Classed Growths and sulk in silent envy at the prices they can charge should look at the example of Chasse-Spleen. Since the mid 1970s, this property (whose name is supposed to come from Lord Byron's claim that the wine chased away his attacks of spleen) has pursued a policy of vigorous quality control in both vineyard and winery, backed up by an astute marketing strategy. The result is that this rich, round, grandly textured wine is now more expensive than many of the lesser Classed Growths, and yet everyone thinks it is splendid value for money. I agree! Second wine: l'Ermitage de Chasse-Spleen.

CHÂTEAUMEILLANT VDQS
UPPER LOIRE
Gamay

If you can find a bottle of this outside the immediate locality, you're a better man than I am. Well, that's not quite fair (on me, that is) because I have cast a rather unenthusiastic palate over the odd bottle of red and rosé and found them rooty, vegetal and one of the least appealing manifestations of Gamay wine I can think of. If you're lost about 37 miles (60km) south of Bourges and in severe need of a thirstquencher, you could give it a go, but I think I'd have a beer.

CHÂTEAUNEUF-DU-PAPE AC
SOUTHERN RHÔNE
Grenache, Syrah, Mourvèdre and others

▲ Harvest-time on a Châteauneuf-du-Pape estate. The AC regulations for red allow 13 grape varieties, including five white ones; which can be blended in.

Châteauneuf-du-Pape is a name we all know, but I wonder how many of us have ever tried a *good* bottle? It isn't that the wine is scarce: this large vineyard area, between Orange and Avignon, covers 7400 acres (3000 hectares) and produces about one million cases every year – 97 per cent of it red. It's just that Châteauneuf-du-Pape ('the pope's new castle') used to be one of the most abused of all wine names: bottles appeared on every wine list at low prices, tasting thick, muddy and coarse. Well, things have changed. Now, the majority of Châteauneuf we drink comes from single estates – it's no longer cheap, and deservedly ranks as one of France's top wines.

Châteauneuf now has very strict AC regulations – which is apt, because it was here, in 1923, that Baron Le Roy of Château Fortia first formulated the rules which became the basis of all French AC laws. A remarkable 13 grape varieties are permitted – eight red and five white – though most growers only use half-a-dozen or so. Five per cent of the crop *must* be left on the vine at harvest – thus reducing the use of poor grapes. And the minimum alcohol level is the highest in France – 12·5 degrees. This is rarely a problem because the broad flat stones which cover the vineyard soak up the sun's heat during the day and release it at night – so the Grenache (the chief grape) often makes 14 degrees! Yield is low at 35 hectolitres per hectare.

There are two styles of Châteauneuf: a light Beaujolais-type which nonetheless has a delicious dusty warmth, juicy spice and raspberry fruit, and the big traditional style. This may need ageing for five years or more and can last for 20. It is fat, weighty, and piled high with fruit – raspberry, blackcurrant, plums – plus a chocolate-coffee-cinnamon richness and the tang of southern herbs. Acidity is low, tannin usually overwhelmed by fruit and the whole effect is a richly satisfying red especially for winter meals in the coldest months. It is *always* worth getting an estate wine, and these are now distinguished by a coat of arms embossed on the bottle above the label. Best years: 1985, '83, '81, '78 (though '84 and '80 are also very' good, if lighter). Best producers: (traditional, to age), Beaucastel, Bosquet des Papes, Chante-Cigale, Chante-Perdrix, Clos des Papes, Fortia, la Nerte, Rayas; (modern, fruitier), Brunel, Clos du Mont Olivet, Font de Michelle, Font du Loup, Grand Tinel, Quiot, Roger Sabon, Vieux Télégraphe; also good, Guigal, Jaboulet.

CHÂTILLON-EN-DIOIS AC
CENTRAL RHÔNE
Gamay, Syrah, Pinot Noir

One of the all-time obscure French ACs – not only because the wines rarely surface, but also because they're grown in a beautiful, isolated outpost on the river Drôme, tucked into the foothills of the Alps and on the road to absolutely nowhere. The village of Die is best known for its excellent Clairette de Die, a Muscat-based fizz. The reds and rosés of Châtillon-en-Diois, grown south and east of Die, are something of an afterthought. Gamay does quite well here, and is often blended with Syrah or Pinot Noir to give a fairly dark wine, quite fruity, but also extremely dry.

CHÉNAS AC
BEAUJOLAIS, BURGUNDY
Gamay

A few years ago a leading Beaujolais merchant stated that the Chénas AC should be abandoned and merged with its neighbour Moulin-à-Vent since the wines were similar anyway and they'd be easier to sell under that label. What cheek! If we pushed that train of thought, all Loire wines would be Sancerre or Muscadet, all Rhône wines would be Châteauneuf-du-Pape – and for that matter his beloved Moulin-à-Vent would disappear too, because adjacent Fleurie is better known, sounds nicer and sells for more money!

So. The facts. Chénas is the smallest of the Beaujolais *crus* and its wines, like those of Moulin-à-Vent, are usually quite tough when young, benefit enormously from two years' ageing and yet reach their peak after five years or more. They. only rarely have the gorgeous juicy fruit of young Beaujolais, but can make up for this with a deep, gently Burgundian flavour when mature – less peaches and redcurrants, more chocolate and strawberries with a lean, dry streak of earthy reserve. Best producers: Champagnon, Château de Chénas, Lapierre, Émile Robin.

CHEVAL-BLANC, CH.
St-Émilion AC, *premier grand cru classé*
BORDEAUX
Cabernet Franc, Merlot

Although Ausone (since 1978) and, to a lesser extent, Figeac contest the position, Cheval-Blanc *is* the leading property in St-Émilion, and likely to remain so for the foreseeable future. It is a large property, right on the border of Pomerol, at the end of a billowing row of gravel humps which run north from Figeac.

Cheval-Blanc derives much of the backbone that allows the wine to mature for longer than most St-Émilions, from this gravelly land; but up by the Pomerol border there are rich veins of clay, mixed with sand and iron, and it is these which give the wine its phenomenal richness and sumptuous fruit. Strangely for St-Émilion, Merlot is the minor grape, occupying only 33 per cent as against 66 per cent for Cabernet Franc. You might expect the wine therefore to lack some of the luscious Merlot fruit, but on the contrary, Cheval-Blanc is one of the grandest, most voluptuous, perfumed St-Émilions. Yet its legendary longevity may well be due to the Cabernet Franc – and those precious hillocks of gravelly soil. Best years: 1986, '85, '83, 82, '81, '80, '79, '78, '75.

CHEVERNY VDQS
CENTRAL LOIRE
Gamay, Cabernet Franc, Cabernet
Sauvignon and others

Cheverny has an absolutely splendid seventeenth-century château with a collection of 2000 antlers on display – which would imply that they're always roasting great haunches of venison and, hopefully, downing great draughts of ruddy-flavoured red wine as they warm themselves by the roaring log fire. Well, if they are, the wine won't be from Cheverny, because although they grow Gamay, Cabernet Franc, Cabernet Sauvignon and Pinot Noir, the wines never perform as well here as they do in warmer areas. They can *smell* rather good – sharp and distinct – but, in general, they taste raw and acid and might be better off marinating the venison rather than accompanying it. The rosés are a slight improvement.

CHINON AC
CENTRAL LOIRE
Cabernet Franc, Cabernet Sauvignon

The best red wine of the Loire valley. Well, the growers of Bourgueil might dispute that, but the wonderful thing about Chinon is that it is so good so young, yet can improve for five, ten, 15, even 20 years to a fragrant, ethereal shadow of the great châteaux of the Médoc, and as such is a rare and precious delight. Good Chinon is doubly precious because the Cabernet Franc grape which normally makes up all, or almost all, of the wine achieves a pure, startling intensity of fruit – the piercing acid/sweetness of blackcurrant juice pressed straight from the bush, sweetened and perfumed with a few drops of juice from ripe raspberries. I've several times bought some to age, only to try a bottle – you know, just to check how it's getting on – and end up slurping the lot because it was irresistibly delicious. Rabelais said it tasted of taffeta, but he had funny ideas about a lot of things. Best recent years: 1985, '83, '82, '78, '76. It's *always* worth buying a single-estate wine, and the best producers are Couly-Dutheil, Gouron, Joguet, Plouzeau, Olga and Jean-Maurice Raffault.

▼ The historic town of Chinon is noted for its hilltop castle and its fruity red wine – one of the top ACs in Touraine.

CHIROUBLES AC
BEAUJOLAIS, BURGUNDY
Gamay

The lightest, most delicately fragrant of the Beaujolais *crus*, and in a way the most 'Beaujolais' of them all because the wine is often little more than deep pink in colour and its perfume is full of strawberries and flowers with just a whisper of cherries. There are only two things wrong with Chiroubles really, there isn't much of it and it costs too much. There's not much wine because at 692 acres (280 hectares) it is one of the smallest of the *crus*. It's expensive because the Parisians go batty about it; restaurants queue up for the privilege of grabbing a bit. Best producers: Domaine de la Grosse Pierre, Duboeuf, Javernand, Georges Passot.

CHOREY-LÈS-BEAUNE AC
CÔTE DE BEAUNE, BURGUNDY
Pinot Noir

One of those forgotten little Burgundian villages we should be thankful for, because they mean that we can still experience the flavour of good, if not great, Burgundy, without having to mortgage the cat. The wine should not by rights be very special, as the village, with its 300 acres (120 hectares) of vineyard, is almost entirely on the flat valley land, just north of Beaune and east of the main N74 road. The general rule in the Côte d'Or is that decent wine only grows *west* of the N74, but Chorey is lucky in having several very committed property owners based there, who, although they also own much more classic land elsewhere, use their considerable skills on their local wine. Without them, Chorey-lès-Beaune wine would merely be sold as Côte de Beaune-Villages and never heard of again. Which would be a pity. Best producers: Drouhin, Jacques Germain, Goud de Beaupuis, Tollot-Beaut.

CINSAUT

A useful rather than exciting grape, Cinsaut (also spelt Cinsault) is grown all over the southern Rhône, Provence and the Midi. By itself, it gives light-coloured wine even at the best of times, with a fresh, but rather fleeting, neutral fruit. However, the one thing Cinsaut *does* have is good acidity and since Grenache acidity is low, it can act as a life-support system to the richer, spicier Grenache fruit, allowing rosés and light reds to age longer than any pure Grenache wine could manage. If it allows the delicious fruit of the Grenache to flower – I'm all for it. But by itself – no thanks!

CISSAC, CH.
Haut-Médoc AC, *cru grand bourgeois exceptionnel*
BORDEAUX
Cabernet Sauvignon, Merlot, Petit Verdot

Sometimes, tasting Cissac, you feel as if you are in a time warp. The tannin is uncompromising, the fruit dark and stubbornly withheld for many years, the flavour of wood more like the rough, resinous edge of hand-hewn pine than the soothing vanilla creaminess now fashionable. Well, it is something of an anachronism. Although not included in the 1855 Classification, it nonetheless doggedly refuses to accept the situation, and makes high quality wines for the long haul by proudly traditional methods: old vines, lots of wood everywhere, and meticulous exclusion of below par wine from the final blend. The wines of the '80s are nowhere near ready yet, the decade of the '70s are hitting their peak – while '64 and '61 are wonderful, dry, cedary claret. You'll have to ask the owner for a bottle of these last two, however.

LA CLAPE
Coteaux du Languedoc AC
LANGUEDOC-ROUSSILLON
Carignan, Cinsaut, Grenache and others

A most attractive seaside region south-east of Narbonne, distinguished by its solitary hill – the *massif*, as they call it – which creates a very effective microclimate for vines, drawing up cool breezes from the water's edge. The result – excellent whites plus good reds and rosés with the Carignan often dominant, but a fair amount of Grenache, and also Cinsaut to ease back the throttle. La Clape is now allowed to use its name along with the Coteaux du Languedoc AC on the label. Although the whites *do* age, reds and rosés are usually best young. Some growers are now experimenting to good effect with Cabernet and Merlot, although current rules condemn such wines to *vin de pays* status. Best producers: Boscary, Hue, Pech-Redon, de St-Exupéry.

CLARKE, CH.
Listrac AC, *cru bourgeois*
HAUT-MÉDOC, BORDEAUX
Cabernet Sauvignon, Merlot,
Cabernet Franc, Petit Verdot

I couldn't exactly leave this one out, could I? Still, only ten years ago I'd have had to, because Château Clarke was just a wistful Anglo-Saxon footnote in the more scholarly books on Bordeaux, and the vineyard looked more like a bomb site. OK, I'll explain. In 1973 one of the numerous Rothschilds (a certain Baron Edmond) decided to recreate from scratch this derelict has-been. He's spent millions on it, totally re-doing the vineyards and their drainage, and building imposing new installations which I first visited one dark April night. In that swamp-black hinterland – lost and two hours late for dinner – I saw a blaze of light filling the sky like some pagan cathedral of wine. I drove up like a moth drawn to flame. It was a stunning sight – sparkling new masonry, gleaming steel and reassuring piles of new oak barrels. It reeked of money and commitment, and since the 1983 vintage it shows in the wines, which have a delicious blackcurrant fruit and a warm oaky richness.

CLOS DE LA ROCHE AC, CLOS DE TART AC, CLOS DES LAMBRAYS AC & CLOS ST-DENIS AC
grands crus
CÔTE DE NUITS, BURGUNDY
Pinot Noir

It is strange that the little-known village of Morey-St-Denis should have five *grands crus* (these four and a sliver of Bonnes-Mares), whereas various far better-known villages like Nuits-St-Georges and Beaune don't have any at all. However, Morey-St-Denis suffers relative obscurity because none of its leading *grands crus* ever caught the imagination as did Chambertin of Gevrey-Chambertin or Musigny of Chambolle-Musigny.

Clos de la Roche is the best and biggest. The wine has a lovely, bright, red-fruits flavour when young which, from a grower like Dujac or Ponsot, may get chocolaty or gamy as it ages. Clos de Tart is unusual in that it is entirely owned by one firm – Mommessin, of Beaujolais fame. The wine, light and dry at first, can build up an unexpected but delicious savoury richness over the years. Clos des Lambrays was made a *grand cru* only in 1981. The quality of the vineyard soil wasn't in doubt, but the vines, averaging 70 years of age, were in disarray! New owners took it over and began renovating the estate in 1979, but it'll be a few years before the exact style of the wine becomes clear. Clos St-Denis is well-made by producers like Lignier and Dujac – red fruit browning gracefully with age – but is rarely seen. Best producers: Dujac, Lignier, Ponsot, Armand Rousseau.

CLOS DE VOUGEOT AC
grand cru
CÔTE DE NUITS, BURGUNDY
Pinot Noir

Clos in Burgundy means a vineyard enclosed by a wall, hence Clos de Vougeot is the 'walled vineyard in the village of Vougeot'. It was founded by Cistercian monks and in the fourteenth century had reached the grand size of 125 acres (50 hectares). So they put a wall round with due proprietorial pride and for more than 600 years this original boundary has stayed intact.

By all accounts Clos de Vougeot wine was then some of the best in Burgundy – but after the French revolution it became fragmented and now has over 80 owners. This multiplicity of ownership has meant it is one of the most unreliable *grand cru* Burgundies. And there's another reason. The Clos runs from the top of the Côte d'Or slope, next to the *grand cru* vineyards of Grands-Échézeaux and Le Musigny, right down to the flat, clay soil on the N74 road – only two cars' width away from dead-end land relegated to the basic *appellation* Bourgogne. Yet it is *all grand cru*. A good owner should be able to make great wine on the upper slopes, but these lower vineyards can *never* produce wine of the fragrance and beauty a *grand cru* label demands.

However, when it's good it is wonderfully soft, fleshy wine, coating your mouth with ripeness, the fruit like perfumed plums backed up by a smoky chocolate richness turning dark and exotic with age – when it's good. The château inside the Clos de Vougeot is used by the Chevaliers du Tastevin to promote the wines of Burgundy with a series of sumptuous dinners, initiation ceremonies and singsongs. It can be great fun and if you're lucky it lets you see the French at their most Irish! Best years: 1985, '83, '80, '78. Best producers: Arnoux, Confuron, Drouhin, Grivot, Gros, Jayer, Lamarche, Rebourseau.

COLLIOURE AC
LANGUEDOC-ROUSSILLON
Grenache, Mourvèdre, Carignan and others

This tiny AC is well into the Pyrenean foothills only a few miles from Spanish Catalonia, and well worth visiting, if only for the thrill of the mountain peaks tagged at their ankles with straggly vines scrambling up the rock, and for the peaceful, historic calm of the little towns-cum-fishing-ports of Collioure and Port-Vendres. The wine is throat-warming, head-spinning stuff – capable of ageing a decade but marvellously, gooily aggressive when young. Hardly seen outside the region. Best producer: Mas Blanc.

CORBIÈRES AC
LANGUEDOC-ROUSSILLON
Carignan, Cinsaut, Grenache and others

Let's get straight to the important thing – the Corbières region is one of the most captivating in France. It is a wild, wind-swept, sun-drenched marvel of stubborn hills and delving valleys, tossed beneath a wide, burning sky and framed to the far south by the snowy majesty of the Pyrenees. It's hardly surprising that consistency was never the watchword in the wines squeezed from these turbulent hillsides and, even though AC status was granted in 1985, a certain amount of the production was still excluded from it.

Carbonic maceration is on the increase, producing a high proportion of big beefy reds – based on Carignan – dusty to the taste but roaring with a sturdy juicy fruit, a whiff of spice and a slap of herbs from the hills. Excellent quality at an excellent price to drink young. The old Corbières, heavy, thick and cloddish in a burnt-jam kind of way, is less and less seen. Some producers are ageing wines in wood and these can be excellent and worth keeping for a few years. Production is around 75 million bottles. Best producers: numerous co-operatives, especially Cascastel, Embres-et-Castelmaure, Mont Tauch; also Fontsainte, les Palais, Surbézy-Cartier (Ollieux), Voulte-Gasparets.

CORNAS AC
NORTHERN RHÔNE
Syrah

The Northern Rhône's up-and-coming star. Ten years ago the Northern Rhône didn't really have *any* star, though Hermitage and Côte-Rôtie were both making splendid wine. But the ballooning prices of Burgundy and Bordeaux made wine-lovers look elsewhere for excellence. Côte-Rôtie and Hermitage are now very expensive wines. So the spotlight turned to the very south of this northern section, where the valley spreads out at Valence, and the western crags return, uncultivated and untamed, to their natural state.

Cornas is the last roar from the great Syrah grape, more a bellow than a roar, since Cornas from the thin terraces clinging doggedly to these granite cliffs can be the most massive of all Rhône reds. People used to say it was too coarse, but I don't agree. Certainly you must be *brave* to drink Cornas, but what's wrong with that? The colour when young is thick, impenetrable red, almost black in the ripest years. Swirl it, and it threatens to stain the glass. Spill it, and no dry-cleaner would accept the challenge. Young, it is tough and chunky, pummelling your mouth with tannin and sheer force of personality. So you wait, five years at least – more like ten. Then you open a bottle: the colour is still deep, but tingling with life; the smell is rich, opulent, blackcurrants and raspberries, heady, exotic; the taste is almost sweet, the fruit bursting through its tannic chains; and *there's* the roar – pure, sensuous fruit, coating your mouth, tannin too, and herbs, and deep chocolaty warmth to sear the flavour into your memory. Cornas means 'burnt earth', and burnt, charred intensity marks the best Cornas wines. Best years: 1985, '83, '80, '78. Best producers: de Barjac, Auguste Clape, Jaboulet, Juge, Michel, Verset, Voge.

CORTON AC
grand cru
CÔTE DE BEAUNE, BURGUNDY
Pinot Noir

Vines have been grown on this flat-topped hill at the northern end of the Côte de Beaune for over a thousand years. The Corton vineyards occupying the sections of the hill mostly facing south and east on red, iron-rich soil are the only red *grand cru* in the Côte de Beaune. The *grand cru* Corton now has 21 sub-divisions spanning the villages of Ladoix-Serrigny to the east, Aloxe-Corton to the south (the most important section) and Pernand-Vergelesses to the west.

I think that's spreading the great name too thin and the taste of the wine bears this out. All 21 sub-divisions can label their wine 'Corton' or use their own name in conjunction, as in Corton-Bressandes, -Clos du Roi, -Renardes and -Pougets. Ideally the wine has the burliness and savoury power of the top Côte de Nuits wines, combined with the super, more seductive perfumed fruit of Côte de Beaune, but a surprising number of examples are rather light and insipid – which is very sad. Corton should take ten years to mature; many modern Cortons never make it. Best years: 1987, '85, '83, '80, '78. Best producers: Chandon de Briailles, Chevalier, Dubreuil-Fontaine, Gaunoux, Rapet, Senard, Tollot-Beaut, Voarick.

COS D'ESTOURNEL, CH.
St-Estèphe AC, *2ème cru classé*
HAUT-MÉDOC, BORDEAUX
Cabernet Sauvignon, Merlot

Cos d'Estournel is a bit of a shock if you're driving out from Pauillac to the north, because it bears more than a passing resemblance to a Chinese temple complete with pagodas and bells. Well, that's just what Monsieur d'Estournel intended. He was a horse dealer in the early nineteenth century who traded extensively with the east, and discovered his wine improved enormously if he took it on the journey with him. So he went 'oriental' in a grand manner as a way of promoting his wine.

If 'chinoiserie' doesn't seem very apt for a leading Bordeaux wine property, don't be deceived, because Cos d'Estournel (you pronounce the 's' in Cos, just like the lettuce) is the best wine in St-Estèphe, and one of the best in all Bordeaux. Although St-Estèphe wines are generally less perfumed than those of neighbouring Pauillac because of the heavier clay soil, Cos d'Estournel makes up for this by having a high proportion of Merlot (40 per cent) and by extensive use of new oak barrels to age the wines. The result is rich, powerful flavours – cherries, blackcurrants and a rather roasted vanilla softness – which really hit you face-on. The wines usually need ten years to show really well, but then build up to a strong, concentrated mouthful, edged by tannin, but perfumed too. Cos is rarely an elegant wine but is marvellously impressive. Best years: 1986, '85, '83, '82, '81, '79, '76. Second wine: Marbuzet.

COSTIÈRES DU GARD AC
LANGUEDOC-ROUSSILLON
Carignan, Grenache, Syrah and others

A large, unmemorable swathe of land running from Nîmes towards Montpellier. I find the reds usually have too much of a meaty, earthy flavour to be that enjoyable, and prefer the rosés – which, if you get them really young, can have more spice and style than many of the Mediterranean pinks.

COTEAUX CHAMPENOIS AC
CHAMPAGNE
Pinot Noir, Pinot Meunier

A surprisingly recent AC (1974) for the still wines of Champagne. They can be red or rosé, but usually pretend to be red. However, these Champagne grapes, even when fully ripe, don't have a lot of colour or sugar so with few exceptions (usually from the villages of Bouzy or Ay) the wine is pale and rather harsh, though it often has a beguiling fresh strawberry or cherry scent. Interestingly, Coteaux Champenois can age a long time. I've had ten-year-old bottles, frail and insubstantial, a kind of chalky seam running through the flavour of the wine, which still had a fetching wistful perfume to them.

COTEAUX D'AIX-EN-PROVENCE AC
PROVENCE
Grenache, Cabernet Sauvignon, Syrah and others

This is the area that broke the mould in the south of France, because it was the first area to acknowledge that Cabernet Sauvignon, the great Bordeaux grape, can enormously enhance the local varieties of Grenache, Cinsaut, Mourvèdre and Carignan, yet it wasn't until 1985 that Coteaux d'Aix gained its AC, purely owing to prejudice against Cabernet Sauvignon.

Some quite good fresh rosé is made, but the best wines are red, and they can have a maximum of 60 per cent Cabernet Sauvignon. I would say the wines are good but could do better, because some enterprising Côtes de Provence estates, as well as many in the nearby Coteaux des Baux-en-

Provence, are achieving richer, more succulent fruit flavours in their wines. Many Coteaux d'Aix wines are marred by a slightly intrusive, earthy toughness – which can be a problem with Côtes de Provence, too. The wines can age, but it's better to catch them quite young with their fruit intact. Production is about 14 million bottles, of which 95 per cent is red or rosé. Best producers: Bas, Beaupré, Fonscolombe, Seuil, Vignelaure.

COTEAUX DE L'ARDÈCHE, VIN DE PAYS
SOUTHERN RHÔNE
Gamay, Syrah, Cabernet Sauvignon and others

▼ The Ardèche, with its rugged rockscapes, is producing good country wines, many of them varietal – Gamay, Syrah, Merlot.

I can't be sure whether my enthusiasm for the Ardèche was kindled by the fact that a steam railway runs from Tournon up to the heavenly hill town of Lamastre, or by the fact that in the value-for-money stakes the region is just about unbeatable. Add to all this the fact that the Ardèche is a wild mountainous paradise, west of the seething Rhône valley, and you have my idea of the perfect place to get away from it all.

The wine comes under the general title of Vin de Pays des Coteaux de l'Ardèche. This applies primarily to the area south of Privas where the large co-operative groups are models of how such organizations should operate. Instead of sticking to lacklustre local grapes, they have planted top varieties like Syrah, Gamay and Cabernet Sauvignon and have succeeded in producing some of France's best-priced and most delicious country wines.

COTEAUX DE PEYRIAC, VIN DE PAYS
LANGUEDOC-ROUSSILLON
Grenache, Carignan, Syrah and others

The most prolific French *vin de pays* covering roughly the same area as Minervois and producing as much as 35 million bottles of wine a year, 99 per cent of which is red or rosé. Although the traditional grapes of the region are widely grown, this *vin de pays* has been one of the leaders in adopting more northern 'classic' grapes. Cabernet Sauvignon, Cabernet Franc and Merlot, in particular, have been planted, primarily at the insistence of the giant Chantovent group.

COTEAUX DE PIERREVERT
VDQS
SOUTHERN RHÔNE
Grenache, Cinsaut, Carignan and others

One of the highest vineyard areas in France (the locals call it *the* highest) – wild, remote and extremely relaxing. The wines are simple and unambitious – but I can think of worse ways of spending the time than sipping a mouthful of the ice-chilled rosé while watching the sun go down over the magnificent Montagne de Lubéron!

COTEAUX DES BAUX-EN-PROVENCE
Coteaux d'Aix-en-Provence AC
PROVENCE
Grenache, Syrah, Cabernet Sauvignon

◄ Provence has been making wine for over 2500 years, ever since Phoenician settlers first introduced the vine to this sun-baked land.

Technically part of the Coteaux d'Aix-en-Provence AC, this is the most exciting new area in the south of France. It's a weird place, though – wild, rock-strewn, unwelcoming. Still, the welcome is in the wines, which can be the best reds and rosés in the south. Fruit is what marks them out, and incredible softness – incredible because the wines are well-structured, full and balanced, and are ideally suited to ageing for several years; yet even when young they seem to soothe your palate and calm your thoughts. The most important grape is the Syrah, which here gets into its joyous, fruit-first mood. The leading estate, Domaine de Trévallon, mixes Syrah with Cabernet Sauvignon – to sensational effect. The AC authorities have decided in their 'wisdom' to down-grade Trévallon, the area's one world-class wine, to *vin de pays* for this heretical improvement with Cabernet. I need hardly add my views on bureaucratic airheads like these. Best producers: Mas de la Dame, Mas de Gourgonnier, Mas de Ste-Berthe, Terres Blanches, Trévallon.

COTEAUX DU GIENNOIS
VDQS
UPPER LOIRE
Gamay, Pinot Noir

This little VDQS's claim to be one of France's most obscure wines is considerably enhanced by the fact that you turn up at Gien, a little town on the Loire about 30 miles (50km) to the north of Sancerre, and no-one seems to know anything about it. So you retrace your steps back south and arrive at Cosne with your thoughts already firmly fixed on a nice cool glass of Sancerre – but alas, you'll have to wait. Your eyes spy the odd scattered vine, and your unenthusiastic inquiries elicit the fact the these are the vineyards of Coteaux du Giennois. In fact, there are a couple of vines at Gien, but most are at Cosne – white Sauvignon, and red Gamay and Pinot Noir, producing about 500,000 bottles of entirely forgettable wine.

COTEAUX DU LANGUEDOC AC
LANGUEDOC-ROUSSILLON
Carignan, Cinsaut, Grenache and others

A recent, but large and increasingly successful AC running across the south of France – approximately from Montpellier to Narbonne. There are 121 villages in the *appellation*, producing about 12 million bottles of red, white and rosé. Although the wines used to have, at best, a rather solid, sturdy kind of fruit, things are now on the move, and it is this area which some experts reckon could be the 'California' of the 1990s. They look forward to a flood of fresh, fruity wines at affordable prices as bad vineyards disappear, better grapes are planted, and up-to-date wine-making techniques are adopted.

I agree, and think the wines will actually be a good deal better than those of California's Central Valley, more closely resembling the highly drinkable bulk wines of Australia. In a new 'incentive and reward' approach to improving quality, 11 leading villages can now add their own names to Coteaux du Languedoc. Best of these are Cabrières, La Clape, Montpeyroux, Pic St-Loup, St-Drézéry and St-Georges-d'Orques. Some of these villages now use oak barrels to mature the best reds, and these can age for several years, though most reds and rosés are best drunk young.

COTEAUX DU LYONNAIS AC
BURGUNDY
Gamay

Good light reds and a few rosés from the area between Villefranche and Lyon. It became an AC in 1984 and, although pretty large, only a million or so bottles are produced annually. A first cousin to simple Beaujolais, the wine is light, quite fruity and very pleasant chilled young, but not too demanding on the old grey matter.

COTEAUX DU TRICASTIN AC
SOUTHERN RHÔNE
Grenache, Syrah, Cinsaut and others

You have to approve of a wine region which shares its promotional headquarters with a truffle-hunters' organization – the 'House of the Truffle and of Tricastin' – it even has a truffle exhibition! This large Rhône area was only created in the 1960s to cater for a flood of displaced wine-growers fleeing from North Africa when Algeria gained its independence. They became VDQS in 1964, and AC in 1974. Right from the start the wines have been good because the new settlers introduced modern methods – formulated to cope with the desert conditions in Africa – on to good virgin vineyard land. Reds and rosés are often quite light, but very fresh, having an attractive juicy fruit livened up with some peppery spice – and rarely marred by excess of tannin or acid. Basically, all the wines should be drunk within three years. Best producers: Grangeneuve, Lônes, Tour d'Elyssas (especially a pure Syrah Cuvée).

COTEAUX DU VENDÔMOIS VDQS
LOIRE
Pineau d'Aunis, Gamay, Pinot Noir and others

One of those miniscule Loire country wines that one is glad to see surviving at all, but which doesn't exactly cause one to dash down to the off-licence in feverish anticipation when the whisper goes round they've got a bottle in. Well, the whisper wouldn't go round. The 50 acres (20 hectares) of vines near the Loir river 25 miles (40km) north of Tours produce hardly enough red and rosé for the locals, let alone export. When the Pineau d'Aunis grape predominates the result can be light, dry and refreshing. Too much Gamay, or indeed Pinot Noir, Cabernet Franc and Cabernet Sauvignon – the other permitted grape varieties – rather spoils it.

COTEAUX VAROIS VDQS
PROVENCE
Grenache, Cinsaut, Mourvèdre and others

A large area to the north of Toulon, and nudging Côtes de Provence to the east, which was promoted to VDQS in 1985. This was largely because a lot of growers were making great efforts, especially with new plantings of Cabernet Sauvignon and Syrah, to upgrade their quality. Good for them! Best estates: Clos de la Truffière, Deffends, St-Estève, St-Jean.

CÔTE CHALONNAISE
BURGUNDY

It's easy to see why the Côte Chalonnaise is the least known of the Burgundy regions. All the other regions have their names enshrined at very least in their overall ACs – Chablis, Côte de Nuits, Côte de Beaune, Mâcon and Beaujolais – but did you ever see AC Côte Chalonnaise? No. There isn't one. Add to that the fact that the region doesn't have any world-famous wines, whereas all the others are thick with them, and the fact that the area considers itself unfairly excluded from the renowned Côte de Beaune. You can almost understand the growers feeling miffed but, frankly, the Côte de Beaune does apply to a single swathe of vines along one single slope of land and the Chalonnaise vineyards are on a different slope. In fact, there isn't a single slope at all here; the hills twist and turn, valleys form and peter out, forests crowd the meadows and vineyards fight for space. It's a different, more traditionally rural world where the vine is merely one part of the texture of rustic life.

Altogether there are five villages with their own ACs in the 15 miles (24km) running south from Chagny. Most northerly is Bouzeron, with its own AC for Aligoté wine since 1979. Over the Montagne de la Folie is Rully, originally known for its sparkling wine but now producing light yet very attractive reds and whites. A run through the woods then takes you to Mercurey, the biggest AC with over 1500 acres (600 hectares). Famous for red wines, its whites are now increasingly good. Four miles (6km) south is Givry with only 300 acres (120 hectares) of vines, but the only Chalonnaise wine to bask in notoriety as yet – Henri IV drank a particularly 'enthusiastic' amount of it and many labels still commemorate this fact. And in the south is Montagny, an all white AC – which is a pity because the neighbouring village of Buxy makes very good red which for some reason only qualifies as simply AC Bourgogne. The growers are lobbying for a more specific AC and they deserve to succeed.

CÔTE DE BEAUNE
CÔTE D'OR, BURGUNDY

The southern part of Burgundy's great Côte d'Or, centred round the town of Beaune. After a quiet start at Ladoix-Serrigny, the Côte de Beaune shoots into top gear at Aloxe-Corton where the great hill of Corton butts into the valley. After this famous villages mingle with the less famous right down to south of Santenay, where the slope suddenly fades away to the west. In general, the best-known wines, Beaune, Volnay, Meursault, come from sites on the broad east-facing slopes, while the less well-known wines – Savigny-lès-Beaune, Monthelie, St-Aubin and so forth, come from little side valleys. Corton is the only red *grand cru*, although *all* the great white *grands crus* of the Côte d'Or are in the Côte de Beaune. The style of reds is softer, more immediately attractive than in the Côte de Nuits, becoming rich and perfumed sooner; but good wines easily last a decade, sometimes two.

CÔTE DE BEAUNE AC
CÔTE D'OR, BURGUNDY
Pinot Noir

There is a Côte de Beaune AC. This covers a couple of vineyard sites around the town of Beaune and is very rare. The wine is usually very dry to start, but does have a good lean fruit which can be delicious at two to three years old. Best producers: Bouchard Père & Fils, Chantal Lescure, Labouré-Roi.

CÔTE DE BEAUNE-VILLAGES AC
CÔTE D'OR, BURGUNDY
Pinot Noir

The general *appellation* covering wine from 16 villages on the Côte de Beaune. These villages have the right to use their own names, but, since some of them are not well-known, merchants may prefer to blend several wines together to sell under the Côte de Beaune-Villages label. This used to be one of the commonest Burgundy *appellations* in the export market, markedly superior to straight Bourgogne Rouge, and having a good deal of the class of some single-village Côte de Beaune wines. But nowadays, even villages like Pernand-Vergelesses, Monthelie and Auxey-Duresses confidently sell wine under their own name and, to be honest, what's left over for Côte de Beaune-Villages usually tastes as though they really had to scrape the barrel to make up the blend.

CÔTE DE BROUILLY AC
BEAUJOLAIS, BURGUNDY
Gamay

One of the Beaujolais *crus* we see least of – perhaps because we see a great deal of Brouilly. Well, that's a pity; the Côte de Brouilly is a volcanic mound rising to 1650 feet (500 metres) in the middle of the Brouilly AC and, because of its steep slopes, the sun ripens the grapes more fully than on the flatter vineyards. This is reflected by the fact that the minimum alcohol requirement for Côte de Brouilly is higher than for any other *cru*. And that extra sun produces a full, juicy, strawberry-and-peach ripeness – a sort of 'super-Brouilly', which is good young, but can age beautifully for several years. Best years: 1987, '86, '85, '83. Best producers: Conroy (Duboeuf), Geoffray, Sanvers, Thivin, Verger.

CÔTE DE NUITS
CÔTE D'OR, BURGUNDY

This is the geographical description of the northern part of Burgundy's great Côte d'Or. It is *not* an AC. Nuits-St-Georges is the main town of this narrow stretch of east- and south-east-facing vineyards which starts in the southern suburbs of Dijon and ends just below the 'pink marble' quarries of Corgoloin and Comblanchien. Between these two points are villages with some of the greatest wine names of France – Gevrey-Chambertin, Vougeot, Chambolle-Musigny, Vosne-Romanée, Nuits-St-Georges itself. I still get a thrill driving down the N74 to see these names slapped on an ordinary signpost without the slightest romance, yet every time I read the names, see the huddled houses surrounded by their sweep of vineyards, and hear the rustle of vine leaves playing in the breeze, my heart beats just a little faster. The Côte de Nuits is almost entirely red wine country, although a little rosé is made at Marsannay in the north.

CÔTE D'OR

The Côte d'Or is Europe's northernmost great red wine area. The name, meaning 'Golden Slope', refers to one single narrow stretch of vines in Burgundy, starting just south of Dijon, and fading out 30 miles (48km) later west of Chagny. It is divided into two sections. The Côte de Nuits in the north encompasses little more than 3460 acres (1400 hectares) of vines, since the slope is often only a few hundred yards wide, and at the Clos Arlot in Nuits-St-Georges it measures less than 700 yards (640 metres) in width!

The Côte de Beaune is the southern section. Beginning at the hill of Corton, it twists and turns a little more than the Côte de Nuits. Beaune is the main town, and as the Côte progresses southwards past Volnay, white takes over from red as the most exciting wine style, until red briefly reasserts itself at Santenay. The less abrupt slopes of the Côte de Beaune possess 7410 acres (3000 hectares) of vines, but again, that isn't a lot of vineyard.

The soil of the Côte d'Or is a mix of clay, marl and limestone. Where the marl is dominant red wines are produced from the Pinot Noir; where the limestone takes over white wines from Chardonnay are best. In the Côte de Nuits where the marl is more prevalent, the slopes are steepest, so the richness of the soil is offset by particularly efficient drainage. In the Côte de Beaune the slopes are gentler, which is fine because in all the best sites, easy-draining limestone is much in evidence.

Over the centuries the best sites have consistently ripened earlier than those too high up the slope or on flatter ground at the bottom. So a minutely accurate system of vineyard classification has evolved. Top of the pile are the *grands crus*, which are allowed to use only the vineyard name. These are almost always at between 820 and 985 feet (250 and 300 metres) in elevation, and facing between south and east. Slightly less well-situated vineyards are accorded *premier cru* status. Their wines should still be excellent, if a little lighter than those of the *grands crus*. Vineyards on the bottom of the slope are less favoured and will usually have the right simply to the village name.

▼ Winter vines at Clos de Vougeot in the village of Vougeot on the Côte de Nuits. Founded by monks in the Middle Ages, Clos de Vougeot is one of Burgundy's best-known *grands crus*.

MAIN WINES	Côte de Nuits-Villages	Pernand-Vergelesses
Aloxe-Corton	Dezize-lès-Maranges	Pommard
Auxey-Duresses	Échézeaux	Richebourg
Beaune	Fixin	la Romanée-Conti
Blagny	Gevrey-Chambertin	Ruchottes-Chambertin
Bonnes-Mares	Grands-Échézeaux	St-Aubin
Chambertin	Griotte-Chambertin	St-Romain
Chambolle-Musigny	Hautes-Côtes de Beaune	Santenay
Chapelle-Chambertin	Hautes-Côtes de Nuits	Savigny-lès-Beaune
Charmes-Chambertin	Ladoix-Serrigny	la Tâche
Chassagne-Montrachet	Latricières-Chambertin	Volnay
Chorey-lès-Beaune	Marsannay	Volnay-Santenots
Clos de la Roche	Mazis-Chambertin	Vosne-Romanée
Clos de Vougeot	Meursault	Vougeot
Corton	Monthelie	
Côte de Beaune	Morey-St-Denis	MAIN GRAPES
Côte de Beaune-Villages	Musigny	Pinot Noir
Côte de Nuits	Nuits-St-Georges	

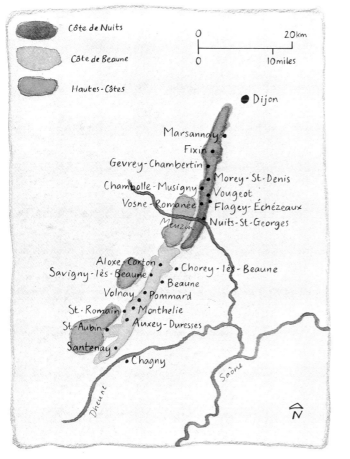

47

CÔTE DE NUITS-VILLAGES AC
CÔTE DE NUITS, BURGUNDY
Pinot Noir

An *appellation* specific to Corgoloin, Comblanchien and Prissey in the south of the Côte de Nuits, and Brochon and Fixin in the north. Fixin wines may also be sold under their own name. The 750 acres (300 hectares) of vines usually produce almost one million bottles, overwhelmingly red. Although not much seen, the wines are often good, not very deep, but with a good cherry fruit, and an attractive resin-bitter edge which can go smooth and chocolaty with age – Côte de Nuits flavours in miniature. Best years: 1985, '83, '80, '78. Best producers: Durand, Julien, Rion, Rossignol, Tollot-Voarick.

CÔTE ROANNAISE VDQS
UPPER LOIRE
Gamay, Pinot Noir

The Côte Roannaise straddles the upper reaches of the Loire river, but the nearest large town is Lyon, capital of Beaujolais, and Roanne does lean towards Beaujolais rather than the Loire. The principal grape is the Gamay, and almost all the wine is red, going from the wispy, but fresh and fruity, to big chocolaty numbers which quite resemble Morgon on a good day. In general, drink them very young, though the Domaine Lapandéry will age for some time. Best producers: Chaucesse, Chargros, Lapandéry, Lutz.

CÔTE-RÔTIE AC
NORTHERN RHÔNE
Syrah, Viognier

Côte-Rôtie – the 'roasted slope' – is the most northerly Rhône vineyard and definitely one of the oldest – it is reckoned there have been vines on these slopes for 24 centuries! Yet it is only very recently that wine-drinkers have realized that this is one of France's greatest red wines – the Syrah grape baking itself to super-ripeness on these steep south-east-facing slopes. What marks Côte-Rôtie out from the heftier Rhône reds like Hermitage is its fragrance, an exotic perfume quite unexpected in a red wine. This is because a little of the heavenly-scented white Viognier grape is allowed in the vineyard (up to 20 per cent, though 5–10 per cent is more likely). The result is damson-juicy, raspberry-sweet, sometimes with a hint of apricot skins and pepper. Lovely young, it is much better aged for ten years. The two best slopes are called Côte Brune and Côte Blonde; they are usually blended but you *may* see the name on a label. Best years: 1985, '83, '82, '80, '78. Best producers: Champet, Dervieux-Thaize, Guigal, Jaboulet, Jasmin, Rostaing, Vidal-Fleury.

CÔTES D'AUVERGNE VDQS
UPPER LOIRE
Gamay, Pinot Noir

The local wine of Clermont-Ferrand. Since this is a large, bustling city pulsating with heavy industry, you'd want your local red to be a good glugger – and it is. Based on the Gamay, with a little Pinot Noir, the red is usually bright, cherry-flavoured and very easy to drink nice and young; the rosé (about 25 per cent of production) extremely pale, slightly sharp but very refreshing when drunk cool. There are 54 villages making the wine, totalling about 2·5 million bottles, and some, making slightly fuller wines, can add their own name.

CÔTES DE BOURG AC
BORDEAUX
Merlot, Cabernet Franc, Cabernet Sauvignon, Malbec

Château Margaux, Château Palmer, and all the other luminaries of the Médoc big-time are just a tantalizing mile or two away on the other side of the Gironde, yet Bourg shares none of their glory. These seemingly perfectly placed vineyard slopes – with such an excellent southerly aspect that the Romans exploited them – are one of Bordeaux's forgotten areas, struggling to regain a place in the sun. Côtes de Bourg is an enclave inside the larger Blaye area; its sloping vineyards are mostly clay, but there is enough gravel to ripen the Cabernet Sauvignon, and the good local co-operative at Tauriac and leading properties are beginning to use new oak as they strive to upgrade their wine. They deserve to succeed. The wines are quite full, fairly dry, but with a pleasant blackcurrant fruit which ensures the earthy *terroir* doesn't dominate; and when they are splashed with the spice of new oak, they can age to a delicious maturity at six to ten years old. Best years: 1985, '83, '82. Best producers: de Barbe, du Bousquet, Haut-Guiraud, Haut-Rousset, la Croix-Millorit, Tauriac co-operative.

CÔTES DE CASTILLON
Bordeaux Supérieur Côtes de Castillon AC
BORDEAUX
Cabernet Sauvignon, Cabernet Franc, Merlot, Malbec

On the Dordogne to the east of St-Émilion is the little town of Castillon-la-Bataille, where defeat at a crucial battle in 1453 lost the English control of Aquitaine – and their supply of Bordeaux wine. We didn't hear much about Castillon after that until the 1980s, when the prices of decent red Bordeaux became so loony that we began casting about for a few understudies while we waited for the primadonnas of the Médoc to calm down. Well, they still haven't calmed down, and the 'replacement' wines are consolidating their reputation with every vintage.

Côtes de Castillon is one of two red Bordeaux Supérieurs (the other is Côtes de Francs) allowed to add its own name on the label. It manages to be more special than simple Bordeaux Rouge, because the vineyards impart flavours of mint, blackcurrant and cedar to the wine – in miniature maybe, but these are the flavours which made the Médoc famous.

They use a high proportion of Merlot – which makes wine more immediately attractive – and some estates now use new oak barrels to age the wine; it is never expensive, but delicious at three to ten years old – depending on the vintage. One feature of Côtes de Castillon wines is that they can be especially good in less ripe vintages. Best years: 1986, '85, '83, '82, '81. Best châteaux: Beau-Séjour, Belcier, Fonds-Rondes, les Hauts de Granges, Moulin-Rouge, Parenchère, Pitray.

CÔTES DE DURAS AC
SOUTH-WEST
Cabernet Franc, Cabernet Sauvignon, Merlot, Malbec

The growers of Côtes de Duras could justifiably feel aggrieved at the legislation fixing AC boundaries. Bordeaux AC covers wines in the Gironde *département*. Côtes de Duras is in Lot-et-Garonne, and so is excluded – despite the fact that it's a close neighbour and only a chartered surveyor could tell where one stops and the other starts.

The result is happy for the consumer, however, because the Côtes de Duras has spawned a very active co-operative movement, which offers extremely good, fresh, grassy reds from traditional Bordeaux grapes, at distinctly lower prices. Drink them young and fresh, though they do have the ability to age if you mislay the odd bottle for a few years. Best years: 1986, '85. Best producers: Conti, Cours, Ferrant, Laulan, co-operatives at Duras and Landerrouat.

CÔTES DE FRANCS
Bordeaux Supérieur Côtes de Francs AC
BORDEAUX
Merlot, Cabernet Sauvignon, Cabernet Franc, Malbec

Now this is *really* something special – so special you can't even find it in most wine atlases – a tiny little area on the eastern fringe of St-Émilion which is going to startle the Bordeaux know-alls in the next decade. Centred on the tiny village of Francs, it is a region of rolling hills, ancient copses and richly verdant meadows. Farmhouses are tumbledown and inviting, cattle doze in the fields, the whole impression is of a rather sleepy, forgotten rural backwater, somewhere to rest and idle away the days. But behind this dreamy facade forces are at work.

Côtes de Francs, this little area with good clay and limestone soil, often on fairly steep slopes, has the warmest and driest microclimate in Bordeaux. It used to be part of St-Émilion but was thrown out when they finalized the St-Émilion AC in the 1920s; for three generations the area stagnated. Then the sons of the famous Cheval-Blanc and Vieux Château-Certan (in neighbouring St-Émilion and Pomerol), eager to spread their wings away from the older generation's influence, saw the amazing potential of the land, bought properties, and began to make wine.

Even the first vintages show that its potential is immense – closely controlled yields plus the use of new oak barrels give the wines a remarkable concentration of fruit; deep plum and blackberry flavours, strengthened by tannin and oak spice. As the vineyards mature the wines will improve with every vintage. Best vintages: 1986, '85, '83. Best producers: la Claverie, de Francs, du Moulin-la-Pitié, Puygueraud.

CÔTES DE GASCOGNE, VIN DE PAYS
SOUTH-WEST
Tannat, Merlot, Cabernet Sauvignon, Cabernet Franc

As the production of Armagnac went into decline during the 1970s, more attention was given to turning the raw base wine into a more pleasant commodity. The majority of the wine is white, but there is a certain amount of rather sharp red – initially from the east of the Armagnac region near Auch but increasingly from the better vineyards in the centre and to the south. The wines should be drunk cool and young. Best producers: Grassa, Plaimont co-operative.

CÔTES DE PROVENCE AC
PROVENCE
Mourvèdre, Grenache, Syrah and others

A few years ago I would have agreed wholeheartedly with the traditionalists who grumbled that Côtes de Provence was grossly overpriced *vin ordinaire*, and deemed Hugh Johnson's verdict – that the reds were like 'tarpaulin edged with lace' – quite brilliant in its horrid accuracy. The reds were fruitless and cloddish and the rosés austere and *far* too alcoholic.

Thank goodness things are changing, because Provence is such a hauntingly beautiful region I feel deprived when the wine doesn't come up to scratch. As far as we can tell the wine *was* up to scratch in Roman times, and an increasing number of small estates, as well as a couple of co-op groups, are now rediscovering the magic in this soil. Rosés are becoming fruitier, and reds are emerging which, along with the powerful pine, thyme and rosemary perfumes of the rugged sun-soaked hillsides, are now displaying other scents (myrtle is one) as well as the one component previously lacking – fruit.

New plantations of Cabernet Sauvignon, Syrah and Mourvèdre are primarily responsible, as are cooler fermentations and restricted yields. This is good news because, though the wines from this large 45,000-acre (18,000-hectare) vineyard – spreading across the coast from past Toulon in the west to

Ste-Maxime in the east and inland to beyond La Motte – have never been cheap, Provence's romantic overtones have 'seduced' people into buying them. An increasing number of wines are now quite good value for money! Vintages do matter in Provence, but basically drink the reds young and rosés *very* young. Best producers: Barbeyrolles, Berne, Commanderie de Peyrassol, Féraud, Gavoty, les Maîtres Vignerons de St-Tropez, Minuty, Ott, Pampelonne, Rimauresq, St-Maur.

◄ Sunflowers and vines colour the Armagnac landscape. The Côtes de Gascogne AC covers all of the Gers *département*.

Some properties use the title *grand cru classé*. This is an old, informal grouping of the self-styled leading properties and is largely irrelevant nowadays.

CÔTES DE ST-MONT VDQS
SOUTH-WEST
Tannat, Cabernet Sauvignon, Cabernet Franc, Merlot

An increasingly good producer of quite sharp but intensely fruity reds and some fair rosé, from a hilly region just to the south of Armagnac and bordering Madiran. If anything the reds are like a lighter version of Madiran, easier to drink young and less tannic. Best producer: the go-ahead co-op group, the Union de Producteurs Plaimont, whose St-Mont wine is now clearly of AC quality.

CÔTES DE TOUL VDQS
ALSACE
Gamay, Pinot Noir, Pinot Meunier

Côtes de Toul doesn't *really* merit a mention, but I have twice turned off the autoroute in north-east France and scoured the wind-swept landscape for a vineyard or two – and discovered a sweet little wine route through just 160 acres (65 hectares) of vines. When I finally tasted a few examples of the very pale rosé, *vin gris*, made from Gamay I actually liked its sharp, lean, but refreshing style. So if you happen to be passing the town of Nancy around lunchtime, the *vin gris*, or even the wispy red Pinot Noir, can make a very pleasant picnic diversion.

CÔTES DU FOREZ VDQS
UPPER LOIRE
Gamay

A kind of mini-Beaujolais, 375 acres (150 hectares) of vines just over the hills from Lyon. The Gamay is the only grape, and most of the wine is red. When the weather is good, the result is a delicious, wispy, cherry and strawberry wine, hardly red enough to stain a napkin, living like a mayfly on its brief summer-surge of simple fruit and fading as the new vintage beckons. That's the good news. In poor years, the wine is just too light and mean and has a raw astringency which requires a hearty plate of Lyonnais *rillettes* to blot it out.

CÔTES DU FRONTONNAIS AC
SOUTH-WEST
Negrette, Cabernet Sauvignon, Cabernet Franc and others

One of the most original red wine flavours in south-west France. The vineyard area isn't very big, clustered round Toulouse on dry, sun-soaked slopes. Negrette is the chief grape and the wine can be superb, positively silky in texture – *very* rare in a red wine – and combining a juicy fruit like raspberry or strawberry, coated in cream, with a lick of anise. They drink almost all of it in Toulouse – sensible fellows – but a little is exported and is well worth seeking out. It is drinkable almost immediately, but can age, although I prefer it in its full flush of youth.

There's a little rosé – good but not *so* good. Best producers: Baudare, Bellevue-la-Forêt, la Colombière, Flotis, Laurou, Montauriol, la Palme.

CÔTES DU JURA AC
JURA
Poulsard, Trousseau, Pinot Noir

The Jura never seems totally dry. Even in the height of summer – with the sun full on these high mountains, meadows and vineyards – there is something refreshing in the air and the ground is faintly damp to the touch. The area is wonderfully relaxing, often hemmed in by forest, always shadowed by the Jura mountain range, and sometimes affording spectacular vistas across the Saône valley to Burgundy.

It would be nice to report that such a mountain paradise had nectar-like wines, but the reds and rosés are rarely special – and often aggressively weird. Côtes du Jura is the general AC but applies in particular to the southern part of the vineyard region, and can produce some lighter red and rosé from the Trousseau and Poulsard grapes which are not too savage, while the Pinot Noir can yield rather good light, perfumed reds. Poulsard also produces a *very* pale pink, *vin gris*. Total production is 1·5m bottles, only 20 per cent of it red or rosé. Best producers: Arlay, Bourdy, Gréa.

CÔTES DU LUBÉRON AC
SOUTHERN RHÔNE
Grenache, Syrah, Cinsaut and others

A lovely lost area to the east of Avignon and north of Aix, running along the Durance valley and sharing the land with the asparagus crops. The whole landscape is dominated by the Montagne du Lubéron and its wine is dominated by co-operatives who produce light, easy reds and rosés to drink as young as possible. However, the recently created Domaine Val Joanis is intent on making more memorable wines, though still for young drinking, and first results are very tasty. Château de l'Isolette red is absolutely delicious.

CÔTES DU MARMANDAIS VDQS
SOUTH-WEST
Abouriou, Fer, Cabernet Sauvignon and others

Another 'me-too' Bordeaux look-alike close to the Entre-Deux-Mers region, but in the Lot-et-Garonne *département*. However, the potential is for a red wine with a definably non-Bordeaux flavour because Bordeaux varieties make up only half or less of the grape mix. Ninety-five per cent of the production comes from two co-ops, of which the Cocumont examples are the better. Price is low, and, so far, the wines are pleasant and light with a Cabernet-influenced flavour.

CÔTES DU RHÔNE AC
SOUTHERN RHÔNE
Grenache, Cinsaut, Syrah and others

Although this general AC covers the whole viticultural Rhône valley – from just south of Lyon at Vienne all the way down to below Avignon – most of the wine comes from the broad southern section of the valley between Montélimar and Avignon. This region is called the Côtes du Rhône Méridional, and is one of the great grape baskets of France. The chief grape is the Grenache, followed by Cinsaut, Syrah, Carignan and Mourvèdre; the last three in particular have lots of warm spicy southern personality to offer to the rich, heady flavours of Grenache.

Côtes du Rhône AC applies to over 80 per cent of the Rhône valley's wines, and over 90 per cent of these are red and rosé. They used to be marked by a rather heavy, jammy fruit and a rough, herby perfume (which the charitable said reminded them of the high, herb-fragrant mountain slopes to the east and the less charitable said didn't – at all). Modern techniques – temperature control, stainless steel installations, some carbonic maceration – have revolutionized the wine style, and Côtes du Rhône nowadays should be juicy, spicy, raspberry-fruited, sometimes almost light as Beaujolais, sometimes juicier and rounder, but as a rule mouth-filling and *very* easy to drink, ideally within two years of the harvest. Single-estate wines can age considerably longer. Best years: 1986, '85, '84. Best producers: Aussellons, Cantharide, Cru du Coudoulet, Duboeuf, Fonsalette, les Goubert, Grand Moulas, Guigal, Jaboulet, Mont-Redon, Mousset, Pascal, de Ruth, St-Estève.

CÔTES DU RHÔNE-VILLAGES AC
SOUTHERN RHÔNE
Grenache, Syrah, Mourvèdre and others

In general the addition of the word 'Villages' to a French *appellation* means that the wine comes from a grouping of villages with better vineyard sites. So Côtes du Rhône is the AC which applies, indiscriminately, to the 100,000 acres (40,000 hectares) of Rhône vineyards, while Côtes du Rhône-Villages is allowed only for 17 different villages which have historically made superior wine. The wine may be labelled Côtes du Rhône-Villages indicating that it is a blend from any or all of these villages, or with its own village name – as in Côtes du Rhône-Cairanne. The best wines will carry a single village name.

There is a move afoot to expand the 'Villages' category and up to 65 different villages are currently under consideration. I hope the authorities think carefully, because the original 17 villages really do produce finer wine. They

have a high minimum alcohol – 12·5 per cent, as against 11 per cent for ordinary Côtes du Rhône. The yield is strictly restricted to 35 hectolitres per hectare as against 50, the Grenache is limited to 65 per cent and the Carignan to ten per cent (many ordinary Côtes du Rhône are almost entirely Grenache and Carignan) while the classier Syrah, Mourvèdre and Cinsaut must make up 25 per cent. The result is splendid wine. For rosé a simple Côtes du Rhône often suffices, but for red with a marvellous, dusty, blackcurrant and spicy raspberry flavour and tannin to support the wine as it matures for up to ten years – you must go to a Côtes du Rhône-Villages. Best years: 1985, '84, '83, '80, '78. Best villages: red – Cairanne, Vacqueyras, Beaumes-de-Venise, Séguret, Valréas, Sablet, Visan; rosé – Chusclan, Laudun, Visan. Best producers: Ameillaud, Boisson, Brusset, Cartier, Combe, Grangeneuve, Pelaquié, Présidente, Rabasse-Charavin, St-Antoine, Ste-Anne.

CÔTES DU ROUSSILLON AC
LANGUEDOC-ROUSSILLON
Carignan, Cinsaut, Grenache and others

Most people only know the Roussillon as the last fractious stretch of autoroute before the Pyrenees and the Costa Brava. But drive up the Tech, the Têt or the Agly valleys to the west and the furious whine of holiday traffic fades blissfully into the sharp, sunny mountain air; you stop at one of the hill-villages, and the chatter of the menfolk breaks into your noon-day thoughts – and it's not French at all, but the strange rasping, convoluted clamour of Catalan. The wine you drink is Côtes du Roussillon – red, dusty as a mountain track, but juicy as fresh orchard fruit – based on the Carignan, but increasingly helped by Cinsaut, Grenache and Mourvèdre.

The co-operatives dominate the production – and for once this is a good thing, because they have an enlightened leadership which managed to gain an AC for the region in 1977, almost a decade before neighbouring Corbières. They emphasize the carbonic maceration method of wine-making, which draws out the juicy flavours of the grape and is crucial when the potentially rough Carignan makes up the majority of the blend. The production is now 25 million bottles, 95 per cent of it red or rosé. The price is never high and so long as the wine is young, both red and rosé are some of southern France's best values. Best producers: Cazès Frères, Corneilla, Jau, Jaubert et Noury, Rey; the Rasiguères co-op makes excellent rosé.

CÔTES DU ROUSSILLON-VILLAGES AC
LANGUEDOC-ROUSSILLON
Carignan, Grenache, Mourvèdre and others

The northern part of the Côtes du Roussillon, centred on the Agly river. The vineyards on the valley sides are especially good, and the Côtes du Roussillon-Villages AC is applicable only to red wines from the best sites. They have a higher minimum alcohol (12 degrees) and a lower yield (45 hectolitres per hectare) than straight Côtes du Roussillon, and the wine, especially from the villages of Caramany and Latour-de-France (which are allowed to add their names to the AC), is full, ripe, wonderfully juicy when young – though still keeping that soft, dusty grain – and capable of maturing for several years. The carbonic maceration technique is largely responsible for this bright, easy character. There are a few wines now aged in new oak, and these too are impressive – drinkable young or at five years old. Best producers: Cap de Fouste, St-Martin; Agly, Bélesta, Latour-de-France, Vignerons Catalans co-operatives.

CÔTES DU VENTOUX AC
SOUTHERN RHÔNE
Grenache, Syrah, Mourvèdre and others

Mont Ventoux is a marvellously impressive peak towering more than 6000 feet (1830 metres) above the Rhône valley away to the east of Châteauneuf-du-Pape and Gigondas. Côtes du Ventoux wines, grown on the slopes which fan out from the mountain, aren't quite as exciting, I'm afraid, but have a lovely fresh juicy fruit – tasting of raspberry and spice – which is bright and breezy and undemanding. There are some fuller reds now made, but the best still keep this lovely simple flavour – they just have a bit more of it per bottle! Best producers: Anges, Jaboulet, Pascal, la Vieille Ferme.

CÔTES DU VIVARAIS VDQS
SOUTHERN RHÔNE
Grenache, Syrah, Mourvèdre and others

These VDQS wines could either be seen as junior Côtes du Rhône or senior Vin de Pays des Coteaux de l'Ardèche. The vineyards are spread along the west bank of the Rhône where the river Ardèche joins at Pont-St-Esprit. When they use the typical southern Rhône varieties – Grenache, Cinsaut, Carignan – the result is light, fresh red and rosé, for drinking as young as possible without further thought. But plantings of grapes such as Cabernet Sauvignon, Syrah and Gamay are producing exciting, deep-flavoured, rich fruity wines of quite surprising quality and irresistible price. About three million bottles; a good co-op movement controls production.

CRÉMANT DE BOURGOGNE AC
BURGUNDY
Pinot Noir

Most Burgundian Crémant is white, but there is a growing amount of pink being made in response to the fad for pink fizz which Champagne has enjoyed. The best wines are made in the Chablis and Auxerre regions at the northern tip of Burgundy where pale, creamy wines of considerable class and fruit are made. The Caves de Bailly is so far the best producer.

CRÉMANT DE LOIRE AC
CENTRAL LOIRE
Cabernet Franc, Gamay, Pineau d'Aunis and others

If there is a way forward for sparkling Loire rosés, Crémant de Loire should provide it. The problem with most Loire sparklers, and especially Saumurs, is a rasping, rather fruitless acidity and an explosive bubble. Crémant de Loire attempts to improve on this by lowering yields – 50 hectolitres per hectare instead of the 60 allowed for Saumur – and requiring that 330lb (150kg) of grapes are used to produce one hectolitre of juice rather than the 287lb (130kg) allowed for Saumur. This produces fruitier, less harsh, base wine. The wine must then lie on its yeast deposit after second fermentation for at least a year, instead of the nine months required for Saumur; and finally the atmospheres of pressure are 7·7lb (3·5kg) as opposed to 11lb (5kg). All this produces a much more attractive wine, with more fruit, more yeast character and a more caressing mousse. More class in other words.

However, all the major producers have created brands based on the Saumur name so there is little incentive to use a more expensive process which you then sell under a less specific name. (Crémant de Loire covers grapes from the entire Anjou and Touraine regions.) Perhaps the name is wrong, but the quality is very definitely an improvement, and it deserves to be a success. Best producers: Ackerman-Laurance, Gratien & Meyer.

CROZES-HERMITAGE AC
NORTHERN RHÔNE
Syrah

The last few years of Rhône wine history have been notable for the succession of rising stars, particularly in the small but high quality northern section. Hermitage and Côte-Rôtie, Cornas and St-Joseph have all been getting the showbiz treatment. Well, there's only one red AC left – and that's Crozes-Hermitage, traditionally thought of as a rather common, unsubtle poor relation, but with the finite amounts of wine available from the terraced hill slopes of the other ACs, people are suddenly discovering that Crozes-Hermitage is rather better than they thought. In fact, the wine from this 2000-acre (800-hectare) AC can be superb – not subtle, but the Syrah grape doesn't need to be subtle to make its mark.

Ideally Crozes-Hermitage should have a full red colour, a rich blackcurrants, raspberries and earth smell, and a strong, meaty but rich flavour. As so often with Syrah, the delicious fruit flavours have to mingle in with strange tastes of vegetables, damped-out bonfires, well-hung meat and herbs – but despite the prose the flavour is strong and exciting. You can drink it young especially if the grapes were grown on flat land, but in ripe years, from a hillside site, it improves greatly for three to six years. Best years: 1985, '83, '82. Best producers: Bégot, Delas, Desmeure, Fayolle, Jaboulet (Thalabert), Michelas, Tain co-operative, Tardy & Ange.

DE LA DAUPHINE, CH.
Fronsac AC
BORDEAUX
Merlot, Cabernet Franc

Fronsac wines have been regarded as the next hot property in Bordeaux for almost as long as I've been out of short trousers. And they *still* haven't managed to progress beyond the 'heir apparent' state. However, Château de la Dauphine is just the kind of property which may give the area the push it needs. The Moueix family, who run many of Pomerol's greatest properties (including Château Pétrus, the world's most expensive red wine) have begun to invest in Fronsac and de la Dauphine is their flagship property. The wine is already changing for the better, with a proportion of new oak barrels being used for ageing. The results are still a little chunky, but the 1985 and '86 vintages show that this château will become one of Fronsac's leading properties.

DEZIZE-LÈS-MARANGES AC
CÔTE DE BEAUNE, BURGUNDY
Pinot Noir

A small village west of Santenay. The wines rarely have much excitement about them, being rather thin and shallow even in the best vintages, although they can sometimes have a pleasant strawberry perfume. In fact, most of the growers declare their wine as Côte de Beaune-Villages – and that is probably the best fate for most of it.

DOMAINE DE CHEVALIER
Pessac-Léognan AC, *cru classé de Graves*
BORDEAUX
Cabernet Sauvignon, Merlot, Cabernet Franc

In years when the sun is hot, but not too hot, when the weather is dry, but not too dry, and when the grapes ripen gently as the autumn evenings close in, rather than race to maturity in the blaze of a late summer heat wave. . . in years like that, Domaine de Chevalier can produce Bordeaux's finest wines. The white is frequently the best dry white in Bordeaux. The red faces far stiffer competition, but always ends up at least in the winning frame. Yet when you finally reach the property after nonchalantly wandering through the woodland and intermittent agriculture of the Pessac-Léognan region, you could be excused for exclaiming, 'Is that all?'.

There's no elegant château, no sense of sombre superiority, just a clearing cut in the forest – covering a mere 45 acres (18 hectares) – and a placid, low, white homestead surrounded by vines. From this unprepossessing source flows a series of red wines which always start out rather dry and tannic but over 10–20 years gain that piercing, fragrant cedar, tobacco and blackcurrant flavour which can leave you breathless with pleasure, and Domaine de Chevalier also adds a slight earthy rub to the taste – just to keep your feet on the ground. Best years: all since 1978, with '78, '81, '83 and '85 excelling.

LA DOMINIQUE, CH.
St-Émilion AC, *grand cru classé*
BORDEAUX
Merlot, Cabernet Franc, Cabernet Sauvignon, Malbec

A superbly situated St-Émilion property next to the great Château Cheval-Blanc. Although not a *premier grand cru classé*, its wine achieves that quality, and is marked by a delicious, rich, almost overripe fruit. Strangely, neither the 1985 nor the '86 vintages match up to this standard, being unbalanced and stand-offish. Hopefully, it's just a passing phase because La Dominique on form is a real delight.

DUCRU-BEAUCAILLOU, CH.
St-Julien AC, *2ème cru classé*
HAUT-MÉDOC, BORDEAUX
Cabernet Sauvignon, Cabernet Franc, Merlot, Petit Verdot

You really do get a feeling of quiet opulence and self-assured confidence as you gaze at the imposing Victorian solidity of this château. If this image also conjures up reliability, then it is accurate enough. But Ducru-Beaucaillou is more than that; much, much more. I can't think of a single bad wine made at this property in more than 20 years, and in the late 1970s this fact was recognized when the wine consistently sold for higher prices than any other Second Growth. We called it a 'super-second' – and though the more showy, extrovert wines of Léoville-Las-Cases and Pichon-Lalande now also rank as super-seconds, many people still prefer the fragrant cedar perfume, the soft, gently blackcurranty fruit and the satisfying round sensation of the Ducru-Beaucaillou. If you wanted to seek out the epitome of St-Julien, mixing charm and austerity, fruit and firmness, this is where you'd find it.

ÉCHÉZEAUX AC, *grand cru*
CÔTE DE NUITS, BURGUNDY
Pinot Noir

Of all the *grands crus* in the Côte de Nuits this is the one with the least reputation. Consequently it is also the least expensive (except from the Domaine de la Romanée-Conti) but this relative cheapness has been taken advantage of for too long by the merchants of the region. It is a big vineyard – 76 acres (30·8 hectares), spread between Clos de Vougeot and Vosne-Romanée – and few of the growers have made a name for themselves, preferring to harvest as many grapes as possible and sell them or their wine without any fuss. However, there is some good Échézeaux and it can be a subtly powerful wine, developing an attractive raspberry and chocolate perfume as it ages. It is rarely a hefty Burgundy, but is rarely the most perfumed either. Best years: 1985, '83, '80, '78, '76. Best producers: Domaine de la Romanée-Conti, Drouhin, Grivot, Jayer, Lamarche, Mongeard-Mugneret.

L'ÉVANGILE, CH.
Pomerol AC
BORDEAUX
Merlot, Cabernet Franc

A reasonably large property by Pomerol's Lilliputian standards – 32 acres (13 hectares) – which has shot to prominence in the last few years by making wines which critics have compared to Château Pétrus. Well, the wine isn't *quite* that good, but the vineyard *is* bang next door to Pétrus, and the wine is made by one of Bordeaux's most talented oenologists, Michel Rolland – a man who not only understands the rule book, but who also knows that for a wine to be great it must gladden your heart, not merely impress your mental faculties. Rich, exciting, expensive wine, worth the price. Best years: 1985, '83, '82, '79, '75.

FAUGÈRES AC
LANGUEDOC-ROUSSILLON
Carignan, Grenache, Cinsaut, Syrah

The first of the communes in the vast Coteaux du Languedoc area to separate itself from the pack and make its own reputation. For a year or two at the beginning of the 1980s it was the new 'buzz wine' of the Paris bistros, and duly got its AC in 1982. Then nothing more was heard about it, and Faugères was left to ponder the fickle finger of fashion – and continue making good wine. Luckily the wine *is* good and well deserves its AC. It's almost entirely red, and comes from hilly vineyards in seven little villages just north of Béziers. Production is about six million bottles.

▶ Winter vines, well-pruned, in Faugères. Pruning, controlled by AC regulations, normally takes place between December and February.

What marks it out from other Languedoc reds is its ripe, soft, rather plummy flavour, and though it's a little more expensive than neighbouring wines, the extra is well worth it. Drink young, but it can age a year or two. Faugères is a compelling proof that there is tremendous quality potential in the hillside vineyards of France's far south, even if much of the wine from the lifeless coastal plains is dire. Best years: 1986, '85. Best producers: Faugères co-operative, Fraisse, Grézan, Haut-Fabrègues, St-Aimé.

DE FIEUZAL, CH.
Pessac-Léognan AC, *cru classé de Graves*
BORDEAUX
Cabernet Sauvignon, Merlot, Petit Verdot, Malbec

An exceptionally good red wine, but one which nobody seems to know about. Usually this would result in a wine priced well below its real value, the owners pleading for custom. Not at Fieuzal. The owners of this 57-acre (23-hectare) estate have invested a lot of money in their property. It is one of the most up-to-date in the region, and their delicious, ripe, oaky wine sells at a high price. Good luck to them; the wine's worth it. Best years: 1986, '85, '84, '83, '82, '81, '78.

FIGEAC, CH.
St-Émilion AC, *premier grand cru classé*
BORDEAUX
Cabernet Sauvignon, Cabernet Franc, Merlot

You have hardly finished shaking hands with Thiery Manoncourt, the delightful though zealous owner of Château Figeac, before he has marched you over into the vineyards, and pointed accusingly to the north. Half-a-mile away sits the small, whitewashed buildings of Cheval-Blanc, acknowledged as St-Émilion's greatest wine. This small section of St-Émilion, to the west of the *appellation*, is called 'Graves' St-Émilion – because the gravel soil gives the wine its special quality. Yet who has the most gravel? Not Cheval-Blanc, but Figeac! Indeed you quickly learn that Cheval-Blanc used to be part of Figeac, was only sold as 'Vin

de Figeac', and derives its name (meaning 'white horse') from the fact that it was there that Figeac had its stables!

Well, it's all true, but luckily there is a twinkle in Monsieur Manoncourt's eye as he berates his mighty neighbour, and luckily his own wine is superb, but in a different way from Cheval-Blanc. In his 100-acre (40-hectare) vineyard he uses 35 per cent Cabernet Sauvignon (rare in St-Émilion) and 35 per cent Cabernet Franc – both varieties which love gravel – and only 30 per cent of St-Émilion's main variety, Merlot. The result is wine of marvellous minty, blackcurranty perfume, with some of the cedar and cigar smoke spice of the great Médocs, and a caressing gentleness of texture. Often more 'beautiful' than Cheval-Blanc, though rarely so grand. It is lovely young yet ideally should age 10–20 years. Best years: 1985, '83, '82, '78, '76, '75.

FITOU AC
LANGUEDOC-ROUSSILLON
Carignan, Grenache, Cinsaut and others

Fitou has become one of the great unexpected success stories of the 1980s. The small *appellation* is virtually submerged by its neighbour, the giant Corbières; and it's not all that cheap. Yet it obviously struck a chord, because there now isn't enough to go round. The wine is a good dark red, and has been recognized as special for quite a while, because the AC was granted in 1948, (almost 40 years before Corbières got its AC). The main Fitou area is a pocket of land around the lagoon of Salses, on the coast between Perpignan and Narbonne, but there are also some villages, where better, tougher wine is made, in the heart of the Corbières hinterland, of which Tuchan is the most important. Fitou's strong, burly flavour comes from the Carignan grape which must constitute 70 per cent of the blend. This makes for a pretty stern basic brew, so there is a minimum ageing requirement of 18 months in wood; the wine itself then ages well to five or six years at least. Best producers: Mont Tauch co-operative, Nouvelles, Vignerons Val d'Orbieu.

FIXIN AC
CÔTE DE NUITS, BURGUNDY
Pinot Noir

Fixin would clearly love to be talked of in the same breath as the great villages of the Côte d'Or. There it sits, looking down indulgently on its great neighbour Gevrey-Chambertin, confident in the knowledge that the Grand Dukes of Burgundy used to spend their summers here, and smug as anything about the imposing Napoleon memorial in its civic park. But Fixin wines, try as they will, never manage to scale the heights. Worthy wines, usually quite full in the mouth, tannic enough to last well, but – perfume, fragrance, the mysterious mix of flavour and fantasy that marks out the greatest Burgundies? No, not in my experience. So trust their worthiness not their magic. There are four *premiers crus* among the 368 acres (149 hectares) of vines but, at the other end of the scale, Fixin wine is often sold as Côte de Nuits-Villages. Best years: 1985, '83, '80, '78. Best producers: Bordet, Durand-Roblot, Gelin, Joliet.

FLEURIE AC
BEAUJOLAIS, BURGUNDY
Gamay

▶ Beaujolais cellars in Chiroubles (left) and Juliénas – two villages which, like Fleurie, rank as Beaujolais *crus*.

If you get me in the right mood – spring flowers bursting free, the bright May-time sun promising an endless summer of warm, dreamy days, the picnic prepared and only ten minutes to go before she arrives – then Fleurie can be my very favourite wine in all the world. Flowery, flowing, flirtatious, fun-filled – yes that's Fleurie, the most Beaujolais of all Beaujolais! The happy carefree flavours of the Gamay grape at their best, plus heady perfumes and a juicy ripe sweetness which can leave you gasping with sheer delight.

I'm not the only one who loves good Fleurie, because it is now the most expensive Beaujolais *cru*. Luckily, there's a fair amount of wine as Fleurie, with 1754 acres (710 hectares), is the third biggest *cru* – and the quality in recent years has been outstanding. I only hope it can cope with its new-found popularity. Best years: 1987, '86, '85. Best producers: Bernard, Chignard, Duboeuf (especially from named vineyards), Fleurie co-operative, la Grande Cour, Montgénas, Paul.

FOURCAS-HOSTEN, CH.
Listrac AC, *cru grand bourgeois*
exceptionnel
BORDEAUX
Cabernet Sauvignon, Merlot,
Cabernet Franc

An important Listrac property of 100 acres (40 hectares), owned by a multinational bunch of Americans, Danes – and French. I used to keep finding stray bottles of this wine in the strangest of places – I had the 1962 and '64 at an abbey lost in a Welsh valley – and they were always dry and cedary, gentle yet austere, in a sort of kind-but-firm-bachelor-uncle way. Nowadays the wines are thoroughly modern, with new wood adding its nuance to the flavour – but the vintages of the '80s have lost a little of that pipe and carpet-slipper charm. Best years: 1985, '82, '81, '78, '75.

FRONSAC AC
BORDEAUX
Cabernet Franc, Cabernet
Sauvignon, Merlot, Malbec

In 1970 people were saying that Fronsac wines would soon be the next star in the Bordeaux constellation. In the late '70s I went to several tastings of Fronsac wines and thought them splendid – full, strong reds, with some of the buttery richness of St-Émilion, the minerally backbone of Pomerol, and more than a whiff of the Médoc's cedar fragrance. But they still didn't appear in the shops. Last year I even went on a trip of the 'lesser' areas of Bordeaux organized by the local wine *comité*. The one area missing in the trip? Fronsac. Lack of organization is the chief problem, and lack of investment – although I would except Château la Rivière and Château de la Dauphine from this criticism. So, we still wait to see how good Fronsac wines may be. There's enough wine to make a mark – the whole area covers 2500 acres (1000 hectares), which is bigger than Pomerol – of which about 70 per cent is Fronsac AC and 30 per cent the enclave of Canon-Fronsac. But, as I said, we're still waiting for the area to take off. Best years: 1985, '83, '82, '79, '78. Best producers: de la Dauphine, Mayne-Vieil, la Rivière, la Valade, Villars.

GAILLAC AC
SOUTH-WEST
Duras, Fer, Gamay and others

Historically, Gaillac – in the Tarn *département* near Albi – was a very important vineyard area, planted by the Romans and famous for centuries. Most of its fame, however, rested on sweet white wine – on whose quality I cannot comment because the modern equivalents I've tasted have been pretty poor. There are 73 villages making wine, producing about seven million bottles, of which less than half are red or rosé. Little of it has any great character, partly because the area is heavily dominated by co-ops (although the Tecou co-op isn't bad). However there are now a few single producers' wines and these can be exciting – sharp, peppery, tangy, unusual but good. In general, drink young. Best producers: Boissel-Rhodes, Jean Cros, Labarthe, Larroze, Mas Dignon, Plageoles.

GAMAY

In most of the world, the Gamay grape is considered as a common kind of creature and, frankly, that's a fair criticism. In general, Gamay wine is rather rough-edged, quite high in raspy acidity – and a bit raw of fruit. But on the granite outcrops of Beaujolais, Gamay has one glorious fling, producing the juicy, peach 'n' pepper, strawberry 'n' cherry happy-juice which at its breeziest is Beaujolais Nouveau, and at its most heady and exciting is a single-domaine wine from Fleurie, Morgon or Moulin-à-Vent. Gamay wine doesn't keep this juicy-fruit quality for long, but good examples can age to a very attractive, slightly farmyardy, but gentle Pinot Noir imitation – toffee and chocolate and plums. In a good vintage, wines from one of the *crus* can make this transformation after two to three years and may drink well for a decade.

Elsewhere in France, the Mâconnais has a lot of Gamay, the Côte d'Or has the odd plot while both Touraine and Anjou make rather dry, occasionally pleasant, light reds and rosés from it. It's also planted among other varieties in the south and south-west, but it is best used on its own in the Beaujolais style: the Côtes du Forez, Côte Roannaise, Coteaux du Lyonnais, and, surprisingly, the Vin de Pays des Coteaux de l'Ardèche, are the most successful at this.

GEVREY-CHAMBERTIN AC
CÔTE DE NUITS, BURGUNDY
Pinot Noir

Gevrey-Chambertin is an infuriating village. Capable, with its *grands crus* Chambertin and Chambertin Clos de Bèze, of making the most startling, delicious red wines of Burgundy, yet maddeningly liable to produce a succession of pale, lifeless semi-reds which really don't deserve the AC at all.

It's the old Burgundian problem of supply and demand. With its world-famous top vineyard, Chambertin, leading the way, all the wines – *grand cru, premier cru* and the village wines – are keenly sought-after. Production increases – Gevrey-Chambertin already has easily the biggest production on the Côte d'Or – less suitable land is planted (some of the Gevrey-Chambertin AC is on the plains side of the N74 road, which is generally seen as the boundary below which good wine cannot be made), and standards slip. So straightforward Gevrey-Chambertin village wine should be approached with circumspection. But good examples are proud, big-tasting Burgundy at its best, usually a bit chewy, jammy even, when young, but gradually getting a fascinating flavour of perfumed plums and dark, smoky chocolates after six to ten years' ageing. Best years: 1987, '85, '83, '80, '78. Best producers: Bachelet, Burguet, Camus, Damoy, Drouhin, Faiveley, Jacquesson, Labouré-Roi, Leclerc, Magnien, Rodet, Rossignol, Armand Rousseau, Varoilles.

GIGONDAS AC
SOUTHERN RHÔNE
Grenache, Syrah, Mourvèdre,
Cinsaut

A large village squashed up into the craggy slopes of the Dentelles de Montmirail on the east of the Rhône valley near Orange, with 3000 acres (1200 hectares) of vines, Gigondas used to be a Côte du Rhône-Villages, but gained its own AC in 1971, and deservedly so, because, even though I don't like all the wines, they certainly have personality. They're sometimes described as poor man's Châteauneuf-du-Pape, but they lack the pure fruit intensity of a good Châteauneuf and instead have a tougher, chewier, jam-rich fruit which takes longer than Châteauneuf to soften and never quite sets the heart aflutter. Production is mostly red with a little rosé. Best years: 1985, '83, '82, '81, '78. Best producers: Beaumet-Bonfils, Faraud, les Gouberts, Guigal, Jaboulet, Longue-Toque, les Pallières, Pascal, Raspail, St-Gayan.

GISCOURS, CH.
Margaux AC, *3ème cru classé*
HAUT-MÉDOC, BORDEAUX
Cabernet Sauvignon, Merlot,
Cabernet Franc, Petit Verdot

It took me quite a while to come round to Château Giscours. I began tasting it with the vintages of the 1960s, which I found hot and rich, almost as though the barrels had been coated in chocolate. Not at *all* like Margaux, I thought snootily, and crossed it off my list. Well, it's back on now! Beginning with a stunning '75 (a very tricky year in Margaux), Giscours has made a string of fabulous wines which certainly do start off with a rather solid, almost tarry quality, but which also have a heavenly perfume just asking for a few years' maturity, and a fruit which is blackberries, blackcurrants and cherries all at once. The wines are already enjoyable at five years old, but good years will last for two decades with ease. Best years: 1983, '82, '81, '80, '79, '78, '75.

GIVRY AC
CÔTE CHALONNAISE, BURGUNDY
Pinot Noir

An important Côte Chalonnaise village of 300 acres (120 hectares) producing 90 per cent red wines. There used to be more vines, but many growers found that you make more money by selling your land to a housing developer from nearby Chalon-sur-Saône. The wines that survive are generally good, not that heavy, but with a full, ripe strawberry perfume and gently plummy flavour. Best years: 1985, '83, '82, '78. Best producers: Baron Thénard, Chofflet, Derain, Ragot.

GRAND-PUY-LACOSTE, CH.
Pauillac AC, *5ème cru classé*
HAUT-MÉDOC, BORDEAUX
Cabernet Sauvignon, Merlot,
Cabernet Franc

Don't be fooled by this wine only being a Fifth Growth. Because Pauillac dominated the awards of First Growth in the 1855 Classifications, one sometimes gets the feeling that several very exciting properties were rather unceremoniously dumped in the Fifth Growths for appearance's sake. However, this 110-acre (45-hectare) estate makes a classic Pauillac. It isn't as weighty and grand as one of two better-known wines like Latour and Mouton-Rothschild, but the purity of its flavour marks it out as special. Although it begins in a fairly rough, dense way, that's just how a Pauillac should start out; as the years pass the fruit becomes the most piercingly pure blackcurrant and the perfume mingles cedar with lead pencils and the softening sweetness of new oak. Best years: 1986, '85, '83, '82, '79, '78. Second wine: Lacoste-Borie.

GRANDS-ÉCHÉZEAUX AC
grand cru
CÔTE DE NUITS, BURGUNDY
Pinot Noir

Always thought of as a Vosne-Romanée *grand cru* – because that village's greatest property, Domaine de la Romanée-Conti, is a major owner and most of the other proprietors also live in Vosne-Romanée – the 22-acre (9-hectare) Grands-Échézeaux is actually in the parish of Flagey-Échézeaux, a hidden and fairly moribund village in the plain well below the vineyard. The wine has never achieved the fame either of Clos de Vougeot, to the east, or of Vosne-Romanée's leading *crus*. But when it is good, it does have a lovely, smoky, plum richness, and a soft caressing texture that ages well over 10–15 years to a gamy, chocolaty depth. Best years: 1987, '85, '83, '80, '78, '76. Best producers: Domaine de la Romanée-Conti, Drouhin, Engel, Lamarche, Mongeard-Mugneret, Sirugue.

GRAVES AC
BORDEAUX
Cabernet Sauvignon, Merlot,
Cabernet Franc

Poor old Graves rather had the stuffing knocked out of it in 1988. The leading properties, all clustered to the south and east of the city of Bordeaux, decided that the Graves AC wasn't good enough for them anymore and they created their own AC – Pessac-Léognan. So now, although the Graves *region* extends for about 37 miles (60km) from the very gates of Bordeaux down the banks of the Garonne to south of Langon, the actual AC will generally be for wine from the less-favoured southern section. This certainly weakens the red wine hall of fame more than the white, because much of the most exciting white is already being created outside the most famous villages, but there is no doubt that the soil isn't so gravelly in the south, (the name 'Graves' means gravel and the area got its name because the area now occupied by Pessac-Léognan is very gravelly indeed!) and consequently the ripening of the grapes and drainage of the land is more difficult. I hope we'll see a resurgence of juicy, quick-drinking reds, and bright, fruit-packed whites because the southern Graves does these extremely well. Best years: 1986, '85, '83, '82. Best properties: Cabannieux, Cheret-Pitres, Ferrande, de Gaillat, la Grave, Magence, Millet, Rahoul, Respide, Roquetaillade-la-Grange, de St-Pierre, Tourteau-Chollet.

GRAVES DE VAYRES AC
BORDEAUX
Cabernet Sauvignon, Cabernet
Franc, Merlot

This does sound rather grand, but it isn't really; just another obscure Bordeaux mini-*appellation* of no renown but, I must say, some potential. The 'Graves' refers to gravel soil, the best soil type in Bordeaux. But this 'Graves' is opposite Libourne, on the edge of the St-Émilion and Pomerol regions, nothing to do with the famous Graves region south of Bordeaux city. The reds *are* quite good, fruity and soft, but I've never had one which seemed any more than a bumped-up Bordeaux Supérieur.

GRENACHE

Grenache can be a brilliant grape or a flabby old plonk-producer depending on what you do with it. It is the world's most widely-planted red variety (the bulk of its acreage is in Spain under the name Garnacha Tinta). It is a hot country grape: in France, you don't find it north of the central Rhône, but it reaches its zenith in the Southern Rhône round Châteauneuf-du-Pape. Here it is the dominant grape variety and in the torrid, pebble-blanketed vineyards it ripens often to 14 degrees of alcohol, resulting in luscious, juicy-rich reds, sometimes almost too voluptuous for their own good and needing to be blended to acquire acidity and tannin.

Indeed, throughout the southern Rhône, Grenache is the most important grape. If overcropped it produces rather pallid empty-tasting wines, but from a normal yield the alcohol is high and the fruit strong and spicy. Carignan becomes more important round the Mediterranean basin, but Grenache is very much in evidence right down to the Spanish border and in Corsica. All the best southern rosés, in particular Tavel, Lirac and Côtes de Provence are based on Grenache, usually blended with Cinsaut. In Rasteau (Côtes du Rhône) and Languedoc-Roussillon (especially Rivesaltes, Maury, Banyuls) Grenache also makes thick, sweet, fortified red.

GRIOTTE-CHAMBERTIN AC
grand cru
CÔTE DE NUITS, BURGUNDY
Pinot Noir

A 'griotte' is a little cherry and, fanciful though it may seem, drinkers really do find the taste of cherries in Griotte-Chambertin. Actually, it's not *too* fanciful, because that's why they called this particular vineyard the 'Cherry-Chambertin' in the first place. In fact, if the locals could discern the taste of cherry in a particular wine hundreds of years before the first modern wine writer mewled and puked his way into print it reassures me that we're not all daft for finding flavours other than 'wine' in wine. What does 'wine' taste of? Well, cherries for a start, in some vineyards, and this little *grand cru* of 13·8 acres (5·6 hectares) in the village of Gevrey-Chambertin is there to prove it. Best years: 1987, '85, '83, '80, '78. Best producers: Drouhin, Pernot-Fourrier, Ponsot, Roty, Thomas-Bassot.

GRUAUD-LAROSE, CH.
St-Julien AC, *2ème cru classé*
HAUT-MÉDOC, BORDEAUX
Cabernet Sauvignon, Merlot,
Cabernet Franc, Petit Verdot

Of all the Médoc's great wines, Gruaud-Larose blows its own trumpet most *sotto voce*. In fact, were it not for American wine critics suddenly going weak at the knees over the quality of the last three or four vintages, Gruaud-Larose might still be trundling along, out of sight, quietly going about the business of making brilliant wine at an affordable price. There is a lot of it – at 203 acres (82 hectares), Gruaud is one of the largest St-Julien estates.

With vineyards set a little back from the estuary, Gruaud used to exhibit a softer, more honeyed style when young than, say, the Léoville trio whose vineyards slope down to the Gironde. This didn't stop the wine ageing brilliantly and gaining a piercing, dry, blackcurrant and cedarwood aroma over 20 years or so. The vintages of the 1980s have been made darker, deeper, thick with the flavours of blackberry and plums, sweetened with wood, toughened with tannin. They're not so easy to drink young nowadays, but I think they'll be even more exciting when they're mature. Best years: 1986, '85, '83, '82, '81, '79, '78, '75. Second wine: Sarget de Gruaud-Larose.

HAUT-BAGES-LIBÉRAL, CH.
Pauillac AC, *5ème cru classé*
HAUT-MÉDOC, BORDEAUX
Cabernet Sauvignon, Merlot, Petit
Verdot

This 64-acre (26-hectare) property, up to now relatively obscure and rarely seen, stands a very good chance of becoming one of my favourite Pauillac wines. Not because it is the most classic – it isn't; not because it has the most beguiling subtleties and nuances of perfume – it doesn't; no, it's the fruit that I love. Big, unbridled bucketsful of delicious plum and blackcurrant fruit, wonderfully unsubtle in a way, but exciting and satisfying. It changed hands in 1980, and it is only the recent vintages which give me such a buzz. They will age, but are already delicious at five years. Best years: 1986, '85 '83 '82.

HAUT-BAILLY, CH.
Pessac-Léognan AC, *cru classé de Graves*
BORDEAUX
Cabernet Sauvignon, Merlot,
Cabernet Franc

The softest and most invitingly charming of the Graves Classed Growths. The 62 acres (25 hectares) of vines are on gravelly soil with rather more sand than usual, just to the east of Léognan, and this contributes to Haut-Bailly becoming agreeably drinkable very early. However, the wines do age fairly well and what is ready to drink at ten years old often seems magically unchanged at 20. Up till 1970 the wines were consistently fine, but there was then a gap till 1979, when the property returned to the top level. Best years: 1986, '85, '82, '81, '79. Second wine: la Parde-du-Haut-Bailly.

HAUT-BATAILLEY, CH.
Pauillac AC, *5ème cru classé*
HAUT-MÉDOC, BORDEAUX
Cabernet Sauvignon, Merlot,
Cabernet Franc

They call this the 'St-Julien' of Pauillac. It's a small property of 49 acres (20 hectares), set back from the melting pot of brilliant wines close to the river, and is in fact owned by one of St-Julien's greatest wine-making families – the Bories of Ducru-Beaucaillou. It gets its 'St-Julien' tag because it doesn't have the concentrated power of a true Classed Growth Pauillac. In recent years, only 1970 and '82 have been 'powerful' wines. This lack of oomph wouldn't matter if the wines had the perfume and cedary excitement of St-Julien, but they rarely do; they're pleasant, a little spicy, but not memorable. Best years: 1985, '83, '82, '81.

HAUT-BRION, CH.
Pessac-Léognan AC, *premier cru classé de Graves*
BORDEAUX
Cabernet Sauvignon, Merlot,
Cabernet Franc

Haut-Brion has been in the news for longer than any other Bordeaux property. It seems to be the first property that got a write-up in the British press for a start when, in 1663, Samuel Pepys wrote that during a session at the Royal Oak Tavern he 'drank a sort of French wine called Ho Bryan; that hath a good and most particular taste that ever I met with'! I don't know whether he always spelt like that – or maybe it was just that he'd got a bit enthusiastic with the flagons of 'Ho Bryan', but either way, it was a good 50 years before other Bordeaux wines began to be known by their own name.

One reason for this is that the excellent gravel-based vineyard which constitutes Haut-Brion is actually in the suburbs of the city of Bordeaux and so was readily accessible to visiting merchants. With the rise in the importance of the Médoc châteaux in the eighteenth and nineteenth centuries Haut-Brion's continued popularity is shown by the fact that when the local merchants decided to classify the top red wines of Bordeaux in 1855 all the wines they chose were from the Médoc – except one, Haut-Brion from the Graves (now Pessac-Léognan) which was accorded First Growth status along with Margaux, Lafite and Latour.

There's no doubt the wine is worth its position. It has all the potential longevity and weight of the Médoc First Growths, and starts out tasting very like them because of the 100-acre (40-hectare) vineyard's deep gravel soil. Yet after a few years the flavour changes course; the tough tannins fade away more quickly, a gentle creamy-edged fruit takes their place and a few years' more maturity brings out all the fruit of plums and blackcurrants mingled with a heady scent of unsmoked Havana tobacco. Frequently Haut-Brion is *not* at its best in the greatest years, but that's OK – the lesser years are always cheaper and more fun to drink. Best years: 1986, '85, '84, '83, '81, '79, '78. Second wine: Bahans-Haut-Brion.

HAUTES-CÔTES DE BEAUNE AC
CÔTE D'OR, BURGUNDY
Pinot Noir

If it wasn't for the fact that the price of decent red Burgundy was pushed through the roof during the 1970s, we probably wouldn't be hearing too much of the Hautes-Côtes de Beaune. But as the supply of affordable Burgundy dwindled, the tumbling, sylvan backwater of little valleys, forests and meadows in the hills to the west of the Côte de Beaune proper came under the spotlight. In the nineteenth century, this area had produced a lot of wine but microclimates were tricky at an average height of 1300 feet (400 metres) and the broad south-east-facing slopes needed to ripen grapes were scarce. A few growers eked out a living, and the new Caves des Hautes-Côtes was beginning to chivvy them along.

Then, in the 1970s, merchants began to prospect land and replant derelict vineyards. Now, the Hautes-Côtes de Beaune are reasonably prosperous and the wines are fairly good. Only in exceptional years like 1976 and '85 will they attain the quality of Côte de Beaune, but in their light, rather chewy or raspberry-fresh way, they often give a purer view of what Pinot Noir should taste like than many supposedly classier offerings. They do age quite well, although I would drink them young and fresh. Best years: 1985, '83, '82, '78.

HAUTES-CÔTES DE NUITS AC
CÔTE D'OR, BURGUNDY
Pinot Noir

The hills behind the Côte de Nuits have been extensively replanted after vine growing had virtually died out in the first part of the twentieth century. The granting of AC to the Hautes-Côtes de Nuits and Hautes-Côtes de Beaune in 1961 acted as a spur, and several growers, in particular Hudelot and Thévenot, planted large estates. They were followed by the merchant houses – Geisweiler have over 200 acres (80 hectares) planted – and the establishment of the Caves des Hautes-Côtes in 1968 gave cohesion to the area. The wines are never weighty and are, if anything, a little leaner to start with than the Hautes-Côtes de Beaune, but with an attractive cherry and plum flavour, and sometimes a pleasing bitter finish. And they can age. The 1978 from Caves des Hautes-Côtes is still good. Best years: 1985, '83, '78. Best producers: Delauney, Dufouleur, Caves des Hautes-Côtes, Hudelot, Thévenot-le-Brun.

HAUT-MARBUZET, CH.
St-Estèphe AC, *cru grand bourgeois exceptionnel*
HAUT-MÉDOC, BORDEAUX
Merlot, Cabernet Sauvignon, Cabernet Franc

I can't believe that Haut-Marbuzet's 94-acre (38-hectare) vineyard between Montrose and Cos d'Estournel is really as good as those of its illustrious neighbours, and yet I freely admit that tasting the wines together I've regularly put Haut-Marbuzet ahead of Montrose and not far behind the mighty Cos. So maybe the energetic Monsieur Dubosq is right because he treats his wine like a top Classed Growth – right up to using 100 per cent new oak for maturing it – and the great, rich, mouthfilling blast of flavour certainly isn't subtle but certainly *is* impressive. Best years: 1986, '85, '83, '82, '81, '78.

HAUT-MÉDOC AC
BORDEAUX
Cabernet Sauvignon, Cabernet Franc, Merlot and others

Haut-Médoc is a geographical entity *and* an AC. The geographical entity is the southern half of the Médoc peninsula. stretching from Blanquefort in the suburbs of Bordeaux, north to St-Seurin-de-Cadourne. All the finest gravelly soil is situated in this section, and it contains six separate village ACs: Margaux, Listrac, Moulis, St-Julien, Pauillac and St-Estèphe.

The *appellation* Haut-Médoc covers all the parts of this geographical area not included in a village *appellation*. There are five Classed Growths within the Haut-Médoc AC including the excellent La Lagune and Cantemerle in the south, but otherwise the wines vary widely in quality and style. If anything they are inclined to lack a little fruit, but may age well in a slightly austere way. Best villages: Ludon, Macau, Lamarque, Cussac, St-Laurent, St-Sauveur, Cissac, St-Seurin-de-Cadourne, Vertheuil. Best properties: d'Agassac, Camensac, Cantemerle, Castillon, Cissac, Coufran, Hanteillan, la Lagune, Lamarque, Lanessan, Larose-Trintaudon, Malescasse, Pichon, Ramage-la-Batisse, Sociando-Mallet, la Tour-Carnet, la Tour-du-Haut-Moulin.

HAUT-POITOU VDQS
CENTRAL LOIRE
Gamay, Cabernet Franc, Cabernet Sauvignon

▼ Haut-Poitou has evolved from a supplier of Cognac-distilling wine into a producer of light, dry table wines.

Thought of as a Loire area, Haut-Poitou is in fact a little island of vine-growing near Poitiers – which is well on the way south to Bordeaux and nowhere near any major Loire towns. Even so, the style is similar to the Loire. The red wine, normally from Gamay, but occasionally from Cabernet, is light and dry, veering towards the raw except in warm years. The rosé, usually Cabernet-based, is also very dry but can be good and refreshing, marked by a nice grassy tang when young. The only important producer is the good co-operative.

L'HÉRAULT
LANGUEDOC-ROUSSILLON

If you needed to find a culprit for the floodtide of mediocre French red which threatens to burst the banks of the EEC wine lake each year, the Hérault *département* would be suspect number one. It produces a positive deluge of rock-bottom gut rot every year. However, things are on the up. Politicians have realized you can't protect sub-standard producers for ever and, between 1976 and 1984 in Hérault and the neighbouring *département* of Aude, over 74,000 acres (30,000 hectares) of unsuitable vineyards were uprooted.

Until the 1980s, Hérault only had one AC – the dull and insipid white Clairette du Languedoc. Since then Faugères, St-Chinian and the widespread Coteaux du Languedoc have joined the AC list. The Vin de Pays de l'Hérault – France's most elephantine *vin de pays* at a giant 200 million bottles annually – is doing sterling work in improving the quality of the non-AC vineyards. Here plantings are heavily loaded in favour of Carignan, which can be coarse and tough, but which, when made by carbonic maceration, can be extremely pleasant. Plantings of Syrah, Mourvèdre, Cabernet Sauvignon and Merlot are increasing. There is one super-star property, Mas de Daumas Gassac.

HERMITAGE AC
NORTHERN RHÔNE
Syrah, Marsanne, Roussanne

▶ The hillside vineyards of Hermitage, overlooking the Rhône, are so steep that a restraining hand is needed on this trailer-load of harvested Syrah grapes.

There was a time, a century or more ago, when Hermitage was regarded by many as the greatest red wine in France. And there was a time, amid the Bordeaux and Burgundy fever of a decade or so ago, when it was dismissed by almost all as a rough-and-tumble Rhône red. And then there's now. Once again Hermitage is revered – rare, rich red wine, expensive, memorable, classic. But these words are too cold to describe the turbulent excitements of a great Hermitage! The boiling cauldron of flavours – savage pepper, herbs, tar and coalsmoke biting at your tongue, fruit of intense blackcurrant-raspberry-and-bramble sweetness – is intoxicatingly delicious and, as the wine ages, a strange, warm softness of cream and liquorice and well-worn leather, all blending in to create one of the world's greatest red-wine taste experiences. Now, not all Hermitage achieves this eccentric but exciting blend of flavours, because the vineyard – flowing down the slopes of this bullish mound above the little town of Tain-l'Hermitage on the banks of the Rhône – only covers 310 acres (125 hectares) and a lot of merchants will take any grapes just to have Hermitage on their list. But the best growers – using the red Syrah, with sometimes a little white Marsanne and Roussane, and carefully blending the wines from different plots of the 'hill' (which do give *very* different flavours) – can make superbly original wine, needing five to ten years ageing even in a light year; but for the full-blown roar of flavours which a hot, ripe vintage brings, then 15 years is hardly enough and 30 years hardly too much. Best years: 1985, '83, '82, '80, '78. Best producers: Chave, Delas, Desmeure, Faurie, Fayolle, Ferraton, Guigal, Grippat, Jaboulet, Sorrel, Vidal-Fleury.

L'ÎLE DE BEAUTÉ, VIN DE PAYS
CORSICA
Nielluccio, Sciacarello, Carignan and others

The *vin de pays* for Corsica. If you don't like the rather warm, vaguely tanniny, vaguely resiny flavours of most mainstream Corsican reds and rosés, you may find a bit of relief here. As is frequently the case in the south of France, the more flexible *vin de pays* regulations allow experimentation with non-traditional grapes, and so far there are encouraging signs from reds based on Syrah and Cabernet and rosés based on Grenache and Pinot Noir. Altogether about 15 million bottles are produced, 95 per cent red and rosé.

IRANCY AC
BURGUNDY
Pinot Noir, César, Tressot

This northern outpost of vineyards, just south-west of Chablis; is an unlikely champion of the clear, pure flavours of Pinot Noir. Frequently – in the vineyards of Burgundy's Côte d'Or, further south – the delicacy of this grape variety is swamped, but in the compact south-facing amphitheatre of 155 acres (63 hectares) which makes up the vineyard of Irancy, the sun gives just enough encouragement to the vines to produce a delicate, clean red wine, lightly touched by the ripeness of plums and strawberries. The wines will also age well, especially if they have an addition of either César and Tressot, two local grapes of diminishing importance. There is a little rosé which can also catch a fleeting glimpse of Pinot Noir fruit. Two other local reds are Bourgogne-Coulanges-la-Vineuse – rougher than Irancy, with a disconcerting rooty taste – and Bourgogne-Épineuil – rare, but a delightful summer red. Best years: 1985, '83, '82. Best producers: Bienvenue, Cantin, Delaloges, Simmonet-Febvre.

IROULÉGUY AC
SOUTH-WEST
Tannat, Cabernet Franc, Cabernet Sauvignon

Yes, I think this gets my vote as the most obscure French AC. Geographically obscure anyway. I eventually found my way to the winery by asking the Spanish customs officer – I'd already crossed into Spain without noticing – but that's what life's like way up in the Pyrenean mountain valleys where they make Irouléguy – wonderful name isn't it? Eeroolegee (hard 'g'). The wine's not as good as the setting but the red is fairly full and peppery with a nice acid streak. The rosé is, well, rosé. Drink them both young – preferably in the meadows by the St-Étienne-de-Baigorry winery, just below the snow line! The co-operative dominates production for the 370 acres (150 hectares).

D'ISSAN, CH.
Margaux AC, *3ème cru classé*
HAUT-MÉDOC, BORDEAUX
Cabernet Sauvignon, Merlot

I've always had a vaguely covetous feeling about d'Issan, because it has an outrageously sumptuous-looking gold label. I had a bottle of 1961 once, and spent so much time drooling over the label that the wine was exhausted by the time I finally pulled the cork. Still, I'm *told* the 1961 was extremely good! We didn't see much of d'Issan during the 1970s but the last few vintages have been some of the most scented and delicious in the whole Margaux commune. The property is a reasonable size at 79 acres (32 hectares), and is unusual for not having any Cabernet Franc in the vineyard, plantings being 75 per cent Cabernet Sauvignon and 25 per cent Merlot. As the deliciously rich vintages of 1982, '83, '85 and '86 mature, the gold label will seem increasingly apt. D'Issan is usually drinkable at only five to six years old, but will be much better after ten. Best years: 1986, '85, '83, '82, '81, '78.

JULIÉNAS AC
BEAUJOLAIS, BURGUNDY
Gamay

A friend of mine once told me that the problem with Juliénas was that it lacked 'humour'. I know what he means. Juliénas. It's rather a serious name; the school prefect rather than the tearaway among the Beaujolais *crus*. The flavour often reflects that too. It frequently lacks the happy-fruit style which we think of as Beaujolais' calling-card. But what it does have is the weight and strength to develop in the bottle: Juliénas *may* have a little too much tannin and acid to be as immediately enjoyable as the others, but in years like 1985 and '87 there is a solid juiciness of peaches and cherry and strawberry which may not make great glugging, but which makes delicious, if slightly more 'serious', drinking. There are 1380 acres (560 hectares), producing about four million bottles. Best years: 1987, '85, '83. Best producers: Duboeuf, Château de Juliénas, Gonon, Juliénas co-operative, Pelletier.

LADOIX-SERRIGNY AC
CÔTE DE BEAUNE, BURGUNDY
Pinot Noir

The most northern village in the Côte de Beaune, and one of the least known since its best wines are usually sold as Corton or Aloxe-Corton *premier cru* and its less good ones as Côte de Beaune-Villages. Even so, wine with a Ladoix label does occasionally surface and can be worth a try – especially since there are several good growers in the village and it is likely to be reasonably priced. The output is overwhelmingly red, and the wine is usually quite light in colour, a little lean in style, but after a few years the rough edges slip away and a rather attractive soft, savoury style emerges. Best years: 1987, '85, '83, '82, '78. Best producers: Capitain-Gagnerot, Chevalier, Cornu, Florent de Mérode.

LAFITE-ROTHSCHILD, CH.
Pauillac AC, *premier cru classé*
HAUT-MÉDOC, BORDEAUX
Cabernet Sauvignon, Merlot, Cabernet Franc, Petit Verdot

Possibly, even probably, the most famous red wine in the world. This First Growth Pauillac of 222 acres (90 hectares), is quoted more often than any other red wine as being the height of elegance, indulgence and expense. If only I could draw near in humble mood to worship at this shrine of perfection but I can't, and the reason is that the wine is so wretchedly inconsistent. I *have* had some wonderful bottles – all cedarwood scent and fragrant blackcurrant, mingled with tobacco and kitchen spice – unnervingly light in the mouth yet entrancingly persistent in their beauty long after the last lingering sip has

drained the glass. Yet in great years like 1970, '66, '62 and '61 – especially '61 which is heaped with paeans of praise – in years like these I feel let down because the expectation was so great and the experience so limp and timid. There does seem to be a new mood in Lafite as far as more serious wine-making in the 1980s goes, but I still find the château and the wine rather distant and aloof. Since Lafite often takes 15 years to weave its subtle strands into cloth of gold, and *can* need 30 years or more to come finally into balance, we won't know for a while yet quite how good the 'new' Lafites are going to be. Even so – these look to be the best years: 1986, '84, '82, '81, '79, '76.

LAFLEUR, CH.
Pomerol AC
BORDEAUX
Merlot, Cabernet Franc

This tiny vineyard of only 9 acres (3·6 hectares) has some of Pomerol's oldest vines, some of Pomerol's most traditional wine-making, and the potential to equal Pétrus for sheer power and flavour. In fact Christian Moueix of Pétrus recognizes the quality of his rival, and now takes charge of operations here. The best of Lafleur is to come, because Moueix only took over in 1981, but vintages like '82, '83 and '85 already exhibit a massive, old-fashioned, unsubtle brute strength loaded with the fatness of oak and soaked in the sweet fruit of plums – unforgettable mouthfuls which will need years to evolve into memorable wines, but I'm confident they'll get there in the end.

LAFON-ROCHET, CH.
St-Estèphe AC, *4ème cru classé*
HAUT-MÉDOC, BORDEAUX
Cabernet Sauvignon, Merlot

I have been a fan of Lafon-Rochet ever since the 1970 vintage, not only for the full, almost honey-edged, dark fruit which usually finds it easy to keep the St-Estèphe earthiness well in check, but also because I can afford it. There weren't many wines I could afford when I bought the 1970 so I was extremely grateful to Lafon-Rochet – and still am – for the chance to possess a case of Classed Growth claret. That said, the owner has been 'improving' Lafon-Rochet since 1960 and nearly 30 years of investment and effort should be showing more regular results. The vineyard is a good one – but perhaps there is just a little too much Cabernet Sauvignon (80 per cent with 20 per cent Merlot) for these heavy clay soils; Merlot ripens more easily on clay and adds crucial richness to wines which can otherwise be a little austere. They need at least ten years to soften up – and that 1970 is absolutely wonderful right now, thank you very much. Best years: 1986, '85, '83, '82, '79.

LAGRANGE, CH.
St-Julien AC, *3ème cru classé*
HAUT-MÉDOC, BORDEAUX
Cabernet Sauvignon, Merlot

Bruno Prats of Cos d'Estournel, one of Bordeaux red's high-flier properties, looked out into the backwoods of St-Julien and told me that Lagrange had potentially one of the finest vineyards in the whole Médoc. He should know, I thought, but I must say that this ramshackle, lumbering estate – 121 acres (50 hectares) of vines at the very western borders of St-Julien – didn't seem a likely candidate for super-stardom. However, since Lagrange was bought by the Japanese Suntory Company in 1983 the leap in quality has been astonishing. No longer an amiable, shambling St-Julien, charming enough yet infuriating in its inconsistency, but instead a clear-eyed, single-minded wine of tremendous fruit, meticulous wine-making and superb quality. Best years: 1986, '85, '83, '82. Second wine: les Fiefs de Lagrange.

LA LAGUNE, CH.
Haut-Médoc AC, *3ème cru classé*
HAUT-MÉDOC, BORDEAUX
Cabernet Sauvignon, Cabernet Franc, Merlot, Petit Verdot

La Lagune has given me more pleasure than any other single wine. A chap who worked for a brewery, Reg was his name, sidled up to me one day and intimated that he might be possessed of something I could find to my liking. Château La Lagune 1961. Thirty bob a bottle. 'Château-bottled?' I was about to enquire, but one look at his 'now don't get cheeky with me, old son' demeanour persuaded me that such questions would not be greeted with enthusiasm let alone candour. 'Er, how many bottles?' 'One hundred and two,' came the reply. Eight and a half cases of 1961 claret? Well, out came the life savings – and I got them. The lot! Now, the experts say that 1961 wasn't a

success at La Lagune, but I can only say that no wine has ever tasted of purer, sweeter, more luscious essence of blackcurrants than that wine did. It's fading now, and I've only a bottle or two left, but if you ever pass by my flat and hear Thomas Beecham's recording of La Bohème blasting at full tilt into the cold night air, you'll know I'm up there with a few of my friends singing, laughing and swigging back the last of my La Lagune '61!

So you can see I find it difficult to think of La Lagune in brass-tack terms – but here are a few facts. It's a Third Growth, Haut-Médoc AC, just to the south of Margaux, and the closest Classed Growth to Bordeaux. The wine is consistently excellent, richer, spicier now than my 1961 was, but full of the charry chestnut sweetness of good oak and a deep, cherry-blackcurrant-and-plums sweetness to the fruit which, after ten years or more, is outstanding Bordeaux, always accessible, yet perfect for the long haul. Best years: 1986, '85, '83, '82, '78, '76, '75.

LALANDE-DE-POMEROL AC
BORDEAUX
Merlot, Cabernet Franc, Cabernet Sauvignon, Malbec

Although Lalande-de-Pomerol is regarded as a Pomerol satellite, with nearly 2500 acres (1000 hectares) of vines it is actually bigger then Pomerol at 1800 acres (725 hectares). The AC covers both Lalande-de-Pomerol and the neighbouring commune of Néac and runs along the northern boundaries of Pomerol. The wines are usually full, soft, plummy and even chocolaty, very attractive to drink at only three to four years old, but ageing reasonably well. They lack the mineral edge and the concentration of top Pomerols, but are nonetheless extremely attractive full ripe wines. They're not cheap, but then nothing with the name Pomerol included in it *is* cheap these days. Best years: 1985, '83, '82. Best properties: Annereaux, Bel-Air, Belles-Graves, Bertineau, Clos des Templiers, Grand-Ormeau, Hautes-Tuileries, la Faurie, Lavaud-la-Maréchaude, St-Vincent, Siaurac, Tournefeuille.

LARMANDE, CH.
St-Émilion AC, *grand cru classé*
BORDEAUX
Merlot, Cabernet Franc, Cabernet Sauvignon

One of those wines which is so creamy, so juicy, so full of coconut spice and gooey fruit that you can't quite take it seriously. But why not? If drinking wine is supposed to be about pleasure, having fun, then Larmande is a very 'serious' wine indeed! The estate is 46 acres (18·5 hectares) situated directly north of the town of St-Émilion, and is a rising star. No-one had heard of Larmande till 1975 when the owners decided to invest and improve. Since then the rich, heady flavours of Larmande have stood out in tastings whenever the wine is shown. Best years: 1985, '83, '82, '81.

LAROSE-TRINTAUDON, CH.
Haut-Médoc AC, *cru grand bourgeois*
HAUT-MÉDOC, BORDEAUX
Cabernet Sauvignon, Cabernet Franc, Merlot

The largest property in the Médoc – 425 acres (172 hectares) in St-Laurent, producing some 65,000 cases of wine! It's a real success story because the Forner brothers who owned it until 1986 had to plant this massive vineyard from scratch in 1966. They had as their aim the production of large amounts of good quality, affordable, red Bordeaux. Direct easy flavours at a decent price is what they were after – and they achieved it almost every year. It's supposed to be the most popular red Bordeaux in the United States – and I can see why. The wines are made to drink at about five years old, but can age for ten. Best years: 1986, '85, '84, '83, '82, '81, '78.

LASCOMBES, CH.
Margaux AC, *2ème cru classé*
HAUT-MÉDOC, BORDEAUX
Cabernet Sauvignon, Merlot, Cabernet Franc, Petit Verdot

A large and important Second Growth which hasn't really managed to match the efforts of its peers for some time. This could be because the remarkable achievement of properties like Léoville-Las-Cases and Pichon-Lalande are due to the dedication of a single owner, whereas Lascombes is owned by the massive Bass-Charrington brewing combine. But that argument doesn't hold water because Rausan-Ségla, one of the most rapidly improving Second Growths, is owned by a large multi-national concern, as is Latour, the most consistent of the First Growths. No, it's a case of the will to excel not being very evident. Hopefully the most recent vintages – promising some of the tantalizing fresh flowers and blackcurrant perfume of which Lascombes is capable – will mark a permanent improvement. I hope so. Otherwise I shall have to go on drinking the Chevalier de Lascombes rosé which is rather good. Best years: 1986, '85, '83, '82.

LATOUR, CH.
Pauillac AC, *premier cru classé*
HAUT-MÉDOC, BORDEAUX
Cabernet Sauvignon, Cabernet Franc, Merlot, Petit Verdot

The first bottle of Château Latour I ever had was the 1954. Or was it '56? It doesn't matter really: they were both lousy vintages in Bordeaux and mercifully few bottles ever surfaced. Lousy vintages? Yes. Although not as lousy as the next two vintages – '63 and '65. Hang on. Why am I talking about one of Bordeaux's greatest properties in these terms? Simple. Firstly, I could afford the '54 and the '56 Latours. Secondly, they were absolutely delicious. *That's* why.

In years when the rest of Bordeaux might as well have packed up and gone home without pressing a grape, Latour stuck to it and produced good wine. All through the fifties, sixties and seventies Latour stood for integrity, consistency and refusal to compromise. The result was that in poor years the wine was good; in adequate years – like 1960, '67, '74, the wine was excellent. In great years like 1966, '70, '75 and '82, Latour's personality – the sheer power of blackcurrant fruit, the temple columns of tannin daring anyone to broach a bottle before its twentieth year, the full-tilt charge of cedar-dry flavours, rich, expensive, but as unconcerned with fashion and fawning as a fifteenth-generation duke – marks it as the most imperious of Pauillac's three First Growths.

Interestingly, the 150-acre (60-hectare) vineyard is on the southern side of the AC, bordering St-Julien. This might lead one to expect a lighter style of wine, but the vineyard, with 75 per cent Cabernet Sauvignon, ten per cent Cabernet Franc, five per cent Petit Verdot and only ten per cent Merlot gives as big and proudly impressive a wine as any in Bordeaux. Strangely, in the '80s, there has been an attempt to make lighter wines. It is by no means a total success – and in any case completely unnecessary because Latour's reputation is built on power and longevity. Hopefully it is only a temporary aberration. Best years: 1986, '82, '81, '79, '78, '75, '70. Second wine: Les Forts de Latour.

LATOUR-À-POMEROL, CH.
Pomerol AC
BORDEAUX
Merlot, Cabernet Franc

I first got to like Latour-à-Pomerol because it made an absolutely fabulous 1973, gorgeously soft and ripe with a delicious hint of mint. This luscious, almost juicy fruit, soft and *very* easy to drink, has been a mark of Latour-à-Pomerol, but the wines do age well. Recent vintages, now directed by Christian Moueix of Pétrus, show a beefier, brawnier style, but the super-ripe softness of fruit is still there, so I'm not worried. The vineyard covers 20 acres (8 hectares). Best years: 1983, '82, '81, '79.

LATRICIÈRES-CHAMBERTIN
AC, *grand cru*
CÔTE DE NUITS, BURGUNDY
Pinot Noir

Yet another of the *grands crus* of Gevrey-Chambertin, this time a 17-acre (7-hectare) stretch of vines at the southern boundary of the commune. Only about 2500 cases are produced and the wine can be very fragrant although not, as some people say, almost the equal of the best wines in Chambertin – it rarely has the intensity of the best Chambertins from the best growers. Best years: 1987, '85, '83, '80. Best producers: Camus, Rémy, Trapet.

LAUDUN
Côtes du Rhône-Villages AC
SOUTHERN RHÔNE
Grenache, Syrah, Cinsaut, Mourvèdre

One of the best Côtes du Rhône-Villages, in particular for whites and rosés. The wines are fresher and fruitier than any other Côtes du Rhône-Villages except those of Chusclan. Rosé and red are for drinking young. Best years: 1985, '83. Best producers: Laudun co-operative, Pelaquie, Vignerons des Quatres Chemins.

LÉOVILLE-BARTON, CH.
St-Julien AC, *2ème cru classé*
HAUT-MÉDOC, BORDEAUX
Cabernet Sauvignon, Merlot, Petit
Verdot, Cabernet Franc

▲ The cellars at Château
Langoa-Barton. Léoville-Barton wine
is made at Langoa, owned by the
same family.

Anthony Barton, whose family has run this Second Growth St-Julien since 1821, has resolutely refused to profiteer in spite of considerable pressure for him to do so, especially in the early to mid-1980s, when every vintage was released substantially more expensive than the last regardless of actual worth. By 1986 he was charging only half what one or two of his more ambitious neighbours thought reasonable. Yet as he freely declares, he runs a profitable business with Léoville-Barton. He knows what it costs to make fine wine, he never stints on quality, and he certainly doesn't intend to make a less than satisfactory profit. So thank you, Mr Barton. And your wine? Old-fashioned, classically proportioned, excellent. This 100-acre (40-hectare) estate – with 70 per cent Cabernet Sauvignon, seven per cent Cabernet Franc, eight per cent Petit Verdot and only 15 per cent Merlot – makes dark, dry, tannic wines, difficult to taste young and therefore frequently underestimated at the outset, but over 10–15 years achieving a lean yet beautifully proportioned quality, the blackcurrants and cedarwood very dry, but pungent enough to fill the room with their scent. A traditionalist's delight. Best years: 1986, '85, '83, '82, '80, '78, '75.

LÉOVILLE-LAS-CASES, CH.
St-Julien AC, *2ème cru classé*
HAUT-MÉDOC, BORDEAUX
Cabernet Sauvignon, Merlot,
Cabernet Franc, Petit Verdot

St-Julien wasn't accorded a First Growth in the 1855 Classification. Any re-evaluation would change all that, because in Léoville-Las-Cases, St-Julien has a property and an owner whose total dedication to quality, whose ruthless, even dour, pursuit of perfection would put most First Growths to shame. Going to meet Monsieur Delon who runs Léoville-Las-Cases is rather like having an audience with your headmaster at school, but I've undergone a couple of these challenging, uncompromising tasting sessions in his cellars, and I can only say, with gratitude, that they've given me more understanding about the passion that is great Bordeaux than any amount of money could buy.

The Léoville-Las-Cases vineyard, at 210 acres (85 hectares), is the biggest of the three Léovilles, and slopes towards the Gironde as the direct neighbour of the great Latour. There are similarities in the wine because Las-Cases, since 1975, has been making wines of startling, dark, depthy concentration. Yet there is also something sweeter, something more enticing right from the start – as the fumes of new oak spice linger over the glass even in the wine's most stubborn adolescent sulks, and the tannins, strong though they are, have a habit of dissolving into smiles in your mouth exactly at the moment you've decided they they're just too much. Las-Cases from a good year really needs 15 years and should happily last for 30. Best years: 1986, '85, '83, '82, '81, '79, '78, '75. Second wine: Clos du Marquis.

LÉOVILLE-POYFERRÉ, CH.
St-Julien AC, *2ème cru classé*
HAUT-MÉDOC, BORDEAUX
Cabernet Sauvignon, Merlot

A glittering name from the distant past, and I mean *distant*. I haven't had a single exciting bottle from this faded famous name, although I was once offered some '66 bottled in Northampton which seemed to have improved with the journey and the '67 I got hold of in Welwyn Garden City wasn't too bad except for a slightly disturbing tarmac smell which may have come from the A1 roadworks. . . It's a big vineyard of 156 acres (63 hectares), situated bang in the middle of the best part of St-Julien, but you'd never know, and if it wasn't for hopeful signs of effort and investment since the 1982 vintage, I don't think I'd have included it in the book at all.

LIRAC AC
SOUTHERN RHÔNE
Grenache, Cinsaut, Syrah,
Mourvèdre

An excellent, but underrated AC between Tavel and Châteauneuf-du-Pape in the southern Rhône, making wines which resemble both its more famous neighbours. There are 1630 acres (660 hectares) of vines producing 2·5 million bottles, more than 95 per cent of it red and rosé. The red has the dusty, spicy fruit of Châteauneuf-du-Pape, without achieving the intensity of the best examples, plus an attractive metallic streak which is unusual but good. Rosés are breezier, more refreshing than Tavel, and can have a lovely strawberry fruit. Reds age very well but are always delicious young. Rosés should be drunk sharpish. Best years: 1986, '85, '83. Best producers: Assémat (Causses et St-Eymes and Garrigues), Devoy, Fermade, St-Roch, Ségriès, la Tour.

LISTRAC AC
HAUT-MÉDOC, BORDEAUX
Cabernet Sauvignon, Cabernet
Franc, Merlot and others

One of the six specific ACs inside the Haut-Médoc area, but not possessing any Classed Growths. All the best Haut-Médoc vineyards are on gravel soil and the majority of them on ridges and plateaux within sight of the Gironde estuary. Listrac is set several miles back from the Gironde, its 1410 acres (570 hectares) of vineyards fashioned on outcrops of partially gravelled heavy soil, encircled by forest. Even so, the wine can be good, near to St-Estèphe in style. Solid fruit, a lightly coarse tannin and an identifiable earthy flavour are the marks of most Listracs. If there is enough fruit the wine can age to an attractive but austere cedarwood maturity; if the fruit isn't there, it can make lean old bones. Château Clarke is the classiest property – and the most expensive. (It makes rosé too!) Best years: 1986, '85, 83, '82, '78. Best properties: la Bécade, Cap-Léon-Veyrin, Clarke, Fonréaud, Fourcas-Dupré, Fourcas-Hosten, Grand Listrac co-operative, Lestage.

LOIRE

▶ Picking red-wine grapes in the Loire. Although the Loire is white-wine country, it also produces some light, fresh reds for drinking young.

The Loire Valley stretches for 620 miles (998km) right across the heart of France, finally sidling out into the Bay of Biscay at Nantes after a journey which began in the southern hills of the Massif Central only 100 miles (160km) from the Mediterranean. The river begins with a series of rapids and thrilling gorges but slows to a positively pedestrian pace by the time it reaches the chief wine areas, and the wines too seem to go from the blandest and most forgettable France has to offer to sharply defined, memorable flavours.

The Loire has about 100 different wines, but the vast majority of them remain disconsolately on the sidelines. And most of them are white, including Muscadet the Loire's most phenomenal success story of recent years. Upriver in Anjou they've found it much more difficult. Their staple, Anjou rosé, has gone out of favour, and Anjou red and white haven't come *into* favour – a pity because an increasing amount of good Anjou Rouge is being made – while Sancerre Rouge is wildly overrated and absurdly overpriced. Touraine makes the Loire's greatest reds – Chinon, Bourgueil and St-Nicolas de Bourgueil mostly from Cabernet Franc beefed up with a little Cabernet Sauvignon. These are oddly harsh, but memorable wines – full of blackcurranty flavour; and they age beautifully – but no-one could call them flavour of the month.

LOUDENNE, CH.
Médoc AC, *cru grand bourgeois*
BORDEAUX
Cabernet Sauvignon, Merlot, Cabernet Franc

In a way, I'd rather write about the *place* Château Loudenne and the people who run it, than the wine. It is a lovely, warm-welcome, pink château set on the banks of the Gironde – fields and vines to the back, paths and croquet lawn to the front. Sounds a bit English? Well, it is! The property was bought by the Gilbeys of London in 1875 and ever since has been an outpost of mild-mannered English hospitality in the Médoc. The wine is mild-mannered too, often so gentle and buttery there seems to be no acid and tannin at all, which doesn't make for exciting drinking. But on the terrace, as the sun goes down after a hard day in the vineyards, and the talk turns to Lords, and Wimbledon, and honey still for tea, well . . . Best years: 1986, '85, '83, '82.

LUSSAC-ST-ÉMILION AC
BORDEAUX
Merlot, Cabernet Franc, Cabernet Sauvignon, Malbec

One of the only ways to get hold of a glass of Lussac-St-Émilion is to fly British Airways a couple of times, because they usually have it as their mealtime red and you can experience the full, round, quite richly fruity style for which Lussac is famous. There are 2700 acres (1100 hectares) of vines, a few miles to the north of St-Émilion town; much of the wine is made by the co-operative at neighbouring Puisseguin, and we see few single-property wines on the export market. The wines are drinkable at two to three years old, but properties like Lyonnat make mouthfillers for a ten-year haul. Best years: 1985, '83, '82. Best producers: Barbe-Blanche, Cap de Merle, Courlat, Lyonnat, Villadière.

LYNCH-BAGES, CH.
Pauillac AC, *5ème cru classé*
HAUT-MÉDOC, BORDEAUX
Cabernet Sauvignon, Merlot, Cabernet Franc, Petit Verdot

Sometimes, tasting this wonderful wine with its almost succulent richness, its gentle texture and its starburst of flavours all butter and blackcurrants and mint, I find myself reflecting that its comparatively lowly position as a Fifth Growth Pauillac can only be because the chaps who devised the 1855 Classification were basically puritans. They couldn't bear to admit that a wine as open-heartedly lovely as Lynch-Bages could really be as important as other less generous Growths. Well, it is. Wine is about pleasure. Great wine is about great pleasure and there are few wines in the world which will so regularly give you such great pleasure as Lynch-Bages. The 175 acres (70 hectares) of vines in the middle of the AC, are planted in the traditional Pauillac mix, with a lot of Cabernet Sauvignon – 70 per cent – a certain amount of Cabernet Franc and Petit Verdot totalling 15 per cent, and only 15 per cent Merlot. This sounds like a tough wine taking a long time to mature – but that's the magic of Lynch-Bages – beautiful at ten years old, even more beautiful at 20. Best years: 1986, '85, '83, '82, '81, '79, '78. Second wine: Haut-Bages-Avérous.

MÂCON AC & MÂCON SUPÉRIEUR AC
MÂCONNAIS, BURGUNDY
Pinot Noir, Gamay

The Mâconnais region produces either Mâcon or Mâcon Supérieur, red and rosé. Mâcon has a minimum alcohol of nine degrees, Mâcon Supérieur of ten degrees, but these figures are almost always exceeded. The flavours are rarely exciting: the red usually has a 'rooty', vegetal rasp, though the fruit is attractive in a coarse, plummy kind of way; and the rosé lacks the fresh, breezy perfume which can make pink wine such fun. Best years: 1988, '87.

MÂCONNAIS
BURGUNDY

The Mâconnais is the large, 14,825-acre (6000-hectare) vineyard area based on the town of Mâcon, south of the Côte Chalonnaise and directly north of Beaujolais. Two-thirds of the area is planted with the white Chardonnay grape, and all of the most interesting Mâconnais wines are white. Gamay accounts for a further 25 per cent of the vineyard, and Pinot Noir makes up the remaining 7·5 per cent. However, the reds have failed to make a name for themselves, primarily because the Gamay is much more exciting in Beaujolais, and the Pinot Noir far more interesting in the Côte Chalonnaise and the Côte d'Or to the north. Lack of perfume, dominant earthy tastes, and a fairly high acid/tannin level are the main problems. Gamay reds will normally be sold as Mâcon and Mâcon Supérieur; Pinot reds will be sold as Bourgogne and, from a good producer, can have a pleasant light strawberry taste. A blend of these two

grapes, with at least one-third Pinot Noir, will be sold as Bourgogne Passe-Tout-Grains. The rosés should be drunk very young, and the reds within a couple of years, because the fruit will usually fade before the toughness softens. The co-operatives at Buxy (in the Chalonnaise), Igé and Mancey make reasonable wines.

MADIRAN AC
SOUTH-WEST
Tannat, Cabernet Sauvignon, Cabernet Franc

I am not one of Madiran's greatest fans. With few exceptions, I find the wines heavy, aggressive and short on personality. It often has the weight of a Médoc or a Graves but never has the complex excitement of flavour and perfume. Tannin is the problem – too much of it, and it comes as no surprise to discover that the tannic Tannat grape is the main variety up to a maximum of 60 per cent; Fer, Cabernet Sauvignon and Cabernet Franc make up the difference. Fans of Madiran will say I haven't waited long enough, that the wine becomes soft and limpid with age. Well, if it does, it will be an amazing transformation. Even so, I'm glad Madiran survives. The vineyards are in the wonderfully relaxing Vic Bilh hills just south of Armagnac; they had virtually died out after World War Two, being down to 15 acres (6 hectares). The reason seems to be that the Tannat grape had become too degenerate to cultivate, but modern botanical science found a way, and now there are 2000 acres (800 hectares). One thing that does help Madiran achieve a more attractive style is the use of new oak and several of the best producers (like Château Montus) are now doing this. Best years: 1985, '83, '82, '81, '79, '78. Best producers: Arricau-Bordes, Aydie, Boucassé, Cru du Paradis, Montus, Peyros, Union des Producteurs de Plaimont.

◀ The medieval château of Arricau-Bordes makes its Madiran wine from 50% Tannat and 50% Cabernet Sauvignon/Franc.

MAGDELAINE, CH.
St-Émilion AC, *premier grand cru classé*
BORDEAUX
Merlot, Cabernet Franc

Very much a wine of two personalities. In lighter years – because of its tremendously high percentage of Merlot (80 per cent) – the wine has a gushing, tender juicy fruit, easy to drink at only four to five years old, which seems to epitomize the indulgent softness of St-Émilion. However, in the grand vintages, Magdelaine changes gear. Those 27 acres (11 hectares) of Merlot-dominated vineyard sit on the steep slopes just south-west of the town of St-Émilion – a plum position for super-ripeness. Because the property is owned by the quality-obsessed J-P Moueix company in Libourne, the grapes are left to hang until the last possible moment, then an army of pickers swoops in. This gives grapes with a significantly higher ripeness than in neighbouring vineyards. Then the wine is fermented long and slow, stalks are added in to impart tannin and structure, and the wine is then aged in predominantly new barrels for a year-and-a-half. The result? Dark, rich, aggressive wines, yet behind the tough exterior there is a whole pile of luscious fruit and oaky spice waiting for release. Lighter vintages such as 1981 and '79 can be enjoyed at five to ten years old; bigger years like '85, '83 and '82 will take 15. Best years: 1985, '83, '82, '81, '79, '78, '75.

MALARTIC-LAGRAVIÈRE, CH.
Pessac-Léognan AC, *cru classé de Graves*
BORDEAUX
Cabernet Sauvignon, Cabernet Franc, Merlot

This is a strange property. It comprises 35 acres (14 hectares), set near the woods just south of Léognan, and is a neighbour of Fieuzal. The vineyard is atypical with only 44 per cent Cabernet Sauvignon, 31 per cent Cabernet Franc and 25 per cent Merlot, and produces more wine per hectare than any other *cru classé*, frequently having to declassify some of the crop. These factors should lead to a light, easy-drinking style. Well, they don't. The owner is adamant that heavy cropping suits his wine, and I can only say that, although Malartic-Lagravière does often start out a little lean and dry, it ages brilliantly. The 1955 is only now fading; the '70 is nowhere near ready. I can't explain it, and, frankly, nor can the owner. But it's a fact! You may find the wine disappointing when young but it gains a delightful cedary fragrance if you give it time. A *long* time! Best years: 1985, '83, '82, '81.

MALBEC

Malbec only really produces exciting wine in Cahors (where it is known as Auxerrois), although it is also planted in the Loire where they call it Cot, as well as in Bordeaux (where the St-Émilion growers call it Pressac!). Its contribution in Bordeaux is to give a slightly squashy softness to reds in areas like Bourg and Blaye, while in the Loire region it can also have a soothing effect when Cabernet Franc is cutting up rough. However, in the warmer climate of Cahors it steps centre stage, comprising a minimum of 70 per cent of the *appellation*'s historic red wine and producing deep, chewy plum-and-tobacco-flavoured wine quite unlike any other in France. Total plantings are about 12,350 acres (5000 hectares).

MARCILLAC VDQS
SOUTH-WEST
Fer, Gamay, Jurançon Noir

Well at least I *have* tasted Marcillac red (though not the rosé), which is more than most people can say because the Aveyron *département*, where it comes from, is an almost totally wineless area and the locals lap up the lot. In fact, there are 275 acres (110 hectares) of Marcillac – though you'd never notice it – and the Fer, at 80 per cent and often more, is the main grape type. The wine is strong and dry, rasping with herbs, grassy freshness and a slightly metallic zing. That may sound a bit off-putting, but you find me another red wine that can cope with the local Roquefort cheese! Best producer: Marcillac-Vallon co-operative.

MARGAUX AC
HAUT-MÉDOC, BORDEAUX
Cabernet Sauvignon, Cabernet Franc, Merlot and others

Margaux is the most sprawling of the six specific ACs in the Haut-Médoc. It covers 2850 acres (1150 hectares), just a little more than the more compact St-Estèphe's 2700 acres (1100 hectares) in the north. The vineyard is centred in the village of Margaux but also takes in the wine of Soussans to the north, and southwards, Cantenac, Labarde and Arsac. The key to Margaux's style is the pale gravel banks which cleave their way through the vineyards, giving little by way of nutrition, but providing perfect drainage so that the wines are rarely heavy and should have a quite divine perfume when they mature at 7–12 years old. The best examples of this style are La Gurgue, d'Issan, Labégorce-Zédé, Margaux, Palmer, Rausan-Ségla. A fuller, rounder but still perfumed style generally comes from the southern part of the AC, and is at its best from d'Angludet, Giscours, Siran, du Tertre. Altogether there are 21 Classed Growths in Margaux AC but many of these were underachieving in the '60s and '70s. Several, like Rausan-Ségla, Brane-Cantenac and Kirwan are only now waking up after a long sleep. There are a large number of non-classified properties – some regularly making Classed Growth quality wine. Most important is d'Angludet, followed by Siran, La Gurgue, Labégorce-Zédé and La Tour-de-Mons. Very occasionally a bottle surfaces simply labelled 'Margaux' (not *Château* Margaux). It shouldn't be taken too seriously since almost all the decent stuff sports a property's name. Best years: 1986, '85, '83, '82, '81, '79, '78.

MARGAUX, CH.
Margaux AC, *premier cru classé*
HAUT-MÉDOC, BORDEAUX
Cabernet Sauvignon, Merlot, Petit Verdot, Cabernet Franc

I first came across Château Margaux in a car park in the Rhône valley. It was lunchtime. I swigged it down with the *charcuterie*, and thought it uncommonly good. It was the 1961! Then a chap turned up one morning at my place for breakfast. He brought some Margaux to wet our whistles; the fruit and perfume in the wine swept aside the Weetabix and Cooper's Oxford marmalade with an imperious toss of the mane. That was the 1962. Then there was. . . in fact I realize I've only once sat down to a sensible dinner in a sensible place and drunk Château Margaux in a vaguely normal way. Even then I ended up having the 1961 poured over my strawberries with a twist of black pepper. Well, yes, it was fantastic but there's obviously something about me and Margaux, and the first thing is that despite all this I think it is the greatest wine in the whole Médoc.

This large 210-acre (87-hectare) property – its awesome Palladian-style

château set back in the trees just outside the village of Margaux – gives a new meaning to the words perfume and fragrance in a red wine, as though an inspired *parfumeur* had somehow managed to combine a sweet essence of blackcurrants with oil from crushed violets and the haunting scent of cedarwood, then swirled them together with more earthy pleasures like vanilla, roasted nuts and plums, and spirited all these into the bottle. Between 1967 and 1977 the property went into serious decline, but since 1978 the Mentzelopoulos family, who bought it in 1977, have produced a flawless series of wines which are as great as any Margaux ever created. At one time everyone was saying that Margaux wasn't worth a place among the First Growths, but it's pistols at dawn for anyone who suggests that to me now. Best years: 1986, '85, '83, '82, '81, '80, '79, '78. Second wine: Pavillon Rouge.

MARSANNAY AC
CÔTE DE NUITS, BURGUNDY
Pinot Noir

Marsannay is north of Fixin, with some if its vineyards virtually touching the suburbs of Dijon. Until 1987 it was famous only for its rosé which was Bourgogne AC but was allowed to include the Marsannay name on the label. Since 1987 Marsannay has been an AC in its own right. I suspect this will mean that we see increasing amounts of red Marsannay. The rosé can be quite pleasant but nowadays is made too dry and austere. The red is a little rough-hewn, and lacks fruit, but can give a reasonable drink at three to four years old. Best years: 1985, '83, '82. Best producers: Clair, Fougeray, Huguenot, Quillardet.

MAUCAILLOU, CH.
Moulis AC, *cru bourgeois*
HAUT-MÉDOC, BORDEAUX
Cabernet Sauvignon, Merlot,
Cabernet Franc, Petit Verdot

Maucaillou shows you don't have to have a 'Classed Growth' tag to make top quality wine. Indeed Moulis has several properties which are showing Classed Growth form at the moment. There are two secrets. Firstly, it does have some excellent gravel ridges especially round the village of Grand-Poujeaux where Maucaillou's vineyards are situated. The fruit that comes from there is every bit as good as that of the inland vineyards of St-Julien to the north and Margaux to the south. Secondly, there is a group of dedicated owners in Moulis of which the Dourthe family at Maucaillou is a leading member. The vineyard is 136 acres (55 hectares), with 45 per cent Cabernet Sauvignon, 35 per cent Merlot, 15 per cent Cabernet Franc and five per cent Petit Verdot. And the wine is expertly made using stainless steel equipment followed by up to two years in oak barrels, at least 75 per cent of which are new. The result is a soft, but classically flavoured wine, the fruit all pure blackcurrant, and oak mixing cedar with creamy coconut and vanilla roundness. It matures quickly but ages beautifully for 10–12 years. Best years: 1986, '85, '83, '82, '81, '79, '78.

MAURY AC
LANGUEDOC-ROUSSILLON
Grenache

A *vin doux naturel* red or rosé, from the Grenache grown north of the river Agly. There are about 5000 acres (2000 hectares) of vineyard producing this strong, sweetish, fortified wine either in a young, vaguely fresh style or the locally-revered but internationally-avoided old *rancio* style. Mas Amiel is a good producer but, frankly, I don't search it out and I don't miss it.

MAZIS-CHAMBERTIN AC
grand cru
CÔTE DE NUITS, BURGUNDY
Pinot Noir

Mazis-Chambertin is the *grand cru* closest to the village of Gevrey-Chambertin. There are 31 acres (12·6 hectares) and, in the infuriatingly unpredictable world of Burgundy *grands crus*, I find Mazis-Chambertin one of the more reliable. It is not usually as tannic and dark when young as its neighbour, Chambertin Clos-de-Bèze, but does have that damson skin, blackberry pip, crunchy fruit to start with, which, at six to eight years, can develop a heady fragrance – plums, blackcurrants and blackberries all perfumed and ripe. Best years: 1987, '85, '83, '82, '80, '78. Best producers: Camus, Hospices de Beaune, Rebourseau, Roty, Armand Rousseau, Tortochot.

MÉDOC

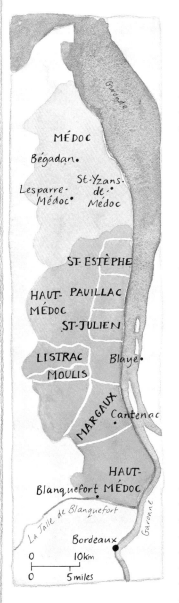

The Médoc produces a good fistful of the world's most renowned red wines, but it was a bit late in getting going, because until the seventeenth century this narrow lip of land running north from the city of Bordeaux between the Gironde estuary and the stormy Bay of Biscay coast was a marsh!

It's the gravel that makes Médoc wines great. Between the villages of Macau in the south near Bordeaux and St-Seurin-de-Cadourne in the north there are great banks of gravel, providing warm ripening conditions and perfect drainage for the Cabernet Sauvignon grape which dominates the vineyards. This whole area is called the Haut-Médoc – the Upper Médoc – and all the best wines come from here, from one of the half-a-dozen villages with the best gravel banks – Margaux, Listrac, Moulis, St-Julien, Pauillac and St-Estèphe – all of which qualify for their own AC.

Further north the land becomes flatter, damper, verdant with pasture and dotted with quiet, welcoming villages. But the gravel isn't there any more, its place being taken by damp clay. The Merlot grape becomes the leading variety; the wines become fruitier, simpler, but drinkable much younger. This is the Bas-Médoc – the Low Médoc. But the AC is plain Médoc – the growers felt 'Low Médoc' was disparaging – and I can see their point.

MAIN ACs
Haut-Médoc
Listrac
Margaux
Médoc
Moulis
Pauillac
St-Estèphe
St-Julien

MAIN CHÂTEAUX	
d'Angludet	Haut-Batailley
Batailley	Haut-Marbuzet
Beychevelle	d'Issan
Calon-Ségur	Lafite-Rothschild
Cantemerle	Lafon-Rochet
Chasse-Spleen	Lagrange
Cissac	la Lagune
Clarke	Larmande
Cos d'Estournel	Larose-Trintaudon
Ducru-Beaucaillou	Lascombes
Fourcas-Hosten	Latour
Giscours	Léoville-Barton
Grand-Puy-Lacoste	Léoville-Las-Cases
Gruaud-Larose	Léoville-Poyferré
Hanteillan	Loudenne
Haut-Bages-Libéral	Lynch-Bages
	Margaux

	MAIN GRAPES
Maucaillou	Cabernet Franc
Meyney	Cabernet Sauvignon
Montrose	Merlot
Mouton-Rothschild	
Palmer	
de Pez	
Pichon-Baron	
Pichon-Lalande	
Pontet-Canet	
Potensac	
Poujeaux	
Prieuré-Lichine	
Rausan-Ségla	
Sociando-Mallet	
Talbot	
du Tertre	

▲ A plane-tree-lined avenue leads impressively to Château Margaux, the top property and only First Growth in the Margaux AC. Lying just north of Bordeaux's industrial suburbs, Margaux is the largest AC in the Médoc and has 21 Classed Growths – more than any other.

MÉDOC AC
BORDEAUX
Cabernet Sauvignon, Cabernet
Franc, Merlot and others

This *appellation* covers the northern half of the Médoc peninsula, starting beyond St-Seurin-de-Cadourne. Frankly the *appellation* should be Bas-Médoc – the area's traditional name reflecting its downstream position on the Gironde estuary. But *bas* means low – and the growers didn't want the connotation of 'low' quality, especially when their neighbours in the southern part of the peninsula could already use the more attractive title 'Haut-Médoc'. The fact that the 'high' Médoc wines were patently superior to the 'low' ones was regarded by them as irrelevant.

The vineyards cover 7350 acres (2975 hectares) and the AC applies only to red wines, which can be very attractive – dry but juicy, with a little grassy acidity to keep them refreshing and quaffable. This easy-drinking style results from there being very little gravel in the Médoc AC and the Merlot grape dominates in the flat, meadow-like clay vineyards. Most wines are best to drink at three to five years old, but the brilliant Potensac takes ten years' ageing with ease. About 40 per cent of production is controlled by the co-operative movement. Best years: 1985, '83, '82, '81. Best producers: Castéra, Lacombe-Noaillac, les Ormes-Sorbet, Patache d'Aux, Plagnac, Potensac, la Tour-de-By, la Tour-St-Bonnet, Vieux Château Landon.

MENETOU-SALON AC
UPPER LOIRE
Pinot Noir

Menetou-Salon is a little AC covering ten villages not far from Sancerre in miles, but light years away in fame and fortune. Although the grapes are the same, and the wine similar, Menetou-Salon is still something of a *recherché* oddity. The vineyards are not yet that extensive – covering only 250 acres (100 hectares) – but the possibility of expansion is considerable and it is happening on a limited scale. White Menetou-Salon is a country cousin of Sancerre, but the reds and rosés from Pinot Noir, making up nearly 30 per cent of the production, can be better than many of Sancerre's rather dull offerings. They quite often have a very attractive, lean but strawberry perfumed style, and can be good and cherry-fresh. Drink them young. Best years: 1986, '85, '83. Best producers: des Brangers, Chavet, Pellé.

MERCUREY AC
CÔTE CHALONNAISE, BURGUNDY
Pinot Noir

Easily the biggest and most important of the four main Côte Chalonnaise villages, its 1500 acres (600 hectares) produce more wine than Rully, Givry and Montagny combined. A measure of its importance, or its self-importance, anyway, is that there is a move afoot to re-christen the Côte Chalonnaise the Région de Mercurey. Whatever the parish pump politics involved, there is a certain amount of sense in this, because Chalon lies away to the east on the banks of the Saône, and Mercurey is bang in the middle of the vineyards. Whereas much of the Côte Chalonnaise is in the hands of smallholders or independent proprietors, over half of Mercurey's vines are owned by merchant houses, so the wines are the most widely distributed of Chalonnaise wines. Production is usually over three million bottles – 95 per cent red from the Pinot Noir. The flavour is usually a pleasant but pale imitation of red wine from the Côte de Beaune just to the north, never very deep in colour, sometimes earthy, but often with a quite attractive cherry and strawberry fruit which can take some ageing. Best years: 1985, '83, '82. Best producers: Chanzy, Faiveley, Juillot, la Mouette, Rodet, Saier, Suremain, Voarick.

MERLOT

Merlot is one of Bordeaux's two main red grapes, the other being Cabernet Sauvignon. In the Médoc and Graves it was traditionally thought of as the secondary grape, since its wine is softer, richer, more precociously attractive – and, in a wine world which idolized longevity in a red wine, Merlot was normally relegated to the subordinate role of softening up the grand, aggressive Cabernet Sauvignon. Only in St-Émilion and Pomerol, where the cool clay soils didn't suit Cabernet, was the easier-ripening Merlot accorded pride of place –

but then traditionalists have never thought as highly of the fleshy, comely Pomerol and St-Émilion wines, as of the cold, haughty beauties of the Haut-Médoc.

Times change, though, and throughout the red wine world – now – there is a demand for wines which have the Bordeaux flavours yet which can be drunk young. Merlot wine fits the bill superbly. It is rich, juicy, often blackcurranty, often minty, sometimes almost sweet and buttery, with a taste of fruit-cake raisins. Pomerol wines are now more sought after than Haut-Médoc ones, and with 80,000 acres (32,000 hectares) of vines in the Gironde *département*, Merlot wines outnumber Cabernet Sauvignon, at 42,500 acres (17,200 hectares), by almost two to one. Merlot's ability to ripen on any soil, and to give high yields, have also encouraged its growth elsewhere in the south-west, especially Bergerac, Duras, Buzet, Cahors and Gaillac. But more importantly, it is a recommended grape for the vast swathes of the Midi. The soft, juicy fruit can make a dramatic difference to simple *vin de pays*, and Merlot has been planted throughout the south and even, with great success, in the Ardèche. If you like soft, full-flavoured reds without complications, these southern French Merlots will suit you fine.

MEURSAULT AC
CÔTE DE BEAUNE, BURGUNDY
Pinot Noir

Red Meursault? Well, there isn't much of it but there is a *little*. Most of it is grown on the Volnay side of the village and if it comes from the *premier cru* Les Santenots vineyard it can be sold as Volnay-Santenots – and it generally is, since the name Volnay means quite a bit in the red wine world, whereas 'Meursault red' tends to confuse. The wine is usually round and earthy – good, but not very 'Volnay'. There is also red wine produced at the southern end of the village, especially around the hamlet of Blagny where it is good, but a little hard, and is sold under the Blagny name. All this gives the impression that Meursault isn't very proud of its red wine; is any sold as Meursault Rouge? Yes, a tiny bit, but since it isn't as good as Blagny or Volnay-Santenots I can understand why most growers stick to white. Best years: 1985, '83, '82, '79, '78. Best producers: Ampeau, Comte Lafon, Matrot, Potinet-Ampeau.

MEYNEY, CH.
St-Estèphe AC, *cru grand bourgeois exceptionnel*
HAUT-MÉDOC, BORDEAUX
Cabernet Sauvignon, Merlot, Cabernet Franc, Petit Verdot

One of those châteaux which has quietly but determinedly been coming up on the inside rails for a number of years. I remember asking the importer a few years ago if I should buy some 1982 *en primeur*, as soon as it was offered, still in barrel. 'Ooh no', he said, 'You don't have to buy wines like Meyney *en primeur.*' So I didn't. But I rather wish I had. You can hardly get it and the price has tripled. Meyney's vineyard is good – 124 acres (50 hectares) with 70 per cent Cabernet Sauvignon, 24 per cent Merlot, four per cent Cabernet Franc and two per cent Petit Verdot, situated on the same riverside plateau as the Second Growth Montrose. But what has made this wine so reliably fine is the effort made by Cordier, the owners: maximizing the quality of the fruit, attaining greater ripeness than surrounding properties, and making ruthless selections of only the best vats to blend as Meyney. The result is big, proud, broad-flavoured wine, generally a little short on nuance but with dark plummy fruit which eventually, often after ten years, or even 15, gives a satisfying hint of cigar-box fragrance. Best years: 1986, '85, '83, '82, '81, '78, '75.

MINERVOIS AC
LANGUEDOC-ROUSSILLON
Carignan, Grenache, Cinsaut and others

Minervois hasn't quite got the wild 'mountain-man' reputation of Corbières. This is partly because – in recent years – the wines have been relatively light, spicy, dusty and deliciously fruity but not in any way challenging, and partly because with Corbières we all dash off into those unfarmed sub-Pyrenean hills and are soon lost in a timeless twilight world, but with Minervois we generally stay in the Aude valley rootling round the co-operatives and large estates within easy reach of civilization.

In fact the high, wind-swept, herb-strewn plateau of the Minervois *is* exciting and some of the old-style reds reflect this dry-earth, hot-resin fruitiness of the far south. But Minervois' great strength is in the rather boring concept of 'organization'. Big companies like Nicolas and Chantovent have worked hard with local co-operatives to produce good quality, juicy, quaffing wine. And at the reasonable prices they charge, that suits me fine. There are 10,000 acres (4050 hectares) of the Minervois AC producing up to 30 million bottles a year, almost all of it red. It is best drunk young, but can age, especially if a little new oak has been used to mature the wine. Most Minervois comes from the co-operatives and is generally good. Other recommended producers: Blomac, Domergue, Festiano, Gourgazaud, Meyzonnier, Paraza, Ste-Eulalie, Vaissière, Villerambert-Julien.

LA MISSION-HAUT-BRION, CH.
Pessac-Léognan AC, *cru classé de Graves*
BORDEAUX
Cabernet Sauvignon, Merlot, Cabernet Franc

One of the properties which, by a show of hands and shouts of 'aye', could be promoted to First Growth. I suppose I'll go along with that but not without qualms, because I always find La Mission wines powerful – almost bullying and hectoring by nature – but never charming, and rarely possessed of that lovely, ruminative flavour-memory which other blockbusters like Latour and Pétrus *do* have. Its strength is in a dark-plums-and-chocolate fruit braided with an earthy dryness which rarely opens out before a decade and often needs 20 years or more to achieve its unsubtle but memorable tangle of tobacco, cedar and herb garden perfumes. The property covers 42 acres (17 hectares). Best years: 1985, '83, '82, '81, '79, '78, '75, '74.

MONBOUSQUET, CH.
St-Émilion AC, *grand cru*
BORDEAUX
Merlot, Cabernet Franc, Cabernet Sauvignon

The only well-known St-Émilion property on the *sables*, the sandy flat lands down by the river Dordogne. The *sables*, generally planted quite recently, have less quality potential than the *côtes* (slopes) or the *graves* (gravel plateau). But Monbousquet makes the best of the conditions and produces a delicious, absurdly soft and soothing wine which hardly seems to have any tannin at all, merely a magical burst of honey and butterscotch and blackcurrant which you would expect to fade away with the evening sun, but which can age well. The 1970 and '75 are still lovely. Best years: 1985, '83, '82, '78.

MONTAGNE-ST-ÉMILION AC
BORDEAUX
Merlot, Cabernet Sauvignon, Cabernet Franc, Malbec

A St-Émilion 'satellite' on the northern borders of both St-Émilion and Pomerol. The wines are rather good and often exhibit quite a bit of the Pomerol plumminess even when quite young. Both Parsac and St-Georges, two small neighbouring communes, have the right to use the Montagne-St-Émilion AC, and in general do so, though some properties in St-Georges, especially the historic Château St-Georges itself, prefer to use the St-Georges-St-Émilion AC. The wines are normally ready in four years but age quite well. Best years: 1985, '83, '82, '81, '79. Best producers: Calon, Corbin, Maison-Blanche, Maison-Neuve, Plaisance, Roudier, des Tours, Vieux Château St-André.

MONTHELIE AC
CÔTE DE BEAUNE, BURGUNDY
Pinot Noir

Monthelie wines have historically been sold as Volnay, the next village to the north-east. That was fine while *appellation* laws allowed it, but when Monthelie had to stand on its own two feet and trade under its own name, things got a bit rough. Nobody knew a thing about Monthelie, so it languished in the shadows while barrels of Volnay reached ever higher prices. Which was bad luck on the growers but good news for us: most of Monthelie's 250 acres (100 hectares) of vines have an excellent south-east to south exposure, many of the vines are old, and the wines generally have a lovely chewy, cherry-skin fruit and a slight piny rasp which make good drinking at a good price. Best years: 1987, '85, '83, '82, '79, '78. Best producers: Bouchard, Deschamps, Leflaive, Parent, Potinet-Ampeau, Ropiteau-Mignon, Suremain, Thevenin-Monthelie.

MONTROSE, CH.
St-Estèphe AC, *2ème cru classé*
HAUT-MÉDOC, BORDEAUX
Cabernet Sauvignon, Merlot,
Cabernet Franc

This leading St-Estèphe property of 166 acres (67 hectares) used to be famous, sometimes infamous, for its dark, brooding, Cabernet Sauvignon-dominated style. Twenty years was regarded as a reasonable time to wait before broaching a bottle, and around 30 years to drink it at its prime. Now I know we used to scoff a bit about how hard it was, how tannic, how slowly it revealed its blackcurrant and pencil-shavings scent, but it *was* a classic and we *did* love it. Maybe we made fun of its burliness once too often, because the wine has undergone a sea change which has markedly reduced its personality. Since 1978 the vintages are lighter, softer and less substantial, certain to be ready for drinking at ten years old, not 20. I really am sorry, because cash-flow accountancy shouldn't affect a famous property like Montrose even if the wine did take 30 years to peak. Montrose used to be thought of as the leading St-Estèphe. Cos d'Estournel now holds this position, and in great years like 1982, '83 and '85 Montrose is regularly outclassed not only by the top Classed Growths of St-Estèphe but also by leading *crus bourgeois* like Haut-Marbuzet, de Pez and Meyney. Best years: 1986, '85, '84, '81, '76.

MOREY-ST-DENIS AC
CÔTE DE NUITS, BURGUNDY
Pinot Noir

After decades of being treated as Cinderella – squashed between Chambolle-Musigny to the south and Gevrey-Chambertin to the north – Morey St-Denis has recently been flexing its muscles, and now commands a price for its wine equal to its more famous neighbours. Certainly the vineyards deserve it. There are five *grands crus* (Bonnes-Mares, Clos des Lambrays, Clos de la Roche, Clos de Tart and Clos St-Denis) as well as some very good *premiers crus*, but the entire extent of the village's vineyards is only 329 acres (133 hectares) – neighbouring Gevrey-Chambertin, for instance, has 1235 acres (500 hectares) – and so the *négociants*, whose promotion of a wine historically made its

▶ Clos de la Roche, the largest of the five *grands crus* in Morey-St-Denis. The word *clos*, widely used in Burgundy, describes a vineyard that is (or was) walled. The *roche* seems to have been a huge stone – long since vanished – which played a part in ancient rites.

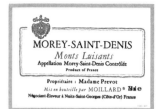

reputation, have paid less heed to Morey, simply because there was less wine to go round. Nowadays most Morey wine does come from *négociants*, often blended by the two small co-operatives which service the village, and much of this is light and dull. However there is better Morey, in particular from the *premier cru* and *grand cru* vineyards and usually from single growers. They generally have a good strawberry or redcurrant fruit, sometimes a little meaty and getting an attractive chocolate and liquorice depth as they age over five to eight years. Best years: 1987, '85, '83, '80, '78. Best producers: Bryczek, Drouhin, Dujac, Lignier, Marchand, Moillard, Ponsot, Tardy.

MORGON AC
BEAUJOLAIS, BURGUNDY
Gamay

Although Moulin-à-Vent is the Beaujolais *cru* which is supposed to age best and come closest in maturity to a fine Côte d'Or Burgundy, Morgon could easily lay claim to that reputation. Indeed they even have a verb *morgonner* – to 'Morgon'! – which is used to describe how the local wine begins to lose its fresh, plummy fruit after two to three years and evolves into something chocolaty, cocoa-ish and strongly perfumed with cherries or even kirsch. Sounds good? It is. But only the best wines behave like this, usually from a single grower, and from the slopes around Mont du Py. You may see Le Py, Les Chaumes or Le Clachet marked as vineyard names, and snap a bottle up if you do. The majority of Morgon, however, is less special, and at 2545 acres (1030 hectares), there is a lot of it, but it still manages a soft, cherry fruit which is very easy drinking. Best years: 1987, '85, '83, '81, '78. Best producers: Aucoeur, Brun, La Chanaise, Descombes, Jambon, Janodet, Lapierre, Longuepierre, Savoye, Vincent.

MOULIN-À-VENT AC
BEAUJOLAIS, BURGUNDY
Gamay

I sometimes feel a bit sorry for poor old Moulin-à-Vent because it would so like to be a big, burly, world-famous Burgundy like Chambertin. But sadly it is in the wrong place – a good 150 miles (240km) too far south – and it grows the wrong grape – the Gamay, rather than the much more vaunted Pinot Noir. Undaunted, it keeps on trying, and while certainly the most un-Beaujolais-like of the Beaujolais *crus*, the wine does in fact do a pretty good job of impersonating a fairly full, chocolaty Burgundy – slightly short on perfume, but good and rich, if you leave it for six to ten years to mature. You won't find a village of Moulin-à-Vent on the map, because *moulin-à-vent* means 'windmill' and that's what the wine is named after – an old building standing in the middle of almost 1750 acres (700 hectares) of vines between the villages of Romanèche-Thorins and Chénas. They say the soil has a streak of manganese in it, accounting for the dark, dry flavour when the wine is young. Best years: 1987, '85, '83, '81, '79, '78, '76. Best producers: Benoit Trichard, Bloud, Brugne, Champagnon, Charvet, Chauvet, Duboeuf (single domaines), Château des Jacques, Janodet, Siffert, la Tour de Bief. Duboeuf is using new oak barrels experimentally and the first wines out are delicious.

MOULIS AC
HAUT-MÉDOC, BORDEAUX
Cabernet Sauvignon, Cabernet Franc, Merlot and others.

One of the six specific ACs within the Haut-Médoc area. It is the smallest, at only 964 acres (390 hectares), and none of its properties are included in the 1855 Classification – but that's to our benefit, because much of the wine is excellent, yet never over-priced. The best vineyards are on a deep gravel plateau centred on the village of Grand-Poujeaux rather than Moulis itself. The wines are beautifully balanced, surprisingly soft behind their early tannin, and delicious to drink at five to six years old, though good examples should age 10–20 years. There's more and more new oak being used to age the wines and you often get a pretty decent mouthful of blackcurrant, vanilla and cedarwood flavours. Best years: 1986, '85, '83, '82, '81, '79, '78. Best properties: Branas, Brillette, Chasse-Spleen, Duplessis-Fabre, Dutruch-Grand-Poujeaux, Gressier-Grand-Poujeaux, Maucaillou, Moulin-à-Vent, Poujeaux.

MOUTON-CADET
Bordeaux AC
HAUT-MÉDOC, BORDEAUX
Cabernet Sauvignon, Cabernet
Franc, Merlot

What's a brand name doing in this book? Well, to leave out Mouton-Cadet would be a bit like writing a history of soft drinks and leaving out Coca-Cola! And in any case, is Mouton-Cadet really a brand name? Lots of people think it's a sort of 'younger brother' – cadet, geddit? – of the great Mouton-Rothschild. Well, that's how it started out. Things were pretty tricky during the Great Depression of the 1920s and '30s. Not only was wine not selling, but the vintages weren't much good. In fact, 1930, '31, and '32 were three of the worst ever. Baron Philippe de Rothschild was determined not to release any wine which might harm the reputation of his beloved Mouton-Rothschild, but he *was* getting strapped for cash. So he blended these three vintages of Mouton-Rothschild and called it Mouton-Cadet. It was a whopping success, and is now the most widely-selling red Bordeaux in the world. But look on the label. It says Bordeaux AC – meaning the wine is blended and comes from anywhere in Bordeaux. They say there's always some Mouton-Rothschild in it. Well, maybe... In the '60s and early '70s it was very classy wine but nowadays it is correct though never inspiring, and never cheap.

MOUTON-ROTHSCHILD, CH.
Pauillac AC, *premier cru classé*
HAUT-MÉDOC, BORDEAUX
Cabernet Sauvignon, Cabernet
Franc, Merlot

Baron Philippe de Rothschild died in 1988 and so ended a remarkable era in Bordeaux's history. For 65 years he had managed Mouton-Rothschild, raising it from a rather capricious and run-down Second Growth to becoming one of the most famous wines in the world, achieving promotion to First Growth status in 1973 – the only promotion ever effected within the traditional 1855 Classification of Bordeaux's top properties! He did this by unremitting commitment to quality, which in great vintages like 1961 and '82 paid off so handsomely that Mouton arguably produced Bordeaux's greatest wine. But you can't rely on quality alone if you're determined to force the Bordeaux establishment into admitting you into the top class. So he did it by flair, imagination and brilliant marketing.

The Mouton-Rothschild he created is a 200-acre (80-hectare) estate planted with 85 per cent Cabernet Sauvignon, ten per cent Cabernet Franc and five per cent Merlot. The high proportion of Cabernet Sauvignon and the perfectly situated gravel banks of the vineyard give a wine which, in most years, is astonishingly exotic and heavy. It manages to transform the cedarwood, cigar-box, pencil-shavings spectrum of dry, restrained fragrances into a steamy, intoxicating swirl of head-turning richness, backed up by a deep, chewy, pure blackcurrant fruit. Mouton is tannic when it's young, often taking 15–20 years to open up fully, but you can always see the richness behind the tough exterior. Each year Mouton commissions a different artist to design the label, and most of the modern greats like Chagall, Miró and Picasso have had a go. Best years: 1986, '85, '84, '83, '82, '81, '78, '75, '70.

MUSIGNY AC
grand cru
CÔTE DE NUITS, BURGUNDY
Pinot Noir

What *is* Musigny, or what has Musigny the potential to be, that is the question. This 27-acre (10·7-hectare) *grand cru* – just to the south of the village of Chambolle-Musigny on the slopes directly above Clos de Vougeot – has the ability to produce red wines of such fragrance, such delicacy of texture, that a French monk called Gaston Roupnel described them as 'of silk and lace', the perfume being 'a damp garden, a rose and a violet covered in morning dew'. Lovely isn't it? And, yes, I *do* know what he means. I've found roses and violets, tainted with that earthy dampness of a garden just after dawn, then running through the thrill of fresh flower scents caught in the breeze of midsummer noons, and later twined through with the autumn smoke of forest bonfires as the wine first breathes, demurely matures and wistfully declines through 20 years or more. Those were Musignys from the '50s, '60s and early '70s. Musigny is nowadays usually too sweet and too thick for romance remembered. I think the producers' hearts have been hardened by commercial reality. So I'll wait awhile, save my money, till its soul returns.

NUITS-ST-GEORGES AC
CÔTE DE NUITS, BURGUNDY
Pinot Noir

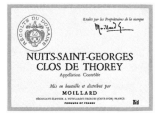

For the UK market, this surely used to be the best-known Côte de Nuits village. In fact, with Châteauneuf-du-Pape and Beaujolais, it was probably the best-known red wine name in the world. That was before 1973, the year EEC regulations took effect in Britain. Suddenly Nuits-St-Georges, which had been on every hotel and restaurant list in the country, disappeared. The reason was simple. British merchants had rather liked the patriotic ring to 'St-Georges' and the vaguely suggestive feel of 'Nuits', and so, untrammelled by French *appellation* laws, had concocted any old stuff from all stations south to Casablanca and called it Nuits-St-Georges. With EEC membership came the application of French AC regulations elsewhere, and the realization that 'brewers Nuits' had nothing to do with what was now a legally protected name.

When it began to creep back on to wine lists in the late 1970s, Nuits-St-Georges was three times the price and half the colour – but it was the real thing. Nowadays it is one of the few relatively reliable 'village' names in Burgundy.

The *appellation*, which includes the village of Prémeaux, is big: 925 acres (375 hectares). Though it has no *grands crus*, it has 38 *premiers crus* – more than any other AC – and many of these are extremely good. The wine can be rather slow to open out, often needing at least five years, but then it gets a lovely dry plumskins chewiness to it which ages to a deep figs-and-pruneskins fruit, chocolaty, smoky and rather decayed. It's delicious, I promise, whatever it sounds like! Best years: 1986, '85, '83, '80, '78, '76. Best producers: Chauvenet, Chevillon, Dubois, Gouges, Grivot, Jadot, Jaffelin, Jayer, Labouré-Roi, Michelot, Moillard, Rion.

PALETTE AC
PROVENCE
Grenache, Mourvèdre, Cinsaut and others

Pine-needles and resin are what I taste in the wines of Palette – a tiny AC just east of Aix-en-Provence. Not that they actually employ these to make the wine, but the slopes on which the 62 acres (25 hectares) of vines grow are covered in pines and herbs, and for once I do see some possible connection between Provençal wines and the herb-strewn hills round the vineyards. Anyway, Palette reds and rosés, usually about 60,000 bottles from a total production of 85,000, are made from Cinsaut, Mourvèdre and Grenache. The rosé is, well, herby and rather dry. The red: well, herby again. I find it tough and charmless. I'm told it does age, and the local market pays high prices for it, but so far I've had no luck. Best producer: Simone.

PALMER, CH.
Margaux AC, *3ème cru classé*
HAUT-MÉDOC, BORDEAUX
Cabernet Sauvignon, Merlot, Cabernet Franc, Petit Verdot

Of all the properties which could justifiably feel underrated by the 1855 Classification, Château Palmer has the best case. Anyone who has the luck to drink this wonderful wine – even in a half-decent vintage – is won over, above all, by its perfume. It is as though every black and red fruit in the land has thrown in a bundle of its ripest flavours: blackcurrant, blackberry, plum, loganberry. . . you'll find them there, but Palmer goes further. There's a rich, almost fat core to the wine; and curling through the fruit and the ripeness are trails of other fragrances – roses, violets, cedar and cigars, all there in abundance. The first time I was offered Palmer I was so captivated by its smell I could hardly bear to drink it!

Named after a British major-general who fought in the Napoleonic Wars, it is an 86-acre (35-hectare) site on excellent gravel right next to Château Margaux. The irresistible plump fruit of Palmer is caused by the very high proportion of Merlot (40 per cent), with only 55 per cent Cabernet Sauvignon, three per cent Cabernet Franc and two per cent Petit Verdot. There was a period during the 1960s and most of the '70s when it was Palmer rather than Château Margaux which held aloft the banner of brilliance in the Margaux AC. Surprisingly the 1980s have been a little more patchy, but there is still no doubt that Palmer is a First Growth in all but name. Best years: 1986, '85, '83, '82, '79, '78, '75, '71, '70. Second wine: Réserve-du-Général.

PAPE-CLÉMENT, CH.
Pessac-Léognan AC, *cru classé de Graves*
BORDEAUX
Cabernet Sauvignon, Merlot

At the moment, Pape-Clément only seems to make good wine about once every decade: 1985 is exciting, 1975 outstanding (in a difficult year), 1966 beautifully mature and classic. But once every ten years isn't much of a record for an expensive and famous Graves Classed Growth. The 67-acre (27-hectare) property, named after the French Pope Clément V – whose brother gave it to him in 1300 – was then well-known for its therapeutic spring. Perhaps the owners have recently taken to dosing themselves with the water, because '86 and '85 are highly promising. Let's hope so, since Pape-Clément can mix ripe, sweet fruit with herby and tobaccoey scents in a most delicious way. Best years: 1986, '85, '75, '66.

PAUILLAC AC
HAUT-MÉDOC, BORDEAUX
Cabernet Sauvignon, Merlot,
Cabernet Franc and others

If there is a king of red wine grapes it has to be Cabernet Sauvignon. In every corner of the world where there is enough sun to ripen the fruit, it makes dark, dense, rather tough but wonderfully flavoured wines. Yet its heartland is the single village of Pauillac in the Haut-Médoc. Throughout the New World – and in much of southern France, Spain and Italy too – if you ask ambitious winemakers what model they take for Cabernet Sauvignon they will say Latour, Lafite-Rothschild or Mouton-Rothschild – one of the three Pauillac First Growths, each of which, in its different way, is an ultimate expression of Cabernet Sauvignon.

There are 2250 acres (900 hectares) of vines in the AC, on deep gravel banks to the north, west and south of the town of Pauillac. This makes Pauillac AC the third biggest community in the Haut-Médoc. Sleepily huddled at the muddy edge of the Gironde – a faded promenade, an idling boat, a few listless fishermen chatting on the quay, the local restaurant specializing in herrings – you'd never guess that for many this is the Mecca of the red wine world. Apart from the three First Growths, there are 15 other Classed Growths, including the world-famous Pichon-Lalande and Lynch-Bages. The wines go from terse, fretful and austere to blooming with friendly fruit, but the uniting characteristic of blackcurrant fruit and cedar or pencil-shavings perfume is never far distant.

Few Pauillacs are ready young and most will last 20 years. Best years: 1986, '85, '83, '82, '81, '79, '78. Best properties: Batailley, Fonbadet, Grand-Puy-Ducasse, Grand-Puy-Lacoste, Haut-Bages-Libéral, Haut-Batailley, Lafite-Rothschild, Latour, Lynch-Bages, Mouton-Rothschild, Pibran, Pichon-Baron, Pichon-Lalande.

PAVIE, CH.
St-Émilion AC, *premier grand cru classé*
BORDEAUX
Merlot, Cabernet Franc, Cabernet Sauvignon

The biggest of the St-Émilion *premiers grands crus* at 91 acres (37 hectares), enjoys a superb site on steep south-facing slopes just to the south-east of the town. Being biggest was obviously a bit more than Pavie could cope with in the '60s and '70s because none of the wines was outstanding; even the potentially strongest vintages had a soft, simple, buttered-brazil kind of flavour – very attractive but totally one-dimensional. Since 1979 things have bucked up dramatically and Pavie is now one of the most improved properties in St-Émilion. The fruit is still there, but the wines are far more concentrated and, while drinkable young, will happily improve for a decade or more to something very good indeed. Best years: 1985, '83, '82, '81, '79.

PÉCHARMANT AC
SOUTH-WEST
Merlot, Cabernet Sauvignon,
Cabernet Franc, Malbec

Lovely red wines from a small enclave in the Bergerac region east of Bergerac town. The soil is relatively chalky, giving wines that are usually quite light in body but with a delicious, full, piercing flavour of blackcurrants and a most attractive grassy acidity. They are rarely very tannic but are, in general, so well-balanced that good vintages can easily age ten years and end up indistinguishable from a good Haut-Médoc. Recommended. Best years: 1986, '85, '83, '82, '81. Best producers: Clos Peyrelevade, Corbiac, Haut-Pécharmant, Tiregand.

PERNAND-VERGELESSES AC
CÔTE DE BEAUNE, BURGUNDY
Pinot Noir

Another of those off-the-beaten-track Burgundy villages which is consequently not much heard about. Yet Pernand-Vergelesses does have one considerable slice of luck: the great hill of Corton comes round from the east, and at its western end a decent-sized chunk lies inside the Pernand-Vergelesses boundary. The red Corton lacks the richness of the wines from the south- and east-facing slopes, and takes longer to mature into a finely-balanced, savoury-rich red. Red sold under the Pernand-Vergelesses AC is immediately softer, easier, very attractive young with nice raspberry pastille fruit and a slight earthiness, though good to age for six to ten years. The 353 acres (143 hectares) of vineyards produce about 85 per cent red wine and, apart from Le Corton, the best vineyards are Île des Hautes Vergelesses and Les Basses Vergelesses, both *premiers crus*. Best years: 1987, '85, '83, '82, '78. Best producers: Besancenot-Mathouillet, Bonneau du Martray, Chandon de Briailles, Dubreuil-Fontaine, Laleur-Piot, Rapet, Rollin.

PESSAC-LÉOGNAN AC
BORDEAUX
Cabernet Sauvignon, Cabernet Franc and others

After years of lobbying, the new *appellation* Pessac-Léognan was born in 1987. Since 1984, wines from this sub-area of the Graves have been able to label themselves Graves-Léognan, or Graves-Pessac. The new *appellation* recognizes that the light gravelly soils which give the Graves area its name have historically provided the finest wines, since below Martillac (the southernmost limit of the Pessac-Léognan *appellation*) the soil becomes sandier, more inclined to clay, and less likely to give grapes of top quality. The AC includes all the Classed Growths of the region. Best years: 1986, '85, '83, '82, '81, '79, '78. Best properties: Domaine de Chevalier, de Fieuzal, Haut-Bailly, Haut-Brion, la Louvière, Malartic-Lagravière, la Mission-Haut-Brion, Rochemorin, Smith-Haut-Lafitte, la Tour-Haut-Brion, la Tour-Martillac.

PETIT-VILLAGE, CH.
Pomerol AC
BORDEAUX
Merlot, Cabernet Franc, Cabernet Sauvignon

Not the wine to get in a blind tasting because, although this property produces one of the top Pomerol wines, the style is much sterner and less sumptuous than that of its neighbours. This may partly be because the owner is Bruno Prats, who makes Cos d'Estournel, the outstanding wine of St-Estèphe, and who perhaps brings a little of his *médocain* instinct to bear on his Pomerol property. However, the soil also plays a part. There was a time when half this 27-acre (11-hectare) vineyard was planted with Cabernet Sauvignon, though now it is 80 per cent Merlot, 10 per cent each Cabernet Franc and Cabernet Sauvignon. Some years, like 1982, *are* luscious and rich, but in general it is worth ageing Petit-Village for eight to ten years, even 10–15 years in vintages like 1975 and '85. Best years: 1985, '83, '82, '81, '79, '78, '75.

PÉTRUS, CH.
Pomerol AC
BORDEAUX
Merlot, Cabernet Franc

Château Pétrus is a small, 28-acre (11·5-hectare) estate with charmingly unimpressive buildings in an area that, 30 years ago, used to merit merely a paragraph or two in 'other Bordeaux wines' sections. Yet Pétrus is now the most expensive red wine in the world. Its AC is Pomerol, so recently acclaimed by critics that it still has no 'classification' of quality, but if it did, Pétrus would stand alone and magnificent at the very head, and for two reasons.

First, the vineyard: this is situated on what is called the 'button' of Pétrus – an oval of imperceptibly higher land which is virtually solid clay, shot through with nuggets of iron. Only Merlot can flourish in this soil and Pétrus is 95 per cent Merlot. These vines are remarkably old, often up to 70 years of age, which is rare in Pomerol and St-Émilion because the great frost of 1956 destroyed most of the vines and caused wholesale replanting. The owner of Pétrus simply waited patiently for several years while the old vines got their strength back. The result is a concentration of pure ripe fruit not found in any other wine.

The second factor in Pétrus' quality is the caring genius of its co-owner, Christian Moueix, and his hugely talented winemaker, Jean-Claude Benouet.

▲ During the grape-harvest at Château Pétrus, a helicopter dries off rain from the vines. Water on the grapes would dilute the juice and so impair quality.

They ensure that only totally ripe grapes are picked (they only harvest in the afternoon to avoid dew diluting the juice and in 1987 a helicopter hovered over the vines to dry off vintage rains!); any portion of the wine which doesn't exude Pétrus quality is rejected and the whole crop is then aged in new oak barrels. The result is a wine of powerful, viscous intensity, a celestial syrup of ripe blackcurrants, blackberries, mulberries, plums and cream, overlaid with mint and tobacco scents and the perilous moist excitement of fresh-dug truffles – these and a dozen other sensations, all in perfect balance. Best years: 1986, '85, '83, '82, '81, '80, '79, '75, '71.

DE PEZ, CH.
St-Estèphe AC, *cru bourgeois supérieur*
HAUT-MÉDOC, BORDEAUX
Cabernet Sauvignon, Cabernet Franc, Merlot

De Pez has been a byword for consistent quality since the 1960s. I have never tasted a poor bottle of de Pez, although nor have I tasted any which made my heart sing, but then ethereal, romantic joys are not St-Estèphe's speciality. Sturdy fruit, slow to evolve, but mouthfilling and satisfying, with a little hint of cedarwood and a good deal of blackcurrant to ride with their earthy taste – that's St-Estèphe's forte. De Pez – for long regarded as St-Estèphe's leading non-classified Growth, but now at least equalled by Meyney and Haut-Marbuzet – adds a leathery, plummy dimension in good vintages. The 57-acre (23-hectare) vineyard, well-placed inland from the Third Growth Calon-Ségur, has a lot of Cabernet Sauvignon (70 per cent), with 15 per cent Cabernet Franc, and 15 per cent Merlot; this goes a long way to explain why good vintages need 15–20 years to mature, and why they have such depth of flavour when they do. Best years: 1986, '85, '83, '82, '79, '78, '76, '75.

PICHON-BARON, CH.
Pauillac AC, *2ème cru classé*
HAUT-MÉDOC, BORDEAUX
Cabernet Sauvignon, Merlot, Malbec

Somehow Pichon-Baron got left behind in the rush. Its Pauillac neighbour, Pichon-Lalande, and its St-Julien neighbours, Léoville-Las-Cases and Léoville-Barton, leapt at the chance offered by the string of fine vintages from 1978. They established a leadership at the top of the Second Growths which now seriously challenges the First Growths for sheer quality and surpasses several of them for consistency. What about Pichon-Baron? Its 74 acres (30 hectares) of vineyards are regarded as superb. Its mixture of 75 per cent Cabernet Sauvignon, 23 per cent Merlot and two per cent Malbec is ideal for making great Pauillac. Yet the wines are medium-weight, correct certainly, and sometimes having an intense blackcurrant and blackberry fragrance – but, just not exciting. I remember thinking how good the 1982 was when I first tasted it – until I tasted the other Pauillac '82s and realized how far behind Pichon-Baron was. Since 1987 the wine-making has been taken over by Jean-Michel Cazes of Lynch-Bages. Committed, opinionated and very talented, he should quickly bring about the revival of one of Bordeaux's potentially great wines. Best years: 1987, '86, '83, '82.

PICHON-LALANDE, CH.
Pauillac AC, *2ème cru classé*
HAUT-MÉDOC, BORDEAUX
Cabernet Sauvignon, Merlot,
Cabernet Franc, Petit Verdot

Of all the top-notch wines in the Haut-Médoc, none has so consistently excited me, beguiled me, and totally satisfied me as Pichon-Lalande. The vineyard is on excellent land next to Latour and Léoville-Las-Cases in St-Julien. In fact some of the vines are in St-Julien and this, combined with the highest proportion of Merlot in Pauillac (35 per cent), may account for the sumptuous, fleshy richness of the wine, and its burst of blackcurrant, walnut and vanilla perfume, and I mean perfume – heady, searching – not just smell. But the vineyards are no better than those of the under-achieving brother Pichon-Baron and the real cause of Pichon-Lalande's sensual triumph over the usually austere Pauillac community is the inspired, messianic figure of Madame de Lencquessaing. She took over the property in 1978 and has since led Pichon-Lalande upwards in a wave of passion and involvement. Quite a woman. Quite a wine. Every vintage seems to be good nowadays. And don't be deceived by the lush caress of the rich fruit – there's lots of tannin and acid lurking, and the wines, though wonderful at six to seven years old, will usually last for 20 at least. Best years: 1986, '85, '84, '83, '82, '81, '80, '79, '78, '75. Second wine: Réserve de la Comtesse.

PINOT NOIR

◀ Pinot Noir stretching as far as the eye can see – a characteristic Burgundian vinescape. France has more Pinot Noir than any other country.

Burgundy's red grape must be a very difficult grape to grow, as anyone who has ever considered giving up Burgundy because the price is so high and the quality so variable will realize. Well, it is. It buds early and ripens early, which makes it suitable for cool climates. But at the same time its tight bunches are seriously prone to rot, it reacts to overcropping by producing wine little better than rosé, and yet because its fruit sets very irregularly, it is often pruned for extra quantity – just in case the fruit doesn't set. When it *does*, of course, you're going to overcrop, which means the vine will object and produce pale juice – and so it goes on.

Pinot Noir is a *very* ancient variety, and was probably one of the first successful attempts to isolate and tame a specific wild vine. That was at least 2000 years ago, and yet the wildness is still there. No other vine mutates so quickly – one authority reckons there are as many as 1000 different Pinot Noir types in Burgundy alone! Yet this savagery is what can make its wine so exciting. Only Syrah has such a variety of flavours to offer. Strawberry, cherry, raspberry and plum predominate in the young wine, but as it ages, the cherry becomes scented, the plums turn to prunes, chocolate and woodsmoke and figs mingle with truffles and over-hung game and the decayed stink of old vegetables. It sounds dreadful but it *is* a shocking flavour, and although many Burgundies never get near it, those that do are more startlingly good than the purer, cleaner flavours of great Bordeaux.

Being a temperamental early ripener, and no good as an 'improver' in the far south, Pinot's sphere of influence is almost entirely in the centre and north of France. It makes either light reds or quite tasty rosés in Savoie, Jura, the Loire – especially Sancerre – and Alsace. But its most important contribution outside Burgundy is as a major component of Champagne, occasionally as a rosé, but usually providing the body to fatten out the leaner flavour of Chardonnay. The juice is run off the skins straight after pressing so has almost no colour at all. Altogether there are over 42,000 acres (17,000 hectares) of Pinot Noir in France, one-third of which are in the only place it really has the chance to set the world alight: Burgundy's Côte d'Or.

POMEROL AC
BORDEAUX
Merlot, Cabernet Franc, Cabernet Sauvignon

When I was at university – not *that* long ago! – there was a restaurant near the river which was a bit on the posh side but was *the* place to take a girl to if you were super-desperate to impress her. There was only one way I could afford to do this – which was to order the cheapest claret on their list with all the self-assured bluster I could manage: I was in luck. It was a bottle simply labelled 'Pomerol' – bottled in Bristol – and I don't think the wine-waiter had any more idea where Pomerol was than I did. But then I didn't care – the wine was so smooth and plummy it should have been twice the price and every sip saw me set my amorous sights a notch higher. Which taught me two things. Firstly, Pomerol has a uniquely smooth, rich taste for a dry red Bordeaux. And secondly, overindulgence in it builds a totally unfounded confidence in one's social skills.

That was Pomerol then. The flavour remains just as seductively rich, but from being a virtually unknown AC 'ooh, somewhere near St-Émilion, I think', it is possibly now the most famous of the Bordeaux regions, in the United States at least; is certainly the most expensive of the Bordeaux ACs across the board, and is the home of the world's most spectacular and exorbitantly expensive red wine – Château Pétrus. Yet Pomerol is the most anonymous of Bordeaux's ACs. You can't tell by looking where it starts – almost in the suburbs of Libourne 25 miles (40km) east of Bordeaux; you can't tell where it ends – a country lane divides it from the vines of St-Émilion – and you certainly can't tell why it's special.

The unique quality lies in that soil – 1800 acres (730 hectares) of deep, close-packed cloddish clay, interspersed with iron, a little gravel, a little sand, but ultimately it is the clay which makes Pomerol great – and the only grape

which relishes clay is the Merlot. Even more than in neighbouring St-Émilion. Merlot dominates Pomerol, with most properties having over 80 per cent and the result is superb, inimitable wine – richer than any dry red wine should be, sometimes buttery, sometimes creamy with honeyed spices too; often plummy, but there's blackcurrant there as well, raisins, chocolate, roasted nuts and the disturbing moist perfume of truffles, mint to freshen it up, and a backbone of minerally strength to keep the flavour from going completely over the top. Phew. All those flavours in one bottle. No wonder it's expensive. Best years: 1987, '86, '85, '83, '82, '81, '79, '78. Best properties: Bon-Pasteur, Certan-de-May, Clos René, la Conseillante, l'Évangile, Feytit-Clinet, Lafleur, La Fleur-Pétrus, Petit-Village, Pétrus, le Pin, de Sales, Trotanoy, Vieux-Château-Certan.

POMMARD AC
CÔTE DE BEAUNE, BURGUNDY
Pinot Noir

I'd be more enthusiastic about Pommard if I hadn't had so many bottles at distressingly high prices which were coarse and rough with sullen, scentless flavours. For that matter I've had some very good Bourgogne Rouge from the same village's producers which is actually better than their Pommard! And a lot cheaper. It does make you wonder what's going on. Now I'm not asking for suave, silky flavours – Pommard has never been good at that – but I am asking for full, round, beefy flavours, a bit jammy when young but becoming plummy, chocolaty and a little meaty with age. In fact, I want old-fashioned flavours. But *fruit* has to be at the core of the flavour – not just alcohol and tannin and jam. When it's good, Pommard ages well, often for ten years or more, and actually needs four to five years to come out of its shell. There are no *grands crus*, but Les Rugiens Bas, Les Épenots and Les Arvelets (all *premiers crus*) are the best sites. Best years: 1987, '85, '83, '80, '78. Best producers: Gaunoux, Lehaye, Lejeune, Monnier, de Montille, Parent, Château de Pommard, Pothier-Rieusset, Pousse d'Or.

PONTET-CANET, CH.
Pauillac AC, *5ème cru classé*
HAUT-MÉDOC, BORDEAUX
Cabernet Sauvignon, Merlot,
Cabernet Franc

Pontet-Canet was, until the mid-1970s, one of the most popular and widely available of the Haut-Médoc Classed Growths. There were good reasons for this. The 185-acre (75-hectare) vineyard next door to Mouton-Rothschild regularly produced (and still does produce) the largest amount of wine of any of the Classed Growths. Added to this, no wine was château-bottled until 1972 and so barrels were freely shipped to every sort of bottler to do what they liked with it. The result was cheap, but hardly authentic, claret in considerable quantities. Since 1979 Pontet-Canet has been owned by the Tesserons of the St-Estèphe Fourth Growth Lafon-Rochet, and gradually we are seeing a return to the big, chewy, blackcurrant and sweet-oak style of which Pontet-Canet is capable. The good vintages of the '80s will need at least 10–12 years ageing, the lighter wines six to eight. Best years: 1986, '85, '83, '82.

POTENSAC, CH.
Médoc AC, *cru grand bourgeois*
BORDEAUX
Cabernet Sauvignon, Merlot,
Cabernet Franc

What a pleasure to be able to give an unreserved thumbs-up to a Bordeaux wine. Thumbs-up for quality, thumbs-up for consistency – and thumbs-up for value for money. And the château cellars are in Potensac's defunct parish church! There are two keys to Potensac's fabulous success. First, there is a ridge of gravel here. These are rare in the northern Médoc AC but crucial to allow a well-drained vineyard capable of fine wine. Second, the 100-acre (40-hectare) estate is owned and run by Michel Delon, the genius of St-Julien's great Second Growth Léoville-Las-Cases. Alone of all the proprietors in the lowly Médoc AC, he draws out a richness, a concentration and a complexity of blackcurrant, vanilla and spice flavour which during the 1980s has regularly surpassed many Classed Growths for quality. Potensac can be drunk at four to five years old, but fine vintages will improve for at least ten, the 1982 for up to twice that. Best years: 1986, '85, '83, '82, '81, '80, '79, '78, '76.

POUJEAUX, CH.
Moulis AC, *cru grand bourgeois*
exceptionnel
HAUT-MÉDOC, BORDEAUX
Cabernet Sauvignon, Merlot,
Cabernet Franc, Petit Verdot

Poujeaux is one of the properties whose ever-improving wine-making standards are propelling the Moulis AC more and more into the limelight. It's a big property – at 125 acres (50 hectares) second only in size to Chasse-Spleen among Moulis' châteaux – and is beautifully located on the gravel banks around the village of Grand-Poujeaux. Although its reputation is for dry, long-lived wines, recent vintages have been richer, more supple, with a delicious chunky fruit, new-oak sweetness and a slight scent of tobacco. This more accurately reflects the very high percentage of Merlot in the vineyard – 35 per cent, with the same amount of Cabernet Sauvignon, 15 per cent Cabernet Franc, and an unusually large amount of the late-ripening Petit Verdot, 15 per cent. Indeed the Petit Verdot may be a major reason why good vintages can easily last 20–30 years. Best years: 1986, '85, '83, '82, '81, '78.

PREMIÈRES CÔTES DE BLAYE AC
BORDEAUX
Merlot, Cabernet Sauvignon,
Cabernet Franc, Malbec

Not one of my favourite Bordeaux regions, but there are definite signs of improvement. Up till now the problems have been a lack of that acid bite and tannic grip which make Bordeaux special and allow the perfumes and fruits of the Cabernet Sauvignon and Merlot to develop. The wines have been smudgy, sludgy things, jammy and sweet to taste and earthy of texture. Premières Côtes de Blaye is nonetheless the supposedly superior AC for reds from the Blayais, a wine area of 6700 acres (2700 hectares) on the opposite side of the Gironde to Lamarque in the Haut-Médoc. (Technically, AC Blaye or Blayais is also allowed in this area. In practice, virtually all the wines are sold as Premières Côtes.) Although vines were planted here long before they were in the Médoc, any wine fame the region once had is long gone. Still, things *are* improving and the following châteaux are beginning to make attractive, rather fresher reds from Cabernet which are ready at two to three years, but can age for two or three more if you want: Bas Vallon, Bourdieu, Charron, l'Escadre, Grand-Barrail, Haut-Sociondo, Jonqueyres, Peybonhomme.

PREMIÈRES CÔTES DE BORDEAUX AC
BORDEAUX
Merlot, Cabernet Sauvignon,
Cabernet Franc

This long, 37-mile (60-km) stretch of the Garonne's right bank, running from the suburbs of Bordeaux down to Verdelais opposite Langon, has always been thought of as sweet white territory, especially since it has three communes – Cadillac, Loupiac, and Ste-Croix-du-Mont – which do specialize in 'Sauternes look-alike' sweeties. However, the market for such wines has been poor, and many proprietors are concentrating on dry whites and reds: there are now 3845 acres (1556 hectares) of red vineyards. In the north, near Bordeaux, a certain amount of *clairet* is made – light red, halfway to rosé for quick drinking. However, as the vineyards mature, a very attractive juicy fruit quality is becoming evident, and the future looks bright. Wines are usually delicious at two to three years old but should last for five to six. Best years: 1986, '85, '83, '82. Best properties: Brethous, Cayla, Fayau, Grand-Mouëys, du Juge, Peyrat, Reynon, la Roche, Tanesse.

PRIEURÉ-LICHINE, CH.
Margaux AC, *4ème cru classé*
HAUT-MÉDOC, BORDEAUX
Cabernet Sauvignon, Merlot,
Cabernet Franc, Petit Verdot

If you're short of something to do on Christmas Day, no problem. Nothing on this Easter? I've the answer. I've also the answer for New Year's Day, Ash Wednesday, Labour Day, May Day, Hallowe'en, or any other day you care to mention. You go to visit Château Prieuré-Lichine in Bordeaux because this property is open 365 days a year! I must say I find it pretty astonishing. But then Prieuré-Lichine is no ordinary château. It is owned by Alexis Lichine, probably the greatest promoter and apostle of French wines this century. This zeal to press the flesh and pop the top of a bottle in persuasive mood is what keeps his property – 143 acres (58 hectares) spread all over Cantenac and Margaux – open all year round. The wine is increasingly good in the '80s, adding a little weight to the gentle, perfumed style typical of the property. It is usually ready quite young, but keeps well for 10–15 years. Best years: 1986, '85, '83, '82, '78, '71.

PUISSEGUIN-ST-ÉMILION AC
BORDEAUX
Merlot, Cabernet Franc, Cabernet
Sauvignon, Malbec

One of the smaller St-Émilion satellites lying to the north-east of the town of St-Émilion. It's situated in charming, gently hilly countryside, and the vineyards cover 1600 acres (650 hectares). The wines are usually fairly solid, without being inspiring; they have an attractive chunky fruit but are a bit short on perfume and excitement. Even so, they're usually good, full-bodied drinking at three to five years. There is an important co-operative. Best years: 1985, '83, '82. Best properties: Beaulieu, Bel-Air, Durand-Laplagne, des Laurets.

PYRÉNÉES-ORIENTALES
LANGUEDOC-ROUSSILLON

▼ The snow-thick peaks of the Pyrenees form a spectacular backdrop to the ancient region of Roussillon (now the Pyrénées-Orientales *département*). Roussillon vineyards, the most southerly in France, produce a distinctive variety of wines, ranging from the ripe raisin-rich *vins doux naturels* to light, fruity-fresh *vins de pays* – increasingly made by carbonic maceration.

The harsh, dry *département* which abuts the Pyrenees and the Mediterranean in France's far south. Total production is usually about 55 million bottles, over half of which are *vin de pays*. The ACs are firstly, the *vins doux naturels* – sweet, fortified rather raisiny wines, usually from the Grenache or Muscat grape, of which Rivesaltes and Banyuls are the best known; the dark red Collioure, based on the Grenache, from near the Spanish border; and Côtes du Roussillon and Côtes du Roussillon-Villages, whose reds and rosés, often with a high proportion of Carignan, are some of the south's best cheap wines. The Vin de Pays des Pyrénées-Orientales designation covers the *département*, though there are five zonal *vins de pays* of which 'Catalan' is the most important. These wines generally resemble lighter Côtes du Roussillon, the reds dusty but attractively fruity and the rosés refreshing if you catch them young enough. Unlike other southern *vins de pays*, there is little experimental vine planting here, and Carignan dominates the vineyards, but there are a few estates, like La Barrera and Mas Chichet, which are making exciting use of Merlot and Cabernet Sauvignon. Co-operatives are the most important producers.

RAHOUL, CH.
Graves AC
BORDEAUX
Merlot, Cabernet Sauvignon

A property which is showing that the unfashionable southern end of the Graves can make exciting wine. Château Rahoul – at Portets, a good five miles outside the new Pessac-Léognan AC – was until 1988 run by Peter Vinding-Diers, one of Bordeaux's most talented and innovative winemakers. Rahoul is only 28 acres (11·5 hectares) in area, planted 60 per cent Merlot and 40 per cent Cabernet Sauvignon. By scrupulous wine-making and considerable use of new oak barrels, Vinding-Diers produced a rich, plummy, vanilla and coconut-scented red which is almost more New World than it is Bordeaux. Lovely at three years old, it will age for ten, and each vintage seems better than the last. Best years: 1986, '85, '83, '82, '81, '79.

RASTEAU
Côtes du Rhône-Rasteau AC
SOUTHERN RHÔNE
Grenache, Syrah, Cinsaut,
Mourvèdre

An important Côtes du Rhône-Village east of Cairanne and north-east of Châteauneuf-du-Pape. Its reds – mostly from the stony slopes at the foot of the Dentelles de Montmirail rocks – are usually fairly old-fashioned, taking several years to soften, and rarely having the fresh burst of spice and raspberry which makes some of the other 'Villages' so attractive when young. Even more old-fashioned is the speciality of Rasteau – a *vin doux naturel*, made from very ripe Grenache grapes which are fermented for three to four days only. Then pure alcohol is added and this remains, giving a rich, raisins-and-grape-skins flavour to the wine.

RAUSAN-SÉGLA, CH.
Margaux AC, *2ème cru classé*
HAUT-MÉDOC, BORDEAUX
Cabernet Sauvignon, Merlot,
Cabernet Franc, Petit Verdot

Before 1983 my comments on Rausan-Ségla would have been sharp and to the point. Something like, 'This is supposed to be the top Second Growth, within spitting distance of Margaux, Mouton-Rothschild and the other greats. So why is it that in most years it is making wine a Fifth Growth would be ashamed of? Lack of care, lack of commitment, lack of respect for the consumer, that's what.' (I would still apply the same kind of remarks to neighbouring Rauzan-Gassies, which explains why it doesn't have its own entry.)

A new broom, in the shape of Monsieur Jacques Theo arrived; he promptly rejected half the crop as totally inadequate, phoned up Bordeaux's most famous wine-doctor Professor Peynaud for advice and then produced one of the finest '83s in the whole Margaux AC. He made a fair stab at the difficult '84, and then produced a superb '85 and a marvellous '86. Rich blackcurrant fruit, almost tarry, thick tannins and weight, excellent woody spice and real concentration. Rausan-Ségla was turned around in *one* year! I wish some of the other under-achievers among the Classed Growths would take note. There are 111 acres (45 hectares) of vines, 55 per cent Cabernet Sauvignon, 32 per cent Merlot, 11 per cent Cabernet Franc, two per cent Petit Verdot. Don't buy any of the wines of the 1970s, but since 1983 Rausan-Ségla is a worthy Second Growth. Best years: 1986, '85, '83.

REGNIÉ AC
BEAUJOLAIS, BURGUNDY
Gamay

'Lucky' is what I call Regnié and its neighbour Durette whose combined vineyards are in effect confirmed as the tenth Beaujolais *cru*. *Cru* is a virtually untranslatable French word, but it means approximately 'a parcel of land and its crop of grapes'. This may be a whole village as in Chénas, or it may be a group of villages as in Brouilly, but what distinguishes each 'patch' of land or *cru* in Beaujolais is that the wines have consistently been of a higher standard than the general run. For this reason the wines can sport their own specific AC. The other nine *crus* without doubt deserve their position, but I'm not yet convinced by Regnié. The vineyards are just west of Morgon and Brouilly, and the light, attractive wine is much closer to Brouilly in style. I *have* had some pleasant bottles, but in poor years like '84 the wines have definitely not rated *cru* status, and even in the great year '85 there were some strangely unattractive attempts. Best years: 1987, '85. Best producers: Cinquin, Crêt des Bruyères, Duboeuf, Durand, Gérarde, Magrin.

RHÔNE

Vienne ● 0   20 km

0   10 miles

CÔTE-RÔTIE

CONDRIEU
CH-GRILLET

White wine AC

Red wine AC

Red and white wine AC

ST-JOSEPH

ST-JOSEPH

CROZES-
HERMITAGE

-HERMITAGE

Tournon ●

Tain l'Hermitage

CORNAS

● Valence

ST-PÉRAY

CHÂTILLON-
EN-DIOIS

CÔTES DU
RHÔNE

Drôme

Roubion

● Montélimar

COTEAUX
DU
TRICASTIN

CÔTES DU
VIVARAIS

CÔTES DU
RHÔNE

● Nyons

RASTEAU

CÔTES
DU
RHÔNE
LAUDUN

VACQUEYRAS

GIGONDAS

● Orange

BEAUMES-
DE-VENISE

CHÂTEAUNEUF-
DU-PAPE

LIRAC

TAVEL

N̂

CÔTES DU
VENTOUX

● Avignon

Rhône

Durance

I t's one of those trick questions: 'What is the most northerly wine grown in the Rhône Valley?' Tricky indeed! It isn't even in France – it's in the Valais high up in the Swiss Alps! We always forget that the Rhône starts out as a Swiss river, ambling through Lake Geneva before hurtling southwards into France. Well, as far as the AC Côtes du Rhône is concerned, we're right. This *appellation* starts below Vienne, which is just south of Lyon, but nowhere near Switzerland, and finishes just south of Avignon. Below this the river sprawls out and fragments into marshlands which soon become the wild Camargue swamps where everything seems to be below sea level, it's so flat and waterlogged. 'Côtes du Rhône' does, after all, mean 'Rhône slopes', or at least 'Rhône banks', and south of Avignon, there isn't much of either. But between Avignon in the south and Vienne in the north there's enough excitement and diversity to show the Rhône as one of France's greatest wine regions.

This central section of the valley splits naturally into two parts. The north doesn't produce much wine, but the little that does appear is of a remarkable individuality. There is only one red grape of any importance – the Syrah. On the vertigo-inducing slopes of Côte-Rôtie at Ampuis, it produces sensuously fragrant long-lasting reds, while at Tain-l'Hermitage the great hill of Hermitage produces what they used to call France's 'manliest' wine. If I understand the term correctly, the stern, imperious flavour of red Hermitage would happily accept the epithet. In between, St-Joseph and Crozes-Hermitage also make excellent reds, while Cornas, a few miles south, makes a marvellous monster red too.

Then there is a gap as the valley widens and flattens, and you can feel the torrid southern heat. The slopes give way to vast expanses of land, rising a little into the hills both east and west but, in general, flat with vines, and sweltering under the sun. Most of these vineyards are either Côtes du Rhône or Côtes du Rhône-Villages, but there are also various specific ACs centred round Orange. Gigondas is to the east, crunched up against the jagged Dentelles de Montmirail peaks. South-west are Lirac and Tavel. But the most well-known of all is directly south of Orange – Châteauneuf-du-Pape – one of the most famous, and ill-used, names in the world of wine.

▶ The uniquely stony soil of Châteauneuf-du-Pape retains the sun's heat, helping the grapes to ripen. Behind stands the ruined papal palace which gives the vineyard its name.

MAIN WINES	MAIN GRAPES
Beaumes-de-Venise	Carignan
Châteauneuf-du-Pape	Cinsaut
Châtillon-en-Diois	Grenache
Cornas	Mourvèdre
Coteaux de Pierrevert	Syrah
Coteaux du Tricastin	
Côte-Rôtie	
Côtes du Lubéron	
Côtes du Rhône	
Côtes du Rhône-Villages	
Côtes du Ventoux	
Côtes du Vivarais	
Crozes-Hermitage	
Gigondas	
Hermitage	
Laudun	
Lirac	
Rasteau	
St-Joseph	
Tavel	
Vacqueyras	

CLOS RENÉ
Pomerol AC
BORDEAUX
Merlot, Cabernet Franc, Malbec

If there's one wine I'd choose to convert a white-wine drinker to Bordeaux, I think it would be Clos René. This 27-acre (11-hectare) estate is on sandy soil in the less fashionable western side of the AC. The result is wonderfully plummy, juicy, fleshy wine – fleshy like the flesh of peaches or pears or lychees – oozing fruit, and slipping down hardly touching the sides. You think it's sweet almost, and as it ages it does acquire a kind of chocolaty, creamy consistency. And, because it's not fashionable, you can afford it – something you can't say about many Pomerols! It is also sometimes sold under the label Moulinet-Lasserre. You can drink Clos René at any age but the wine ages well for at least ten years. Best years: 1985, '83, '82, '81 '78.

REUILLY AC
UPPER LOIRE
Pinot Noir, Pinot Gris

A tiny area, well away from the mainstream, west of Bourges. White, red and rosé are produced from the 150 acres (60 hectares) of vines on the banks of the river Arnon. There is a little rather pallid red from the Pinot Noir, but the speciality is rosé from either Pinot Noir or Pinot Gris. The best are from Pinot Gris, very pale pink, quite soft but with a lovely, fresh, slightly grapy fruit. Good young, you could age them a year or two to gain richness but you'd lose the freshness. Best years: 1986, '85. Best producers: Beurdin, Cordier, Lafond.

RICHEBOURG AC
grand cru
CÔTE DE NUITS, BURGUNDY
Pinot Noir

What a name! It has resonances of tremendous opulence, of sumptuous velvet and silk-smooth flesh, of scents dark and musky, of dishes based on fatted calves and cream served to corpulent prelates and princes. This 20-acre (8-hectare) *grand cru* at the northern end of Vosne-Romanée, just as the slope curves imperceptibly away towards the north, does produce a rich, fleshy wine, its bouquet all flowers and sweet, ripe fruit and its flavour an intensity of spice and perfumed plums which fattens into chocolate and figs and cream as it ages. Because the name is so evocative, there are occasionally bottles – usually with a Beaune or Nuits-St-Georges merchant's name on them – which really don't do justice to the vineyard; but most domaine-bottlings are exceptional. Best years: 1987, '85, '84, '83, '82, '80, '78. Best producers: Domaine de la Romanée-Conti, Gros, Jayer, Noëllat.

RIVESALTES AC
LANGUEDOC-ROUSSILLON
Grenache

A small town on flat land just north of Perpignan in the Côtes du Roussillon area. Its fame lies in two wines. Firstly, the local firm of Cazès Frères makes an outstanding red *nouveau*, using the carbonic maceration method of vinification, similar to that employed in Beaujolais. Secondly, it is the home of some of the south's best *vin doux naturel* – fortified wine made by partially fermenting the grape juice, then adding a proportion of pure alcohol, which increases the strength up to about 20–21 degrees and at the same time stops any further fermentation, thereby preserving the sweet fruitiness of the half-converted grape juice. The most famous of these are deep and gold, from the Muscat grape, but red and rosé wines·are made from Grenache. If stored for several years in barrel they take on a barley sugar, burnt toffee taste along with the Grenache's original plummy grapiness which is strangely attractive but not exactly thirst-quenching. The Rivesaltes AC covers 86 of Roussillon's 118 communes, and about five million bottles of Rivesaltes VDN are produced. Best producers:·Cazès Frères, Sarda-Malet, Vignerons Catalans.

RIVIÈRE, CH. LA
Fronsac AC
BORDEAUX
Merlot, Cabernet Sauvignon, Cabernet Franc, Malbec

You have to hand it to Monsieur Borie, who owns this 109-acre (44-hectare) Fronsac estate with its truly magnificent château building – he knows how to market his wine. He is always setting up tastings against wines like Classed Growth St-Émilions and Haut-Médocs – and walking off with the plaudits. But totally independent arbiters have also included La Rivière in blind tastings and it has consistently bested more expensive, more renowned wines. Monsieur

Borie is always the first to let you know. Actually the wines *are* good, and they do age remarkably well. Use of at least one-third new oak barrels each year and a good number of very old vines must play a part in this. Best years: 1985, '83, '82, '78.

LA ROMANÉE AC
grand cru
CÔTE DE NUITS, BURGUNDY
Pinot Noir

The smallest AC in France covering a touch over 2 acres (0·84 hectares). This tiny little scrap of magic dirt is on the slope just above Romanée-Conti but doesn't produce wines of the class of the other Vosne-Romanée *grands crus*. While the wines made by its neighbour Domaine de la Romanée-Conti are all rich flavours and exciting perfumes, La Romanée, wholly owned by Liger-Belair, is strangely lean and glum. Best years: 1985, '80, '78.

ROMANÉE-CONTI AC
grand cru
CÔTE DE NUITS, BURGUNDY
Pinot Noir

This is the cloud-capped pinnacle of Burgundy for many extremely wealthy Burgundy lovers. They tell me it has an almost satiny texture, that its bouquet shimmers with the fragrance of sweet-briar and its orgy of wonderful scents and exotic opulence has been known to strike wine-writers dumb and imbue sommeliers with solicitous friendliness. That's what they tell me. I'm not really the chap to comment on all that, because I've only had Romanée-Conti once. It was the 1985 and I thought it was delicious, but Romanée-Conti is only 4½ acres (1·8 hectares) in the heart of the Vosne-Romanée *grands crus*. It only produces 7000 well-heeled bottles in a good year, and since there are sure to be at least 7000 well-heeled Burgundy fanatics desperate for a slurp at any price, it was actually jolly nice of the owners to open a bottle of '85 for me at all. It's wholly owned by the Domaine de la Romanée-Conti, and I must say, even with my fleeting gaze into the crystal ball of the '85's future I knew that its almost sweet, yet surprisingly delicate flavour, which I could still taste a good half-hour later, must bode something pretty special.

ROMANÉE-ST-VIVANT AC
grand cru
CÔTE DE NUITS, BURGUNDY
Pinot Noir

Of all the great *grands crus* of Vosne-Romanée this is the one I got most excited about first and yet the one which has proved most troublesome to love in recent vintages. I first came across it in the early '70s. I kept being offered it really young, hardly off the vine, and I thought it was fantastic, rich, unctuously soft with that heavy-lidded decadence of fresh *foie gras* and Sauternes. This, mark you, in a dry red wine! Well, I was hooked, and after a long barren period when I had to do things like work for a living and pay the rent, I was reintroduced to Romanée-St-Vivant with the vintages of the '80s. Maybe it's me, but the wine doesn't seem so rich any more, that absurdly hedonistic thrill of excitement which great Burgundy can impart I just don't get. Perhaps it is simply that this 24-acre (9·54-hectare) vineyard, crunched up to the houses of Vosne-Romanée below Richebourg, is no longer having to pander to the instant gratification market and at 10–15 years these wines *will* show the keenly balanced brilliance of which the vineyard is capable. I hope so. Best years: 1987, '85, '84, '83, '80, '78, '76. Best producers: Arnoux, Latour, Noëllat, Domaine de la Romanée-Conti.

ROSÉ D'ANJOU AC,
CABERNET D'ANJOU AC &
ROSÉ DE LOIRE AC
CENTRAL LOIRE
Groslot, Cabernet Franc, Cabernet Sauvignon and others

Rosé d'Anjou is usually somewhere between off-dry and reasonably sweet. It is produced predominantly from the Groslot grape – a pretty ordinary performer that doesn't give much colour or much flavour. When the wine is fresh, not too sweet, and not ruined by a gross over-application of the antiseptic sulphur dioxide (which is the case with most cheap Anjou rosé), it has a lovely, slightly nuts-and-apple flavour, with a slight blue cast to its bright pink colour. Drier rosés, usually made from Cabernet Franc grapes and higher in alcohol than Rosé d'Anjou, are called Cabernet d'Anjou. This can be delicious if it is fresh, with a rather smoky, grassy flavour. There is also a Rosé de Loire which is drier than Rosé d'Anjou. This can come from Anjou, Saumur or Touraine and must contain 30 per cent Cabernet. This can be a lovely, grassy drink but, again, get it as young as possible and chill it well down.

ROSÉ DES RICEYS AC
CHAMPAGNE
Pinot Noir

A real oddball rosé. It comes from Les Riceys in the very south of the Champagne AC region. It is made from Pinot Noir as a still wine – but only in the ripest years. The wine is a strange sort of dark golden pink, and tastes full, rather nutty, or, if the locals are to be believed, 'of gooseberries'. There's hardly any of it – only about 7500 bottles. And it's fiendishly expensive. So why do they make it? They probably get fed up with drinking Champagne and like the change. Best producers: Bonnet, Horiot.

RUCHOTTES-CHAMBERTIN AC
grand cru
CÔTE DE NUITS, BURGUNDY
Pinot Noir

The smallest of Gevrey-Chambertin's *grands crus* at less than eight acres (three hectares), squeezed up into the hillside directly north of Clos-de-Bèze. The result is that Ruchottes is often intensely coloured and full of deep, slow-evolving fruit, but also with a good tannin and acidity. After ten years it does show that mix of perfumed plum and dark, figgy prune richness which is at the heart of Gevrey-Chambertin *grands crus*. Best years: 1987, '85, '83, '82, '80, '78. Best producers: Mugneret, Roumier, Rousseau.

RULLY AC
CÔTE CHALONNAISE, BURGUNDY
Pinot Noir

In reputation, more of a white wine village with a tradition of making Champagne-method sparkling wine. In fact the amounts of red and white produced are roughly equal, and Rully – at the northern end of the Côte Chalonnaise – is one of the few areas in Burgundy where there is room for expansion, with some very promising steep slopes facing east to south-east, recently planted and coming into full production. Red Rully is light, with a pleasant, if fleeting, strawberry and cherry perfume. Certainly I'd like a bit more body in the wines, but at two to four years they can be very refreshing. You may see *premier cru* on some labels but such epithets have nothing like the importance in the Côte Chalonnaise that they would in the Côte d'Or, and several of the best vineyards are not *premiers crus*, so I shouldn't worry about it. Best years: 1987, '85, '83. Best producers: Chanzy, Cogny, Delorme, Duvernay, Noël-Bouton.

ST-AMOUR AC
BEAUJOLAIS, BURGUNDY
Gamay

What a lovely name. The Love Saint. Obviously this northernmost of the Beaujolais *crus* has missed its vocation: it ought to be a honeymoon retreat. The calf-eyed couples would certainly find it quiet: there isn't even a village inn! So perhaps the inhabitants are better off making a particularly juicy, soft-fruited Beaujolais, perfumed, peachy, ready to drink within the year, but lasting well for two or three.

The village is just inside the Saône-et-Loire *département* (all the others are in the Rhône *département*) and so is theoretically in the Mâconnais. Indeed any white wine from its 568 acres (230 hectares) can legally be called St-Véran, but the red is so delicious, and the vineyard area so restricted, that I wouldn't like to see white plantings increase. There is no co-operative at St-Amour, and several *négociant* offerings are better than average. Best producers: Billards, Domaine du Paradis, Duboeuf, Patissier (Guy and Jean), Poitevin, Revillon, Saillant, Château de St-Amour.

ST-AUBIN AC
CÔTE DE BEAUNE, BURGUNDY
Pinot Noir

This is my sort of Burgundy village! It's not actually on the Côte d'Or's Golden Slope but in its own cleft, just up the hill from Puligny-Montrachet, which means that prices are fairly low, and despite recent replanting, there are lots of old vineyards producing quite big, chewy-fruited reds. In fact most of the 300 acres (120 hectares) of vineyards are on good east to south-east facing slopes, and two-thirds of them are classified *premiers crus* – and they deserve it. Les Frionnes and Les Murgers des Dents de Chien (love that name) are two of the best. You can drink St-Aubin at two to three years but good years will age six to ten. Best years: 1987, '85, '83, '82. Best producers: Bachelet, Clerget, Colin, Lamy, Prudhon, Roux, Thomas.

ST-CHINIAN AC
LANGUEDOC-ROUSSILLON
Carignan, Grenache, Cinsaut and others

With Faugères, this was the first of the red wines of the Hérault *département* to break away from the pack and start making a name for itself. In the hill villages back from the coast, the rocky slopes can produce strong, spicy reds with a fair amount of fruit and *far* more personality than the run of the Hérault mill – particularly when carbonic maceration has been employed at least partially. St-Chinian and Faugères (which gained their ACs in 1982) are the best examples of this. About 14 million bottles of St-Chinian are produced from around 25,000 acres (10,000 hectares) of vines in the hills above Béziers, but the potential is for twice that. Carignan is the main grape, but increasingly Grenache, Syrah and Mourvèdre are being planted. The wines can be drunk very young but age happily for two to three years. Though they have a good, strong taste, they are usually a little lighter-bodied than neighbouring Faugères, and as yet not quite so consistent. Best years: 1986, '85. Best producers: Calmette, Clos Bagatelle, Coujan, Jougla, co-operatives at Rieu-Berlou and Roquebrun.

ST-ÉMILION AC, ST-ÉMILION
grand cru AC
BORDEAUX
Merlot, Cabernet Franc, Cabernet Sauvignon, Malbec

If William the Conqueror had decided to take some Bordeaux wines to England with him when he laid low poor old Harold at Hastings in 1066, there's a good chance his triumphant tipple would have been St-Émilion, because the Brits have been drinking it for over 800 years. And I can see why it became so popular so quickly, because the one thing that marks the flavour of St-Émilion is a gorgeous softness, a buttery, toffeeish sweetness, and a fruit whose flavour owes more to the dark, chewy richness of raisins in a fruit cake, than to the leaner more demanding tastes of the great classic red wines of the Graves and Médoc.

The *appellation* is centred on the Roman town of St-Emilion on the right bank of the Dordogne, east of Bordeaux. The vines cover 130 acres (52,000 hectares) in eight different communes, although the best lie within the boundaries of the St-Émilion commune itself. It is a region of smallholdings, with over 1000 different properties, the smallest being Château le Couvent actually in the town of St-Émilion. Consequently, the co-operative is of great importance, and vinifies over 20 per cent of the entire St-Émilion crop to a consistently high standard.

There has been a classification system for St-Émilion wines since 1954, which allows for promotion and demotion every ten years. St-Émilion *premier cru classé* applies to the top 11 properties, and St-Émilion *grand cru classé* covers 64 wines, although both figures are re-appraised each decade. Below this level comes 200 or so St-Émilion *grands crus*, and the rest are straight St-Émilion.

The classification used to be enshrined in the AC, but since 1985 there are only two ACs – St-Émilion *grand cru* for the top 90 wines and St-Émilion for the rest. Now I can add up – just – and this looks to me as though a wine not in the top 90 can call itself *grand cru* although its AC is merely St-Émilion. Yes, that's *exactly* what it looks like!

Best years: 1988, '87, 86, '85, '83, '82, '81, '79, 78. Best producers: l'Angélus, l'Arrosée, Ausone, Balestard-la-Tonnelle, Belair, Berliquet, Canon, Cheval-Blanc, la Dominique, Figeac, Fonplégade, Franc-Mayne, Larmande, Magdelaine, Monbousquet, Pavie, la Gaffelière, Pavie Decesse, la Tour du Pin Figeac, Tertre Rôteboeuf, Troplong Mondot.

ST-ÉMILION
AND POMEROL

S t-Émilion and Pomerol make the greatest red wines on the right bank of the Dordogne in Bordeaux. Indeed St-Émilion is the most historic wine region in Bordeaux. Over 1700 years ago the Romans were planting the steep south-facing slopes just outside the town, and leading properties, like Château la Gaffelière and Château Ausone (whose vineyards once belonged to the Roman poet Ausonius) can trace their records as far back as the second century. The hill town of St-Émilion, huddled in the clefts of rock above the vineyard is a true Roman town, timeless and magical.

The finest vineyards with most of the famous names are on the steep slopes round the town, the *côtes* vineyards ('the slopes'). But there is a second large area of St-Émilion to the west towards the town of Libourne called the *graves* which contains two of St-Émilion's greatest properties – Château Cheval-Blanc and Figeac. The *graves* refers to a gravel ridge occupied by both of these properties on a plateau which is otherwise noted for heavy clay soil. Although Cheval-Blanc and Figeac both use a high proportion of Cabernet Sauvignon and Cabernet Franc due to the warm, well-drained gravel soil, St-Émilion's characteristic soft, juicy flavour is

essentially imparted by the Merlot grape.

The clay comes into its own in Pomerol – a flat, featureless expanse of vines that doesn't even boast a village called Pomerol – which begins right next to Cheval-Blanc and continues westward to the outskirts of Libourne. There are no fancy buildings, no signs of affluence and renown here, yet the world's most expensive wine – Château Pétrus – is made in a tiny building in the heart of Pomerol, and the rich, sumptuous flavours of the Merlot-based wine are echoed by numerous other properties crammed into the tiny space, none as great as Pétrus, but many giving more than just a suggestion of the power and succulence which make Pétrus so exciting.

Both Pomerol and St-Émilion have 'satellite' ACs – employing a hyphenated version of the famous name. Lalande-de-Pomerol produces good soft wines directly to the north of Pomerol. North of St-Émilion there are a group of ACs all producing sturdy but fruity reds – Lussac-St-Émilion, Montagne-St-Émilion (also the preferred AC for most wines in neighbouring Parsac-St-Émilion and St-Georges-St-Émilion) and Puisseguin-St-Émilion.

◀Château Fonplégade, a *grand cru classé* situated on *côtes* vineyards south-west of the town of St-Émilion.

MAIN ACs	Figeac
Lalande de Pomerol	Fonplégade
Lussac-St-Émilion	la Grave-Trigant-de-Boisset
Montagne-St-Émilion	Lafleur
Pomerol	Latour-à-Pomerol
Puisseguin-St-Émilion	Magdelaine
St-Émilion	Monbousquet
St-Georges-St-Émilion	Pavie
	Petit-Village
MAIN CHÂTEAUX	Pétrus
l'Angélus	de Sales
l'Arrosée	Siaurac
Ausone	Trotanoy
Balestard-la-Tonnelle	Vieux-Château-Certan
Belair	
Canon	MAIN GRAPES
Certan de May	Cabernet Franc
Clos René	Cabernet Sauvignon
la Dominique	Merlot
l'Évangile	

105

ST-ESTÈPHE AC
HAUT-MÉDOC, BORDEAUX
Cabernet Sauvignon, Cabernet
Franc, Merlot and others

The wines of St-Estèphe are frequently accorded only grudging praise. I can understand this if the wines are being judged on their perfume and elegance: St-Estèphe's four-square style is no match for St-Julien and Margaux here. I can also understand if it is sheer concentration of fruit and personality that matter: St-Estèphe's broad-shouldered, tweedy character is far less memorable and less dignified than that of Pauillac. Yet, in this very same old-fashioned tweed and plus-fours way, St-Estèphe is the most reliable and the least overpriced of the Haut-Médoc's specific ACs.

It is a large AC at 2700 acres (1100 hectares), but the most recently established of the great Haut-Médoc areas, partly because the gravel soil which gives all the finest wines in Pauillac, St-Julien and Margaux is much less prevalent here – clay clogs your shoes as you wander these vineyards. It also has a cooler climate than the other main villages and the vines may ripen a week later than those in Margaux. This means that most of the properties have a fairly high proportion of the earlier-ripening Merlot, though Cabernet Sauvignon is still the leading grape. The clay soils are also a reason why St-Estèphe has only five Classed Growths; but the late development of the area also meant that many vineyards were not fully established by 1855 when classification took place. There are now several non-classified properties which year in year out make fine wine of Classed Growth quality.

St-Estèphe wines are not the most likeable wines straight off. They have high tannin levels, and a definite earthy scratch in their texture. Give them time, however, and those sought-after flavours of blackcurrant and cedarwood do peek out – but rarely with the brazen beauty of a Pauillac or a St-Julien. There is some evidence of a softer style of wine-making being tried out, but although this is fine for the lesser properties, for the leading châteaux the end result is a bit half-hearted and St-Estèphe's best efforts are still in the brawny mould, demanding 10–20 years ageing for full development. Best years: 1986, '85, '83, '82, '79, '78, '76, '75. Best properties: Andron-Blanquet, Calon-Ségur, Cos d'Estournel, Haut-Marbuzet, Lafon-Rochet, Meyney, Montrose, les Ormes-de-Pez, de Pez.

ST-GEORGES-ST-ÉMILION AC
BORDEAUX
Merlot, Cabernet Franc, Cabernet
Sauvignon, Malbec

Probably the best of the satellite St-Émilion ACs. The wines can be the epitome of Merlot softness – all buttered brazil nuts and fruitcake and soft plums, but well able to age for six to ten years if called on to do so. Best years: 1985, '83, '82. Best properties: Bélair-Montaiguillon, Calon (sometimes sold as Montagne St-Émilion), Cap d'Or, Château St-Georges (one of the most impressive buildings in the whole region as well as lovely wine), Maquin St-Georges, Tour-du-Pas-St-Georges.

ST-JOSEPH AC
NORTHERN RHÔNE
Syrah, Roussanne, Marsanne

If ever the Syrah wished to show the smily side of its nature in the northern Rhône it would have to be at St-Joseph. I have never had an unfriendly St-Joseph, and most of them have been an absolute riot of rich, mouthfilling fruit and an irresistible blackcurrant richness. I was at a Paris Wine Fair with Jean Lenoir who has invented a system of identifying wine smells called Le Nez du Vin (the nose of wine). 'Show me the purest example of blackcurrant', I cried recklessly, expecting to be shunted towards some wonderful Cabernet Sauvignon-based Classed Growth red Bordeaux. Not a bit of it. He parked me down in front of Monsieur Coursodon's stand and ordered a glass of his 1980 St-Joseph. Pure, heavenly blackcurrants, *crème de cassis*, blackcurrant jam, blackcurrant sorbet – all there. Mmmm!

St-Joseph used to be limited to the granite slopes of half-a-dozen right-bank villages centred on Mauves just south of Hermitage. All the best St-Joseph still comes from there. But in one of those infuriating administrative decisions the AC was extended in 1969 to take in another 20 communes on flat land north of Tournon and Hermitage. Their wine isn't anything like as good, although it's still a jolly nice drink. Ah well. St-Joseph is brilliant at only one to two years old; it can age for up to ten from the area round Mauves, but you'll be gradually losing that wonderful fruit, so I'd drink it before five years old. Best years: 1985, '83, '82, '80. Best producers: Chave, Coursodon, Gonon, Gripa, Grippat, Jaboulet (le Grand Pompée), Marsanne, St-Désirat-Champagne co-operative (for the lighter style).

ST-JULIEN AC
HAUT-MÉDOC, BORDEAUX
Cabernet Sauvignon, Cabernet
Franc, Pinot Noir

If someone said to me 'show me the perfect red Bordeaux', this is where I would look first. Not because they are the most fragrant. Margaux often has a more beguiling perfume. Not because they are the most sumptuous – Pomerol and St-Émilion regularly produce richer reds. And not because they are the grandest – the great Pauillacs have a massive concentration of flavour St-Julien rarely approaches. No, it is because St-Julien wines have the perfect balance between substance and delicacy, between opulence and austerity of aroma, between the necessary harshness of youth and the lean-limbed genius of maturity. Although it is the great Pauillacs which winemakers across the world set out to copy, if it was the perfect Bordeaux they sought to emulate, St-Julien should be their target.

There's not very much of it – at 1850 acres (750 hectares) it is the smallest of the four main Haut-Médoc communes, snugly tucked into the southern boundary of Pauillac, but almost all of it is vineyard land of the highest class, with 75 per cent of the land being taken up by the 11 Classed Growths. The Second Growths, Léoville-Las-Cases, Ducru-Beaucaillou and Gruaud-Larose are the leaders, making wine as fine as First Growths in most years, and not far behind are Léoville-Barton and Beychevelle. The third group, also making excellent wine, is Talbot, Branaire-Ducru, St-Pierre, Langoa-Barton and the recently revived Lagrange. Only Léoville-Poyferré continues to be erratic, but despite that, the overall quality in St-Julien is higher than in any other Bordeaux AC. Best years: 1986, '85, '83, '82, '81, '79, '78, '75.

ST-NICOLAS-DE-BOURGUEIL AC
CENTRAL LOIRE
Cabernet Franc

A little enclave of 1250 acres (500 hectares) inside the Bourgueil area of Touraine producing two million bottles of red and rosé wine. Cabernet Franc is usually the sole grape used although sometimes a bit of Cabernet Sauvignon creeps in. Almost all the wine is red and it has the sharp, piercing, raspberry and blackcurrant flavours of neighbouring Bourgueil and Chinon, but in less striking tones, because the wines are generally pretty dry, prone to be a little tannic and with an earthy background which is pleasant enough. They are drinkable young – two to three years – and will last seven to ten years from warm vintages. Best years: 1986, '85, '83, '82. Best producers: J-P Mabileau, Joël Taluau.

ST-PIERRE, CH.
St-Julien AC
HAUT-MÉDOC, BORDEAUX
Cabernet Sauvignon, Merlot,
Cabernet Franc

After a century of anonymity, Château St-Pierre (previously known as St-Pierre-Sevaistre) has stepped forward to claim its place in the sun. It was bought in 1982 by Monsieur Henri Martin, owner of the nearby Château Gloria, and suddenly is becoming sought-after – and pricy. It used to be undervalued, and in years like 1970, '75, '79 and '81 you got superb quality at half the price of the better-known St-Juliens. But I really can't complain – it was too cheap for too long. It isn't a big property, only 50 acres (20 hectares), but the vines, close to Branaire and Beychevelle, are well-sited and old, with 70 per cent Cabernet Sauvignon, 20 per cent Merlot and ten per cent Cabernet Franc. The wine often lacks the startling beauty of the best St-Julien – twining cigar-box and cedar perfumes endlessly in the glass – but makes up for this with a full, gentle, almost honeyed weight of flavour, plums and blackberries and soft vanilla backed up by unassertive but effective tannins. It is often ready quite young, and since 1982 there is a lusher feel to the wines, but top vintages can easily improve for 20 years. Best years: 1986, '85, '83, '81, '79, '75.

ST-POURÇAIN-SUR-SIOULE VDQS
UPPER LOIRE
Gamay, Pinot Noir

This tiny VDQS sits inside the great loop of the Loire river as it turns south towards its source. The reds and rosés, based on Pinot Noir and Gamay, can have quite a pleasant fruit to them, although it may take more than a single glass to get used to the rather smoky, earthy taste that accompanies the fruit. Don't go out of your way, but they can be nice enough to drink young.

ST-ROMAIN AC
CÔTE DE BEAUNE, BURGUNDY
Pinot Noir

St-Romain is better known for barrels than wine, since François Frères, barrel-makers to the Domaine de la Romanée-Conti and a whole string of other top estates, are situated here. Actually there isn't much room for vines, since St-Romain is at the rocky head of a little side valley running up through Auxey-Duresses from Meursault, and the difficult growing conditions mean there are more trees than vines around. Even so, there are 350 acres (140 hectares), but the poor geological situation results in its being the only Côte de Beaune AC to have no *premiers crus*. About 55 per cent of production is red, and though they often have a slightly unnerving earthiness which can verge on the resinous, they also have a firm, bitter-sweet cherrystone fruit – and can age very well for five to seven years. Best years: 1987, '85, '83, '82. Best producers: Bazenet, Buisson, Thévenin, Thévenin-Monthelie.

DE SALES, CH.
Pomerol AC
BORDEAUX
Merlot, Cabernet Franc, Cabernet Sauvignon

At 117 acres (47·5 hectares), this is Pomerol's biggest property, with a lovely château building – commonplace in the Haut-Médoc, but almost unheard of in artisanal Pomerol where every square inch of land is occupied by precious vines. This spaciousness is assisted by the fact that de Sales is right at the north-western tip of the AC, away from the brilliant centre with its superstar châteaux clustered round Château Pétrus, and the soil is sandier with a fair sprinkling of gravel too. The wines never have the tingling excitement of the best Pomerols, but they don't have a blood-pressure-raising price tag either. They are full, round, plummy, rather luscious and smooth for a red wine, quick to mature, but able to age ten years. Best years: 1985, '83, '82, '81, '79, '78.

SANCERRE AC
UPPER LOIRE
Pinot Noir

Sancerre is much better at growing white wine than red or rosé (a point emphasized by the fact that red and rosé Sancerre only gained their AC in 1959, 23 years after the white). Still, it certainly must be profitable because many of the new plantings in the region are for Pinot Noir, the only permitted red grape. I suspect one can blame the 'modishness' of Paris restaurateurs who love to find some new wine 'phenomenon' and flog it to death. They've certainly done this with Sancerre red and rosé and an ice-cold bottle of one or the other seemed at one time to be the only wine ever recommended at some 'nouvelle cuisine' establishments.

With very few exceptions, Pinot Noir doesn't ripen enough here to give interesting red wine, partly because it is usually planted on the less successful north-facing slopes. A couple of growers have planted Pinot Noir on good slopes and their wine is noticeably fuller, but rarely does it achieve more than an attractive, fleeting cherry and strawberry fruit – which would be rather good at half the price. The rosé is usually very dry, sometimes with a hint of fruit, but I can't see a lot of point to it. About 20 per cent of the 3700 acres (1500 hectares) are devoted to Pinot Noir, and the production is about 1·5 million bottles out of a total of 7·5 million. Drink it young. Best years: 1986, '85, '83. Best producers: Bailly-Reverdy, André Dezat, Fouassier, Roger, Vacheron.

SANTENAY AC
CÔTE DE BEAUNE, BURGUNDY
Pinot Noir

You can almost taste the Côte de Beaune winding down in the wines of Santenay. The challenging, powerful fruit of the wines of Aloxe-Corton or Pommard is missing, the soft, perfumed beauty of Volnay and Beaune doesn't seem to surface with any regularity, yet the village *is* an important one, and

there *are* good wines. In fact, Santenay is really a little town, well-known since Roman times for its therapeutic springs. There are 939 acres (380 hectares) of vines, mostly to the north-east and south-west, and 99 per cent of them are Pinot Noir. The vineyards to the north-east, well sloped towards the morning sun, give the best wine – rarely heavy and sometimes a little stony and dry, but reasonably fruity and reasonably priced. Though Santenay reds often 'feel' good, and promise a good ripe flavour, the final result is usually just a little disappointing. Occasionally a full, rather savoury style appears from a vineyard like Les Gravières and it is worth ageing Santenay for at least four to six years in the hope that the wine will open out. Sometimes it does: sometimes it doesn't. Best years: 1987, '85, '83, '82, '78. Best producers: Belland, Clair, Fleurot-Larose, Girardin, Lequin-Roussot, Mestre, Bernard Morey, Pousse d'Or, Prieur-Brunet, Roux.

SAUMUR AC
CENTRAL LOIRE
Cabernet Franc, Cabernet Sauvignon, Pineau d'Aunis

Best known for its sparkling white wines, but quite important as a producer of light, rather sharp reds. Thirty-eight villages around Saumur have the right to the AC. Cabernet Franc is the main grape, sometimes blended with Cabernet Sauvignon or Pineau d'Aunis and the result is usually a fairly thin wine, slightly earthy, but with a fairly good, direct, raw blackcurrant fruit. The wine softens with age but doesn't particularly improve. There is a little off-dry rosé made, generally sold under the title Cabernet de Saumur. Best years: 1985, '83, '82. Best producers: Fourrier, Pérols, St-Cyr-en-Bourg co-operative.

SAUMUR-CHAMPIGNY AC
CENTRAL LOIRE
Cabernet Franc, Cabernet Sauvignon, Pineau d'Aunis

Saumur's best red wine area deservedly sports its own AC. The vineyards are to the east of Saumur on a chalk and limestone plateau 200 feet (60 metres) above the left bank of the Loire. Cabernet is the dominant grape, and in hot years the wine can be superb, never heavy but with a piercing scent of blackcurrants and raspberries easily overpowering the earthy finish. Absolutely delicious young, it can happily age six to ten years, losing some of its sharpness and seeming to get sweeter with maturity. Best years: 1985, '83, '82, '78. Best producers: Chaintres, Duveau, Filliatreau (especially his Vieilles Vignes cuvée – unbelievably delicious), Legrand, St-Cyr-en-Bourg co-operative, Sanzay.

SAVIGNY-LÈS-BEAUNE AC
CÔTE DE BEAUNE, BURGUNDY
Pinot Noir

Although Savigny-lès-Beaune is off the main 'Côte', in the side valley through· which the Autoroute du Soleil now leaps southwards, its parish boundaries are far flung, spreading right down to Beaune, and across to Aloxe-Corton. The 1000 acres (400 hectares) of vines in the AC represent the third largest red wine production on the Côte de Beaune, after Beaune and Pommard. The vines follow the cleft in the hills, facing both north-east and south to south-east. This less than perfect aspect does show in the wines, which are usually fairly light with a slightly minerally streak, but there is also a very pleasant strawberry fruit, often enriched with the vanilla of new oak, and despite their lightness of texture, they can age extremely well, though they never achieve the standard of their more famous neighbours Aloxe-Corton and Beaune. Best years: 1987, '85, '83, '82, '80, '78. Best producers: Bize, Camus-Bruchon, Écard-Guyot, Fougeray, Girardin, Guillemot, Pavelot-Glantenay, Tollot-Beaut.

SAVOIE
Mondeuse, Gamay, Pinot Noir

Savoie's high, alpine vineyards, tumbling down from the snow-capped peaks, are obvious candidates for making fresh, snappy whites, and certainly this is what they do best. However they also make a fair number of very attractive light reds and rosés, and one deep, strong red which could happily hold its head up in the Rhône valley. This is chiefly possible because the general title Vin de Savoie covers the wines of the whole Savoie and Haute-Savoie *départements*,

▲ Mountains surround the scattered vineyards of Savoie. In this mainly white wine area, the AC/*vin de pays* regulations permit the addition of 20% white grapes to some red wines.

as well as a few little patches of Ain and Isère, and this gives widely differing growing conditions. Most of the best reds come from a group of villages near Chambéry, where the mountains curve round into the Isère valley. The grapes are Gamay, Pinot Noir and Mondeuse. The Gamay isn't special and often ends up as rosé whereas the Pinot Noir can make lovely, fragile reds, scented with flowers and strawberry fruit. But the true star is Mondeuse, which makes an improbably deep, chewy red full of plum and mulberries and a slightly tarry darkness. Buy it only in hot years like 1982, '83, and '85, but then it can age for up to ten years. Best villages are Chignin, Montmélian, Arbin and Cruet. Chautagne, north of Chambéry makes light, smoky reds from the Pinot Noir and Gamay which can be good. The better Savoie wines can carry their village name on the label as well as the *appellation* Vin de Savoie. Best years: 1985, '83, '82. Best producers: Magnin, André Quenard, Raymond Quenard, and the co-operatives at Cruet, Chignin and Ruffieux (for Chautagne Gamay and Pinot Noir).

SIAURAC, CH.
Lalande-de-Pomerol AC
BORDEAUX
Merlot, Cabernet Franc, Cabernet Sauvignon

A leading Lalande-de-Pomerol property of 57 acres (23 hectares). The wines are full, rounded but reasonably tannic – excellent to drink young for their rather soupy richness, but much better to age for five to ten years. I've got half bottles of the 1966 and '67 which still have a delicious delicate blackcurrant scent, going a little musty like old lace in a shuttered room, but still lovely. Best years: 1985, '83, '82, '78, '75.

SMITH-HAUT-LAFITTE, CH.
Pessac-Léognan AC, *cru classé de Graves*
BORDEAUX
Cabernet Sauvignon, Merlot, Cabernet Franc

The property is one of the region's biggest at 111 acres (45 hectares), producing about 250,000 bottles of red (and a little white) from a vineyard of 73 per cent Cabernet Sauvignon, 11 per cent Cabernet Franc and 16 per cent Merlot. The soil is good and gravelly on a swell of ground to the north of Martillac, but the wine just doesn't 'sing', and is always a bit short on personality and a little lean. It lasts well enough, but it never seems to get very exciting and if anything is marked by a persistent streak of green gooseberryish acidity. It is owned by Eschenauer, a Bordeaux shipping company and the same group which has revolutionized Rausan-Ségla in the last few years. Certainly the 1985 and '86 vintages show distinct signs of improvement. Best years: 1986, '85, '83, '82, '78.

SOCIANDO-MALLET, CH.
Haut-Médoc AC, *cru grand bourgeois*
HAUT-MÉDOC, BORDEAUX
Cabernet Sauvignon, Merlot, Cabernet Franc

A rising star if ever I saw one. When I first visited the château at St-Seurin-de-Cadourne, holding lonely vigil over the last really decent gravel outcrop of the Haut-Médoc, I was not prepared for the beady-eyed, furious passion of the owner, Monsieur Gautreau, for his wine. And I wasn't prepared for the magnificent quality of this wine whose name I'd hardly even heard before. Dark, brooding, tannic, dry, but with every sign of great, classic claret flavours to come if you could hang on for 10–15 years. So hats off to Monsieur Gautreau for his dedication and for believing in his wine which now easily attains the quality of a Classed Growth, and is rapidly approaching Classed Growth prices too. The vineyard is 75 acres (30 hectares), 60 per cent Cabernet Sauvignon, 30 per cent Merlot, 10 per cent Cabernet Franc and produces up to 220,000 bottles. Fifty per cent of the oak barrels used to mature the wine are new – *very* rare for a non-Classed Growth. Best years: 1986, '85, '83, '82, '78, '76, '75.

SYRAH

I adore this grape and have done ever since I first tasted a Hermitage 1972 bottled by Nicolas years ago. Hermitage is usually made entirely from Syrah and it was the startling mixture of flavours which got me hooked. So savage to start with – the tannin tugging at your gums, the tarry, peppery brashness overlaid with a thick, hot jammy fruit – that you feel sure the wine will never be remotely civilized. Yet the change does come. The tar and pepper subside into a smoky, leathery perfume, while the tannins drop away to reveal a wonderful sweet fruit – blackberries, blackcurrants, raspberries and plums – the black chewiness of dark treacle and liquorice, the slightly bitter edge of pine, the soothing texture of cream. All this may take five years, it may take ten or even 20, but it is one of wine's great conjuring tricks.

Its home base is the northern Rhône, in particular the ACs of Hermitage, Côte-Rôtie, Cornas, St-Joseph and Crozes-Hermitage, in which it is the only red grape permitted. Its other traditional role has been as an improver vine in the southern Rhône and especially Châteauneuf-du-Pape, where it is used to add backbone and toughness to the fleshier Grenache. And it has now found a new role – as an improver to all the lifeless vineyards of the far south. The dark, tannic character and good plummy fruit can make a massive difference to a dull Midi blend, and many of the southern ACs as well as the burgeoning *vins de pays* use Syrah to great effect. Syrah now accounts for almost two per cent of French red grape plantings, with nearly 50,000 acres (20,000 hectares).

LA TÂCHE AC
grand cru
CÔTE DE NUITS, BURGUNDY
Pinot Noir

With Romanée-Conti, La Tâche is at the very peak of Vosne-Romanée *grands crus*, and similarly owned by Domaine de la Romanée-Conti. But there's a lot more La Tâche – 15 acres (6·1 hectares) as against 4½ acres (1·8 hectares) and production is generally around 24,000 bottles. The vineyard's position is superb, just yards south of Romanée-Conti, fractionally more south-east, at the perfect altitude between 800 and 1000 feet (250 and 300 metres). For me, it is the greatest of these marvellous Vosne-Romanée *grands crus*. It has the rare ability to provide layer on layer of flavours, different scents and sweetnesses endlessly satisfying yet challenging, an exotic richness of fruit as heady as ripe plums soaked in brandy, and a spice of smoke, cinnamon, mace, the blackest of dark chocolate. . . La Tâche is a great sensation for the palate, the brain, but especially for the heart because it is the most sensuous and emotional of all Burgundy's great wines. Unless you keep it for ten years you'll only experience a fraction of the pleasures in store and since you're paying outrageous prices for La Tâche, keep it nearer 20 years to appreciate its full glory. Best years: 1987, '85, '84, '83, '82, '80, '79, '78.

TALBOT, CH.
St-Julien AC, *4ème cru classé*
BORDEAUX
Cabernet Sauvignon, Merlot, Cabernet Franc, Petit Verdot

Poor old Château Talbot never seems to be judged on its own merits: because it is a sister-château of Gruaud-Larose, it is endlessly compared, normally being worsted in the process. Well, Talbot isn't quite as good as Gruaud-Larose, but then it is a Fourth Growth not a Second, and whereas Gruaud-Larose is a brilliant Second Growth which should be upgraded to a First, Talbot is a superb Fourth Growth which should be upgraded to a Second. You see, I'm doing it too; compare, compare! Right. Talbot is a *very* big estate – 250 acres (100 hectares), planted 71 per cent Cabernet Sauvignon, 20 per cent Merlot, five per cent Cabernet Franc and four per cent Petit Verdot. It occupies a single chunk of land bang in the middle of the AC. The wine is big, soft-centred but sturdy, capable of ageing extremely well for 10–20 years, going from rather rich, almost sweet beginnings to a maturity of plums, blackcurrants and cigar-box scent – yet never to quite the same extent as Gruaud-Larose. Sorry! Best years: 1986, '85, '84, '83, '82, '81, '79, '78. Second wine: Connétable Talbot.

TAVEL AC
SOUTHERN RHÔNE
Grenache, Cinsaut, Clairette and others

An oddity for southern France in that the Tavel AC applies only to one colour of wine – pink. Tavel was once considered France's best rosé, but this opinion was held largely by those who thought that the closer a rosé tastes to a red wine the better. Tavel is big wine and certainly boasts a hefty degree of alcohol as well as a big, strong, dry taste. But if rosé is supposed to be bright, cheerful and refreshing I'm afraid Tavel misses the mark because it just takes itself too seriously; it's too adult – which reminds me: it's also generally too old by the time it gets to the shops. One year old is fine, but frequently I come across examples at nearer three years old which have lost their pretty pink bloom and gone orange at the edges! The vineyards are quite extensive at 1900 acres (750 hectares), to the north-west of Avignon. Grenache is the dominant grape, giving ripe juicy flavours to the young wine, as usual kept from getting really fleshy and exciting by its side-kick Cinsaut. Altogether nine grapes are allowed, including Syrah and Mourvèdre, but these two are the important ones. Colour can be gained by giving the grapes a very strong pressing, but this seems merely to harshen the taste; the best producers allow the grapes to soak with the juice for a few hours before fermentation to add colour as well as perfume and flavour. Best years: 1986, '85. Best producers: Aqueria, Génestière, Trinquevedel, Vieux Moulin.

DU TERTRE, CH.
Margaux AC, *5ème cru classé*
HAUT-MÉDOC, BORDEAUX
Cabernet Sauvignon, Cabernet Franc, Merlot

When I first started banging the drum about how wonderful Château du Tertre was I found so little agreement that I thought perhaps I should send my palate in for an overhaul. Well, at last du Tertre is gaining recognition – which it really does deserve, because stuck out in the wilds of Arsac, on the edge of the Margaux AC, you're not exactly going to benefit from any passing trade. But this 120-acre (48-hectare) vineyard is atop a knoll (*tertre* means 'knoll') on the highest ground in the AC, with extremely gravelly soil. The mixture of 80 per cent Cabernet Sauvignon, 10 per cent Cabernet Franc and 10 per cent Merlot could be expected to produce hard, difficult, slow-maturing wine, but in fact du Tertre shows wonderful fruit – strawberries, blackcurrants and mulberries right from the start – with tannin, certainly, but also a glycerine ripeness coating your mouth and a marvellous cedar, strawberry and blackcurrant scent building up after a few years. It's usually delicious at five to six years old, but will happily age 10–15 years, maybe more. Best years: 1986, '85, '83, '82, '80, '79, '78.

TOURAINE AC
CENTRAL LOIRE
Gamay, Cabernet Franc, Cabernet Sauvignon and others

All the best red wines in Touraine have their own specific *appellations* – Chinon, Bourgueil and St-Nicolas-de-Bourgueil. However, there is still a large amount of red and rosé made which merely qualifies for the Touraine AC, a fairly general AC covering 60 miles (97km) of the Loire valley around Tours.

The grapes used reflect Touraine's position on the Loire, between the wine cultures of Bordeaux and Burgundy. The Loire grapes Grolleau and Pineau d'Aunis are used for rosé only, whereas the Bordeaux grapes Cabernet Sauvignon, Cabernet Franc and Malbec (here known as Cot), the Pinot Noir from Burgundy and the Gamay from Beaujolais are used for rosés and reds. Most of the reds are from Gamay and in hot years can be juicy, rough-fruited wines, but they usually have a rather rooty overtone which can spoil the pleasure. Cabernet, too, is often a bit green, but can give quite pure-tasting wine. A new departure is a wine called Tradition – blending Gamay, Cabernet Franc and Malbec – which works rather well. The rosés are in general drier than those of Anjou and on a visit you may find a rather attractive, peachy-flavoured, pale rosé called Vin de Noble Joué, though none is exported. In general all Touraine wines are best drunk within two years of harvest.

There are three villages which can add their names to the Touraine AC. Touraine-Amboise is a surprisingly good red from the Cot and some fair rosé from an area of high chalk cliffs on the river just east of Tours. There are 914 acres (370 hectares) of vines. Touraine Azay-le-Rideau is a merely adequate rosé based on the Grolleau, which can be raspingly dry or slightly sweet; there are 245 acres (100 hectares) south-west of the city of Tours. Touraine-Mesland has 1530 acres (620 hectares) of good vineyard on the north bank to the west of Blois that produces red wines from the Gamay which, especially when made with at least partial carbonic maceration, can be Touraine's best. The Bordeaux grapes produce good, full-tasting red. Rosé is fair. Best years: 1988, '87, '86, '85. Best producers: Brossillon (Mesland), Charmoise, Corbillières, Denay (Amboise), Girault-Artois (Mesland), Octavie, Oisly-et-Thésée co-operative.

LA TOUR-MARTILLAC, CH.
Pessac-Léognan AC, *cru classé de Graves*
BORDEAUX
Cabernet Sauvignon, Merlot, Cabernet Franc

A Classed Growth, which seems to have been left behind by the wave of improvement sweeping through the region. This is a pity, because the owner Monsieur Kressmann stubbornly refuses to uproot old vines simply because their yield has fallen. Some of his vines date from the 1920s. He also determinedly follows organic practice in the vineyard and such an attitude should bring about deep, dark, well-structured wines for the long haul, but somehow they just lack chutzpah – their flavours are rather full and blank and their chunky feel is never matched by good dollops of fruit. But Monsieur Kressmann's heart is obviously in the right place, and there does seem to be an improvement in the '80s. Best years: 1986, '85, '83, '82.

TOURTEAU-CHOLLET, CH.
Graves AC
BORDEAUX
Cabernet Sauvignon, Merlot

Another example of how the less fashionable parts of the Graves, south of Pessac-Léognan, are taking up the quality banner and running with it. This 75-acre (30-hectare) property is in Arbanats, on the river Garonne to the south of Portets. Since the beginning of the 1980s (including the difficult years '80 and '84) the wines have been full, dry, slightly earthy but with good compact fruit – ready at three to four years old, but much better after six or seven. Best years: 1986, '85, '83, '82, '81.

TROTANOY, CH.
Pomerol AC
BORDEAUX
Merlot, Cabernet Franc

Trotanoy puts itself up as Pétrus' main challenger for the title King of Pomerol but, except in vintages like 1978 (when Pétrus was inexplicably disappointing) and 1962 (when Trotanoy was an enormous, broad-flavoured wine, smacking of chocolate and hazelnuts, brown sugar and blackberry jam), it is going to have to content itself with a crown prince's role. It's tremendous stuff, though, and another example (along with Pétrus, Lafleur, Latour-à-Pomerol and a gaggle of others) of the brilliant touch of Jean-Pierre Moueix and his son Christian. They own this 19-acre (7·5-hectare) property to the west of Pétrus on slightly more gravelly soil, and though the plantings of 85 per cent Merlot and 15 per cent Cabèrnet Franc do give a rich, massively impressive, Pétrus-like wine, they are also likely to have a tempering of leather and tobacco scents, and just lack the magic mingling of sweetness, spice and perfume which make Pétrus so memorable. One of the great Pomerols, not *the* greatest. Best years: 1985, '83, '82, '81, '79, '78, '76, '75.

TURSAN VDQS
SOUTH-WEST
Cabernet Franc, Tannat, Cabernet Sauvignon

Adequate reds and rosés from south of the Adour river on the edge of Landes. The district backs on to Côtes de St-Mont and Madiran, and the Tannat grape – which makes Madiran so dour and charmless when it is young – is also evident in Tursan, backed up by Cabernet Franc and Cabernet Sauvignon. So it isn't surprising that the reds resemble a rather shadowy Madiran. The rosés, too, have the 'lack of fruit' problem of Madiran and although I'd drink them if I were passing through, I wouldn't seek them out anywhere else.

VACQUEYRAS
Côtes du Rhône-Villages AC
SOUTHERN RHÔNE
Grenache, Syrah, Cinsaut, Mourvèdre

▼ The dramatic profile of the Dentelles de Montmirail rising above the terraced vineyards of Vacqueyras.

The most important and consistently successful of the Côtes du Rhône-Villages communes, now edging its way towards its own fully fledged individual AC. The village itself is rather a large one liable to be raucous in summer and silent as a tomb in winter, and is on the flat land just south of Gigondas. However the vineyards sweep up towards the jagged Dentelles de Montmirail and produce red wines of a lovely dark colour, a round warm spicy bouquet and a fruit which happily mixes plums and raspberries with the wind-dried dust of the south. Lovely at two to three years; good producers' wines from good vintages will age well for ten years or more. Best years: 1986, '85, '83, '81, '80, '78. Best producers: Couroulu, Fourmone, Jaboulet, Lambertins, Montmirail, Pascal, Roques, Vacqueyras co-operative.

VIEUX-CHÂTEAU-CERTAN, CH.
Pomerol AC
BORDEAUX
Merlot, Cabernet Franc, Cabernet
Sauvignon, Malbec

If Trotanoy now disputes the title of runner-up to Pétrus in the Pomerol hierarchy, traditionally that position has always been occupied by Vieux-Château-Certan. But whereas Trotanoy often seems to ape Pétrus, Vieux-Château-Certan goes out of its way to be different. It is owned by the Thienpont (not Moueix) family, for one thing. And, although it is only a few hundred yards down the road, its soil is obviously different, mixing sand and gravel with its clay. But most important it has only 50 per cent Merlot as against Pétrus' 95 per cent. The rest of the 34-acre (13·6-hectare) vineyard is 25 per cent Cabernet Franc, 20 per cent Cabernet Sauvignon and five per cent Malbec, and it is this unusually strong presence of Cabernet for Pomerol which makes Vieux-Château-Certan drier, leaner, less gushing, less sumptuous, less Rubens flesh and sheer indulgence. What you do get is a slow-developing, tannic wine, which gradually builds up over 15–20 years into an exciting 'Médoc' blend of blackcurrant and cedarwood perfume just set off by the brown sugar and roasted nuts of Pomerol. A bottle of '52 was the first blind wine-tasting prize I won. (I don't know why they gave it to me – I said the wine was a Latour!) Best years: 1987, '86, '85, '83, '82, '81, '75.

VIN DE CORSE AC
CORSICA
Nielluccio, Sciacarello, Grenache
and others

Corsica has been slower than mainland southern France to catch on to the new wave of wine technology – and with it the tremendous possibilities of making good wine even where the sun is baking the ground dry long before noon. The problems lie in the dogged traditionalism of most of the owners of the best-sited vineyards, and the carpet-bagging mentality of many of the vine-growers from French North Africa who re-settled during the 1960s on to the flat eastern plains. With commendable agricultural skill, but little oenological interest, they turned eastern Corsica into a grape basket of grand proportions. As a wine venture it was a disaster – the heavy, unsubtle reds were merely shipped north to add a little beef to the feeble Midi brews, and since 1976 one-third of the vineyards have been uprooted.

However, on this heavenly island which effortlessly lives up to its title Île de Beauté (the name of its *vin de pays* too), there are many fine hillside vineyards, producing good fruit – primarily the local Nielluccio and Sciacarello varieties. What is lacking is good wine-making. Most reds are volatile and oxidized, most rosés flabby and dull, and the famed *maquis* herb perfume more likely to be a polite description of the pong left by a dirty wooden barrel. Things are improving, but very slowly. At a recent tasting, the fruit was obviously good on most of the estates, but the wines all turned out unbalanced and past it – except for the expensive but highly proficient Comte Peraldi. Corsican wines are supposed to age well, but except from a producer like Peraldi, I'd drink them as young as possible. The better areas – Calvi, Cap Corse, Figari, Patrimonio, Porto Vecchio, Sartène – are allowed to add their name to Vin de Corse. Outside the AC areas, co-operative groups and in particular Sica UVAL are planting mainstream French grapes like Cabernet and Syrah. I'm not one to support the dilution of traditional grape types, but maybe the Nielluccio and Sciacarello just aren't terribly brilliant. Best producers: Cantone, Dominique Gentile, Peraldi, Sica UVAL, Torraccia.

VIN DE L'ORLÉANAIS VDQS
UPPER LOIRE
Pinot Noir, Pinot Meunier, Cabernet
Sauvignon

Vin de l'Orléanais is a bit lucky to get into this book at all, because Orléans is really best known as France's vinegar capital! But what wine there *is* is *unique* – and that's why it's in. The leading Orléans wine is a very pale rosé or very pale red from the Pinot Meunier (one of the three Champagne grapes) – the only time in France it appears under its own name unblended. They call it Gris Meunier d'Orléans, and it's not too bad – light and thin, but then slightly creamy and smoky all at once. Not bad at all; but drink it young. They also grow Pinot Noir and Cabernet Franc, but I think I'd go elsewhere for them. Best years: 1986, '85. Best producer: Clos de St-Fiacre.

VINS DE PAYS

The phrase '*vins de pays*' implies that these are the traditional wines of the country districts of France which have been created and enjoyed for centuries by the locals. The reality is a little different. The vast majority of *vins de pays* are impressively modern and forward-looking.

The idea of '*vin de pays*' was conceived as a dependable category of French wine only in 1968. Until then, in many parts of the country – especially the far south – there was a serious problem of overproduction of very mediocre wine and no incentives available to the grower to improve quality since all the wines were consigned to the anonymity of the blending vats of various shippers and merchants.

The aim was to encourage quality, and to provide a specific guarantee of geographical origin for the wines. In this the *vin de pays* system follows the example set by the two top quality tiers in French wines (see page 8). In effect, *vin de pays* became the third tier of quality control, following similar guidelines based on geographical origin, yield of grapes per hectare, minimum alcohol levels and choice of grape varieties.

There are three geographically defined categories, each one becoming more specific. *Vins de pays régionaux* cover whole regions, encompassing several *départements*. There are only three of these and any wine grown in the region concerned may qualify, if desired, for this designation. *Vins de pays départementaux* cover the wines of an entire *département*. There are 35 of these. *Vin de pays de zone* is the most specific category, and relates only to the wines of a particular community or locality. Altogether these account for about 14 per cent of French wine production.

Yield is higher than for ACs since the *vins de pays* are only beginning to create a reputation and cannot as yet command high prices, and alcoholic strength is generally lower.

The grape varieties are specified to eliminate the worst sorts, but the crucial element here is that excellent varieties excluded from a region's ACs but capable of producing high-quality wine are included. Consequently, for example, we are seeing excellent white Chardonnay from the Loire and Languedoc-Roussillon, red Cabernet Sauvignon and Gamay from the Coteaux de l'Ardèche, and Merlot from the Hérault – grape varieties previously virtually unknown there. Increasingly the *vin de pays* is labelled with the grape variety – and these are now the source of some of France's best-value flavours.

REGIONAL WINES
Vin de Pays du Comté Tolosan
Vin de Pays du Jardin de la France
Vin de Pays d'Oc

DEPARTMENTAL WINES
Aude
Bouches-du-Rhône
Gard
l'Hérault
Pyrénées-Orientales

ZONAL WINES
Charentais
Coteaux de l'Ardèche
Coteaux de Peyriac
Côtes de Gascogne
l'Île de Beauté
Sables du Golfe du Lion

▶ Timeless terraces of vines and olives in the Hérault, which has more vineyards than any other *département* in France. Although it has several AC and VDQS wines, the Hérault is primarily *vin de pays* country. Its own departmental *vin de pays* is traditionally based on the rough, sullen Carignan grape but is being improved by planting other varieties – including the Bordeaux classics Cabernet Sauvignon and Merlot – and by the use of carbonic maceration.

VIN DE PAYS DES BOUCHES-DU-RHÔNE
PROVENCE
Grenache, Cinsaut, Carignan

This *département*, which stretches across the wide Rhône delta, produces about 15 million bottles a year of Vin de Pays des Bouches-du-Rhône – mostly red, with some rosé. The best wines come from the area round Aix, although the mysterious, wild marshes of the Camargue contribute about a quarter of the total. The wines are rarely very exciting, although when made by an up-to-date co-operative, they can have a pleasant, dusty, strawberry fruit.

VIN DE PAYS DES SABLES DU GOLFE DU LION
LANGUEDOC-ROUSSILLON
Cabernet Sauvignon, Cinsaut, Grenache and others

This splendid title translates as 'the Sands of the Gulf of the Lion'. Well, the Gulf of the Lion is the whole of the gentle loop of shore-line that swings round from Marseille to Béziers, and the *vin de pays* comes from the coastal vineyards through most of that area, covering three *départements* – Bouches-du-Rhône, Gard and Hérault – and producing in total about 16 million bottles: 35 per cent red, 40 per cent rosé or *gris* (very pale rosé) and 25 per cent white. By far the most important producer is the Domaines Viticoles des Salins du Midi – which uses the brand name Listel. Basically a salt company producing enormous amounts of salt from the Rhône delta marshes, the Salins du Midi are also, astonishingly, the biggest vineyard owners in France with a staggering 4700 acres (1900 hectares). Among numerous claims to fame – like, how you grow anything on sand in the middle of a salty swamp – they are France's largest producer of Cabernet Sauvignon! Listel wines probably are the best in the area, though they are by no means memorable – but they're not expensive either. The very pale *gris* can be good but *must* be drunk ultra-young and I prefer the slightly darker rosés. Grenache, Cinsaut and Carignan are the main grapes in the region, but there are good plantings of Syrah, Merlot – and obviously, Cabernet Sauvignon.

VIN DE PAYS D'OC
LANGUEDOC-ROUSSILLON
Carignan, Cinsaut, Grenache

In the olden days, one part of France expressed 'yes' by saying *oui*; another part, spread round the Mediterranean basin said *oc*. 'Some more wine, Asterix?' 'Oc please.' Well, sort of. But that's how the Languedoc region got its name. The Vin de Pays d'Oc therefore covers the whole Midi region, but *départements* like the Hérault and Aude either use their own names, or one of the numerous 'zonal' *vin de pays* names available. Which is fair enough, because the Vin de Pays d'Oc is by far the least specific.

Most of the wine which uses the title comes from down by the Pyrenees. There's a fair amount – about ten million bottles – of which 90 per cent is red and rosé, mostly from Carignan, Cinsaut and Grenache. Cheap and cheerful. Drink it young.

VIN DE PAYS DU COMTÉ TOLOSAN
SOUTH-WEST
Cabernet Sauvignon, Cabernet Franc, Merlot, Malbec

Technically this is a highly important regional *vin de pays* title, since it covers all the *départements* in the south-west of France. So far, however, the vast majority of the *vins de pays* from this large and very interesting area are exported under more specific local titles. Total production averages about 2½ million bottles.

VIN DE PAYS DU GARD
LANGUEDOC-ROUSSILLON
Carignan, Cinsaut, Grenache and others

The smallest of the 'big three' departmental *vins de pays* in France's Midi, producing about 30 million bottles. Because the Gard *département* takes in the southern end of the Rhône valley as it fans out into the Mediterranean, the reds and rosés are often supposed to have something of a Rhône quality. That would be flattering them.

There is a lot of Carignan planted and not enough of the top grapes Syrah, Mourvèdre, Cabernet Sauvignon and Merlot – although plantings are increasing. Consequently, most Gard red is light, slightly spicy, but often with a gamy earthiness flattening the fruit. The rosés are often better and, drunk young and fresh, can be very attractive.

VIN DE PAYS DU JARDIN DE LA FRANCE
LOIRE
Cabernet Franc, Cabernet Sauvignon, Cot and others

The largest of the French regional *vins de pays*, covering the whole Loire valley. Thirty million bottles are produced, but mostly of white wine. The few reds and rosés – usually from the Gamay, but occasionally from Pinot Noir or Cabernet – are generally light and sharp; fine drunk young and chilled on the banks of some Loire tributary like the Layon or the Cher, but not to be sought out for more 'substantial' experiences.

VOLNAY AC & VOLNAY SANTENOTS AC
CÔTE DE BEAUNE, BURGUNDY
Pinot Noir

Until the eighteenth century, Volnay produced Burgundy's Nouveau, much the same way as Beaujolais does now. The wine was extremely pale and was snapped up for high prices as soon as it had settled down after fermentation. French kings drank quite a bit of it, which is always good for trade. The main reason for this lightness has to be the soil structure, which has a fair bit of chalk and limestone, particularly in the higher vineyards. There are, in fact, two main styles of Volnay. One *is* light, or perfumed in a delicious cherry and strawberry way, but there are also some wines of tremendous, juicy, plummy power, particularly from the lower vineyards like Champans and Santenots. Drinkable at three to four years old, but unless the wine is very light this is usually a pity, because lovely flavours can develop between seven and ten years. Best years: 1987, '85, '83, '82, '80, '78. Best producers: Blain-Gagnard, Clerget, Comte Lafon, Delagrange, Glantenay, Lafarge, Marquis d'Angerville, de Montille, Potinet-Ampeau, Pousse d'Or, Vaudoisey-Mutinde.

VOSNE-ROMANÉE AC
CÔTE DE NUITS, BURGUNDY
Pinot Noir

They call it the greatest village in Burgundy – simply because it has an incomparable clutch of five *grands crus* at its heart. I'd only go so far as saying the greatest village in the Côte de Nuits – partly because the Côte de Beaune has Puligny-Montrachet, home of the greatest dry white wines in the world, and partly because the Côte de Nuit's other contender – Gevrey-Chambertin, with its large string of *grands crus* – is relentlessly failing to realize its potential at the moment. There are 600 acres (240 hectares) of vineyards of which just under 66 acres (27 hectares) are Vosne-Romanée's *grand cru* itself, but this figure rises to 163 acres (66 hectares) if the *grands crus* of Échézeaux and Grands-Échézeaux are included in the total, as is usual. There are also 119 acres (48 hectares) of *premiers crus* which match other villages' *grands crus* in quality. Best of these are Malconsorts and Suchots. And the fact that all of Vosne-Romanée's other AC land is on the slopes to the west of the N74 road, rather than slipping across to the inferior plains beyond, also helps to keep the wine quality high. The mix of exciting, red-fruit ripeness with a delicious tangle of spices and smoke, sometimes even showing a distinctly savoury edge and a whiff of mint and eucalyptus, and finally ageing to the deep, decaying pleasures of prunes, brown sugar and chocolate, moist autumn dampness and well-hung game – all these make Vosne-Romanée red wine one of the world's really exciting experiences. In good years the wines should have at least six years' age. Ten to fifteen would be better. Lighter years still need five to eight. Best years: 1987, '86, '85, '84, '83, '82, '80, '78, '76. Best producers: Domaine de la Romanée-Conti, Engel, Grivot, Gros, Hudelot-Noëllat, Jayer, Lamarche, Martin-Noblet, Moillard, Mugneret-Gibourg, Rion.

VOUGEOT AC
CÔTE DE NUITS, BURGUNDY
Pinot Noir

When I first saw a bottle of Vougeot I thought the label was faulty because I was so accustomed to seeing Clos de Vougeot, that plain Vougeot just didn't look right. But there are 30 acres (12 hectares) of Vougeot vines outside the walls of the famous Clos, producing about 70,000 bottles of wine, divided six to one in red's favour. It's not bad stuff – full and slightly solid to start but gaining a really good chocolaty richness with a few years age – and it's a *lot* cheaper than Clos de Vougeot – but then, what isn't? *Premiers crus* Clos de la Perrière and Les Petits Vougeots are best. Best years: 1987, '86, '85. Best producer: Bertagna.

BOTTLES, CORKS AND LABELS

COLOUR Dark green glass is traditional for Bordeaux red wines.

COLOUR Burgundy bottles are made of olive-green glass.

SHAPE The classic Bordeaux bottle has high, shoulders.

SHAPE The classic Burgundy bottle has low, sloping 'shoulders'.

Neck label showing the vintage; many wines do not have a neck label.

The estate – although *château* means 'castle', in Bordeaux it applies to any wine-producing property.

Classed Growth, as listed in the 1855 classification of top Médoc properties. The label doesn't specify, but this is a Fifth Growth.

Village name – Vosne-Romanée is one of the most famous communes on Burgundy's Côte d'Or.

Vintage.

Pauillac is a leading commune in the Haut-Médoc with its own AC.

Vineyard name – Beaux Monts is a *premier cru*, First Growth – the second-best quality level for vineyards in Burgundy.

Name of company owning the property.

Cork stamped with the estate name.

Cork stamped with 'estate-bottled'.

Contents in bottle.

Name of the producer owning the vineyard.

Estate-bottled – obligatory for *cru classé* wines in the Médoc.

Bottled on the estate.

CHATEAU GRAND-PUY DUCAS

CRU CLASSÉ EN 1855

1980

PAUILLAC

APPELLATION PAUILLAC CONTROLEE

STE CLE DE GRAND-PUY DUCASSE
PROPRIÉTAIRE A PAUILLAC (GDE)
FRANCE

MIS EN BOUTEILLES AU CHÂTEAU

1984

GRAND VIN DE BOURGOGNE

VOSNE-ROMANÉE 1er CRU

BEAUX-MONTS

APPELLATION CONTROLEE

Mis en bouteille au Domaine
DOMAINE DANIEL RION & FILS
PROPRIÉTAIRE-RÉCOLTANT
PREMEAUX 21 NUITS-ST-GEORGES (COTE-D'OR)
PRODUCE OF FRANCE

You can learn something about a wine simply by looking at the bottle – certain regions have traditional shapes and colours (which have often been adopted by similar style wines in other parts of the world). And you can learn a great deal more by understanding the label, which carries a range of essential information, some of it required by law, and some at the discretion of the winemaker or *négociant*.

COLOUR Like Burgundy, Rhône wine is bottled in olive-green glass.

The neck label shows the vintage and that the wine is estate-bottled.

SHAPE Rhône wines use a Burgundy-style bottle with smoothly tapered 'shoulders'.

In Châteauneuf-du–Pape, the name and papal coat of arms embossed on the bottle indicate that the wine is estate-bottled.

Wine-producing property – Château de Beaucastel.

The *appellation controlée*.

Name of company owning the estate.

Cork stamped with the estate name.

COLOUR Clear glass is used for rosé wines.

SHAPE Tall, slender bottles are conventionally used for rosé wine; Côtes de Provence comes in a distinctive curved bottle.

The *appellation contrôlée*.

Name of co-operative making the wine.

Contents in bottle.

Vintage.

Alcoholic strength.

STORING
AND SERVING
WINES

STORING Most wine, unless it's really getting on in years, is pretty resilient stuff. Although it won't *like* being stored next to the central heating boiler it'll probably survive for a few weeks at least. But if the wine is at *all* special, it's worth taking a few precautions.

That is, if you need to store the stuff at all! Despite the feeling that the older the bottle the better, this just isn't the case with most modern wine: nowadays nearly all wine is ready to drink the moment it appears on the shop shelf. Reds *may* benefit from a little ageing, especially those based on the Cabernet Sauvignon and Syrah grapes, but – except for the top wines of Bordeaux and the northern Rhône – these also are generally ready to drink by the time they are put on sale.

However, if you still want to store a few bottles – find somewhere with an even temperature which is fairly quiet and not too dry. The traditional basement cellar is ideal for this, but few houses have one nowadays, so a broom cupboard, a disused fireplace, or the space under the stairs may have to do. Lay the wines on their sides to stop the corks drying out, and preferably shield them from direct light. The cooler the place is, within reason, the

slower the wines will develop: somewhere between 50°F and 55°F (10°C and 13°C) is ideal. But avoiding sudden changes in temperature is the most important thing.

SERVING Most red wine is best served at room temperature – but that's 60°F (15°C) or so – cooler than many centrally-heated houses. It's better to serve reds slightly too cool than too warm because you can always warm wine up by cupping the glass in your hand. *Don't* do anything dramatic to change a wine's temperature like leaving it in front of the fire. It'll probably blow its cork and taste like grape soup. Light, new reds such as Beaujolais can take up to an hour in the fridge, but that's not essential. Rosés should be well-chilled to very chilled indeed!

Any wine can be decanted just for the fun of it, and some wines do get softer and rounder after a couple of hours' decanting. But no wine *demands* it. Even an old wine which has thrown a sediment can be poured out successfully from the bottle – do it slowly, avoiding any sudden movements which might make the wine slop about. But if you do decide to decant, stand the bottle upright for a couple of days to let the sediment settle. Just before you want to drink it – within an hour or two – open it, and with a candle or torch under the neck of the bottle, pour gently in one single motion until you see an arrowhead of sediment arrive at the lip. If you do it carefully you'll only waste about half a glass – and that can go into the gravy.

There's one final thing – use nice big glasses which you fill to between one-third and one-half.

And after you've finished with them, hand-wash them in very hot water, taking particular care to rinse away any traces of washing-up liquid.

TASTING Well, we're going to drink it rather than swish it round our mouths and spit it out like the wine buffs do. But take a moment to look at the colour – some reds have a lovely hue – and do register the smell, which is often memorable. Then take a decent mouthful, and hold the wine in your mouth for a few moments, breathing through your nose. As the wine warms up in your mouth and the aromas rise into your nasal cavity, you'll get at least ten times the pleasure than if you'd just glugged it back!

FOOD AND WINE The last thing I intend to do is start laying down laws about what you must or must not drink with this or that food. No, that's up to you to decide, and if you like Burgundy with your fish course – why not! The thing to remember is – it's *your* palate doing the tasting, so if the flavours seem to go well together – then they do. For you at least!

Even so, let's look at a few guidelines which may help us decide what we're *likely* to enjoy most. Take rosés first. So long as they're fresh and young and well chilled, these are the perfect all-purpose wines. Their slight hint of red-wine fruit makes them happy with meat dishes, yet the absence of red-wine toughness makes them good partners for salads or fish. A really nice rosé is the perfect picnic choice when a single wine has to accompany the entire contents of the hamper.

Red wines are *not* quite as adaptable – largely because of their tannin. Tannin is the tough, rather cold-tea bitter edge that most reds have, especially from areas like Bordeaux and the northern Rhône, and especially from the Cabernet Sauvignon grape. Tannin makes most fish taste metallic, and becomes drier and more rasping with sweet things. So red wine with dessert doesn't usually work and tannic reds are unlikely to suit meat dishes in sweet sauces like duck *à l'orange*.

On the other hand, tannin does cut through fat so the fattier cuts of lamb and beef are often good with quite tough reds (though pork goes better with a white). And if you want to drink red with spicy food, a rough young red can become positively mellow. Cheese, too, softens a red wine and makes it seem bland, which is why I wouldn't use an expensive wine with the cheese course – you won't be able to taste why it was expensive!

Bordeaux-type reds, with their tannins and acidity, often act as appetite-whetters. Burgundy and Beaujolais have far less tannin and react differently with food. If you've got some well-hung game, or well-hung red meat, the slightly gamy and plum-perfumed flavours of Burgundy will often complement it perfectly. And if you want the one really all-purpose and affordable French red which will go with anything from omelette to oxtail, turkey to taramasalata – it's Beaujolais. The reason is its gush of fresh fruit – the most unquenchable of flavours in a wine. Beaujolais, young Côtes du Rhône, and an increasing number of southern *vins de pays* have it in abundance.

VINTAGES

BORDEAUX	88	87	86	85	84	83	82	81	80	79
Margaux	7⌂	5⌂	8⌂	8⌂	5⌂	9⌂	8●	6●	4★	7★
St-Julien	7⌂	6⌂	8⌂	8⌂	5⌂	8⌂	10⌂	7●	4★	7★
Pauillac	6⌂	6⌂	8⌂	8⌂	5⌂	8⌂	10⌂	7●	4★	7★
St-Estèphe	6⌂	5⌂	8⌂	8⌂	4⌂	8⌂	9⌂	6●	4★	7★
Listrac/Moulis	7⌂	5⌂	7⌂	8⌂	4●	8⌂	9●	6●	4★	6★
Graves/Pessac-Léognan	7⌂	5⌂	7⌂	8⌂	5●	8⌂	9●	8●	5★	7★
St-Émilion	8⌂	6⌂	7⌂	10⌂	3●	8●	10●	6●	4★	7★
Pomerol	8⌂	6⌂	8⌂	10⌂	3●	8●	10●	6●	4★	8★
BURGUNDY	88	87	86	85	84	83	82	81	80	79
Côte de Nuits	8⌂	9⌂	7⌂	10●	6★	7●	6★	3★	6★	5⌄
Hautes-Côtes de Nuits	6⌂	8⌂	6●	8★	4⌄	7★	6★	3⌄	4⌄	5⌄
Côte de Beaune	8⌂	8⌂	7⌂	9●	5★	7●	6★	3⌄	6⌄	6⌄
Hautes-Côtes de Beaune	6⌂	7⌂	6●	8★	3⌄	6★	6⌄	3⌄	3⌄	6⌄
Beaujolais Cru	9●	9★	6★	10★	4⌄	8★	5⌄	7★	4⌄	7⌄
Côte Châlonnaise	8⌂	7●	5●	8★	5★	6★	6⌄	3⌄	5⌄	5⌄
LOIRE	88	87	86	85	84	83	82	81	80	79
Anjou Rouge	8●	6●	5★	9★	3⌄	8★	7★	6⌄	2⌄	4⌄
Bourgueil	9⌂	6⌂	6●	9●	3●	8●	7★	6★	3⌄	5⌄
Chinon	9⌂	6⌂	7●	10●	4●	9★	8★	6★	3⌄	5⌄
Sancerre	8⌂	5●	6★	9★	4⌄	8⌄	7⌄	6⌄	3⌄	5⌄
RHÔNE	88	87	86	85	84	83	82	81	80	79
Hermitage	9⌂	7⌂	7⌂	9⌂	5●	10⌂	7●	4★	7★	6★
Côte-Rôtie	8⌂	7⌂	6⌂	10⌂	4●	9⌂	7●	4★	6★	6★
Châteauneuf-du-Pape	8⌂	4⌂	7●	8●	6★	7★	5★	6★	6★	6⌄
Cornas	8⌂	6⌂	6⌂	9●	4●	9●	7●	5★	5★	6★
St-Joseph	8⌂	6●	6●	9★	4★	9★	7★	4⌄	8⌄	6⌄

HOW TO READ THE CHART　　⌂ = not ready　● = just ready　★ = at peak　⌄ = past its best

The numerals represent an overall rating for each year, bearing in mind that such measures can only ever be broad generalizations. There will be many variations with individual wines and producers.

GLOSSARY

ACIDITY Naturally present in grapes, it gives red wine an appetizing 'grip'.

AGEING Essential process for fine wines and for many everyday reds. It usually takes place in wooden barrels then often continues in bottles; can last months or years.

ALCOHOLIC CONTENT Alcoholic strength of wine, usually expressed as a percentage of the total volume.

ALCOHOLIC FERMENTATION Process whereby yeasts convert grape sugars into alcohol, transforming grape juice into wine.

APPELLATION D'ORIGINE CONTRÔLÉE Official designation in France guaranteeing a wine by geographical origin, grape variety and production method; abbreviated as AC or AOC.

CARBONIC MACERATION Wine-making method traditional to Beaujolais. The grapes, whole and uncrushed, are fermented in a closed vat to give a well-coloured, fruity wine for early drinking.

CAVE French for 'cellar'.

CHAMBRER To bring (red) wines to room temperature, ready for drinking.

CHAPTALIZATION Legal addition of sugar during fermentation to increase alcoholic strength.

CLARET English name for red Bordeaux.

CLOS Term for a vineyard that is (or was) wall-enclosed; traditional to Burgundy.

CO-OPERATIVE Winery run collectively by growers.

CÔTES, COTEAUX Slopes. Hillside vineyards generally produce better wine than low-lying ones.

CRU French for 'growth'. Used to describe a single vineyard, normally with an additional quality reference as in grand cru.

CRU CLASSÉ Literally 'classed growth', indicating that a vineyard is included in the top-quality rating of its region.

DOMAINE Estate, especially in Burgundy.

ÉLEVAGE Term covering all wine-making stages between fermentation and bottling.

EN PRIMEUR Wine offered for sale immediately after the vintage, still in cask.

ESTATE-BOTTLED Wine bottled on the premises where it has been made.

FINING Clarifying wine by adding coagulants, traditionally egg-whites, to the surface. As these drop through the wine they collect all impurities.

LEES Coarse sediment – dead yeasts, etc – thrown by wine in a cask and left behind after racking.

NÉGOCIANT Merchant or shipper who buys in wine from growers, then matures, maybe blends and bottles it for sale.

OAK Traditional wood for wine casks. During ageing it gives important flavours, such as vanillin and tannin, to the wines. The newer the wood, the greater its impact.

OXIDATION Over-exposure of wine to air causing bacterial decay and loss of fruit.

PHYLLOXERA Vine aphid which devastated viticulture worldwide in the late 1800s. Since then, the vulnerable European vitis vinifera has been grafted on to phylloxera-resistant American rootstocks.

RÉCOLTANT Grower. He may either make his own wine or sell the grapes to a merchant.

RACKING Gradual clarification of wine by transferring it from one barrel to another, leaving sediments behind.

SECOND WINE Wine from a designated vineyard which is sold separately from the main production, under a different name, for a variety of technical reasons. Usually lighter and quicker-maturing than the main wine.

TANNIN Bitter element in red wine, derived from grape skins, stems and oak barrels; softens with ageing and is essential for the wine's development.

VIN DÉLIMITÉ DE QUALITÉ SUPÉRIEURE Second category of French quality control for wines, below AC; abbreviated as VDQS.

VIN DE PAYS French 'country wine'. Third and bottom category for quality, but includes some first-class wines which don't follow local AC regulations.

VIN DOUX NATUREL Sweet wine fortified with grape spirit; abbreviated as VDN. Mostly from the Midi.

VIN GRIS Very pale rosé made by lightly pressing red grapes and then drawing off the juice before fermentation.

INDEX

A page reference in *italics* indicates main entry.

ACKNOWLEDGEMENTS

Photographs supplied by Jon Wyand 7 left, Patrick Eagar 7
right, Michel Guillard/Scope 9, Jean-Paul Ferrero/Explorer 10,
Jacques Guillard/Scope 12, Mike Busselle 15, Francis
Jalain/Explorer 16, Mike Busselle 18, Michel Guillard/Scope
22, Landscape Only 26, Patrick Eagar 30, Luc Girard/Explorer
34, Michel Guillard/Scope 36, Mick Rock/Cephas 41, Jacques
Guillard/Scope 42, Mike Busselle 46 and 50, Jean-Daniel
Sudres/Scope 57, Christian Errath/Explorer 59 left, Anthony
Blake 59 right, Mick Rock/Cephas 65, Jacques Guillard/Scope
67, Patrick Eagar 72, Richard Platt 75, Mike Busselle 76,
Francis Jalain/Explorer 81, Mick Rock/Cephas 85, Patrick
Eagar 91, Henri Veiller/Explorer 92, Jean-Daniel Sudres/Scope
96, Mike Busselle 99, Anthony Blake 104, Manix/Explorer
110, Jacques Guillard/Scope 114, Jean-Paul Ferrero/Explorer
117.

Editor Sandy Carr; **Art Editor** Ruth Prentice; **Deputy
Editors** Catherine Dell, Fiona Holman; **Deputy Art Editor**
Alison Shackleton; **Editorial Assistants** Mary Pickles, Mary
Hitch, Ray Granger; **Design Assistant** Alison Leggate;
Production Manager Rupert Wheeler; **Consultant**
Rosemary George MW; **Indexer** Naomi Good; **Maps** Diane
Fisher; **Illustrations** Peter Byatt, Robina Greene.